THE

DARK

SIDE

OF

LOVE

The Positive Role
of Negative Feelings

THE

DARK

SIDE

OF

LOVE

Jane G. Goldberg
WITH A NEW INTRODUCTION
BY THE AUTHOR

TRANSACTION PUBLISHERS
NEW BRUNSWICK (U.S.A.) AND LONDON (U.K.)

Third printing 2007

Copyright © 1999 by Transaction Publishers, New Brunswick, New Jersey. Originally published in 1993 by G.P. Putman's Sons.

This book is printed on acid-free paper that meets the American National Standard for Permanence of Paper for Printed Library Materials.

Library of Congress Catalog Number: 99-20547
ISBN: 0-7658-0610-X
      978-0-7658-0610-9
Printed in the United States of America

Library of Congress Cataloging-in-Publication Data

Goldberg, Jane G. (Jane Gretzner), 1946
    The dark side of love: the positive role of negative feelings Goldberg;
with a new introduction by the author.
        p. cm.
    Includes bibliographical references and index.
    ISBN 0-7658-0610-X (pbk. : alk. paper)
        1. Title.
[BF575.L8G643 1999]
152.4'1—dc21   99-20547
                                                                          CIP

I dedicate this book to the memory of my mother, my first teacher about love. She was a woman who loved me enough to recognize the maturational gaps in her own mothering ability, because of her own pained childhood, and who bravely found her way to a psychoanalyst at a time when such things were not yet done, or at least, not openly. She loved me enough to allow the full gamut of feelings to come into our relationship. She loved me enough to encourage me to talk and helped me learn to listen with empathy and sensitivity. My greatest pain is that she did not live long enough to witness the full flowering of my personality. I miss her prideful boasting of me (which never ceased to embarrass me); I miss her warmth and easy openness; I miss our long talks. I miss her.

To Madeleine Malvina Levy Goldberg

Contents

ACKNOWLEDGMENTS

I thank Connie Zweig and Jeremy Tarcher for participation in this book, from early conceptualization to polished end, above and beyond the call of duty: Jeremy, especially for recognizing that there was a book to be written before I knew there was; Connie, especially for recognizing that I could write such a book before I knew I could.

I thank my editor, Nellie Sabin, whose editorial contributions to the book are seamless, and without which this book would have been a much less good book.

I thank Theresa deGeronimo for her valuable contributions in many, many ways; George Ernsberger for his story of Alicia and Marty; Michael Shapiro for help early on in the conceptualization of the book; Michal Ginach for her comments on chapter 1.

I thank Sydelle Engel for her consistent support and interest in the project.

I also want to thank two people who, more than anyone, have helped me to dream my dreams: Phyllis Meadow, for helping me to believe that no dream is unreachable; and Gregg Lalley, who helps me by putting nuts and bolts into my sometimes ethereal mind and makes my dreams come true.

We are never so defenseless against suffering as when we love, never so helplessly unhappy as when we have lost our loved object or its love.

SIGMUND FREUD

A rabbi had a conversation with the Lord about Heaven and Hell. "I'll show you Hell," said the Lord and led the rabbi into a room in the middle of which was a very big round table. The people sitting at it were famished and desperate. In the middle of the table there was a large pot of stew, enough and more for everyone. The smell of the stew was delicious and made the rabbi's mouth water. The people around the table were holding spoons with very long handles. Each one found that it was just possible to reach the pot to take a spoonful of the stew, but because the handle of the spoon was longer than a man's arm, he could not get the food back into his mouth. The rabbi saw that their suffering was terrible. "Now I will show you Heaven," said the Lord, and they went into another room exactly the same as the first. There was the same big round table and the same pot of stew. The people, as before, were equipped with the same long-handled spoons—but here they were well nourished and plump, laughing and talking. At first, the rabbi could not understand. "It is simple, but it requires a certain skill," said the Lord. "You see, they have learned to feed each other."

HASIDIC TALE

Introduction to the Transaction Edition

Since the initial publication of *The Dark Side of Love*, we have borne witness to children bearing shotguns and killing their fellow children. We have seen public role models, men and women who should be inspirational to us—Bill Clinton, as well as both Charles Windsor and his wife, Diana—all admitting to extramarital affairs. We have watched as a whole nation—Bosnia—divided itself, and people who had been life-long neighbors and friends became mortal enemies, ready and willing to kill each other.

Some would say that it seems as though love and decency have taken a back seat to destructive forces. Love, they would say, has taken flight, leaving us to flounder around with our most heinous, most dark sides. Yet, any student of history knows that aggression, and its myriad manifestations—murder, adultery, jingoistic patriotism—have been around for eons. Children have always been capable of deeds as destructive as any adult. Adultery has occurred for as long as man has been coupling, even in cultures where punishment for the infraction was death. We have never been far from war. Scarcely a generation passes in any nation without some exposure to war. And until this century, war was extolled as a necessity and virtue. Surely we must conclude, with Freud, that aggression is innate within us—that its manifestations are not anomalies, but rather representative of an essential, inescapable part of ourselves. Yet, unless we heed Freud's warning that our urge to destruction must be brought out of the darkness of unconsciousness, we will be forever at the mercy of forces that may well prove to be our ultimate undoing.

REGARDING CHILDREN AS MURDERERS

Recently there was an episode on a television show called *The Practice* about a thirteen-year-old boy who had killed his mother. He killed her merely because he was angry at her. The defending attorney was pleading with the judge to not try the boy as an adult because doing so presented the possibility of putting him away for life. The attorney argued that the boy was still a child, and that we surely should have more hope than imprisoning a child for the rest of his life would suggest. The judge, after deliberating on the issue for a while, concluded before rendering her verdict that the boy would be tried as an adult: "I have to believe that a child couldn't do that (kill; kill his own mother). If a child could—*that* is the death of hope."

This television show could not have been written by a psychoanalyst. Psychoanalysts know that children are fully capable of acts of murder and mayhem. Freud's most revolutionary finding was not the existence of childhood sexuality; rather, it was his belief in the death instinct and its corollary, the aggressive drive—his notion that we each harbor a killer within. This theory is still widely disputed, even among psychoanalysts. Yet, even a cursory glance at human development reveals the killers we all are. We begin, as infants, in our self-absorbed narcissism, as killers. Infants want what they want, when they want, and the needs of the other person be damned. It is only the size and the ineffectualness of infants in carrying out most behaviors that prevents them from actual destructiveness.

In observing British children during World War II, psychoanalysts were at first concerned that exposure to the atrocities of war conditions would horrify and repel the children. Yet, they discovered the contrary: rather than repelling the violence that surrounded them, the children embraced acts of violence with glee, joyfully playing on bombed sites, throwing bricks from crumbled walls at one another. Anna Freud concluded that the destructiveness raging in the outer world may meet the very real aggressiveness which rages in the inside of the child. Children have to be safeguarded against the primitive horrors of war, not because the horrors and atrocities are so strange to them, but because we want them, at this decisive stage of development, to overcome and estrange themselves from the primitive and atrocious wishes of their infantile nature.

Children can, and do, kill. It is only when they are helped to "estrange themselves from (their) primitive and atrocious wishes"—from their inherent murderousness, from the innate murderousness of which we are all, child as well as adult, comprised—that the civilizing force of love and decency becomes the stronger force.

REGARDING ADULTERY

Simultaneous to the publication of *The Dark Side of Love*, Helen Fisher published her important research on love and coupling in *The Anatomy of Love*. In combining anthropological and epidemiological data, she has come up with a startling theory that gives us a new perspective on monogamy and why extramarital affairs are so common.

Fisher initially looked at the animal world, and found that in many animal species where monogamous mating occurred, the coupling lasted only as long as it took for the progeny to become independent. She cites ornithologist Eugene Morton who has estimated that in at least 50 percent of all monogamous bird species, males and females pair only through a breeding season—just long enough to raise their young through infancy. Fisher found the same phenomenon in foxes and other wild dogs.

Fisher wondered if this could be a clue to human mating habits. Epidemiological evidence shows that the highest rate of divorce, and this is true cross-culturally—is in the fourth year of marriage. She was struck by the remarkable correlation between the length of human infancy in traditional societies, about four years, and the length of many marriages. She developed her theory: "Like pair-bonding in foxes, robins and many other species that mate only through a breeding season, human pair-bonding originally evolved to last only long enough to raise a single dependent child through infancy, the first four years...."

Fisher has effectively re-cast the folklore of the seven-year itch into a scientific hypothesis of a four-year itch, and has rendered it a biological phenomenon. She has suggested that the notion of "being in love," or, the chemistry of love is a biological, evolutionary phenomenon, and this chemistry of love has a half-life of about four years. It is serial monogamy rather than life-long monogamy that is programmed into our genes.

Yet, many couples do, in fact, stay together longer than four years. Many, of course, stay together for life. Fisher concludes that when couples decide to stay together for longer than this initial four years, they do it for reasons other than the feeling of being in love. There are, indeed, many compelling reasons to stay together for long stretches: companionship, a sense of having a place in a community, friendship, the desire to have support through old age, financial dependency.

Extramarital affairs, from Fisher's perspective, may be simply the fulfillment of our biological destiny. Yet, even with the power of this urge, some of us resist fulfilling our biological imperative. Why do some people permissively give themselves license to act according to biologic dictates, and why are others able to over-ride the alluring pull of biology in order to live their lives based on psychological, as opposed to biological principles? The answer to these questions is a complicated issue. It's an answer that is addressed in *The Dark Side of Love*. One might say that *The Dark Side of Love* begins where *The Anatomy of Love* ends.

ON NATIONALISM AND WAR

Psychoanalysts beginning with John Bowlby have studied the attachment that infants make to their mothers. Toward the end of the first six months of life, an infant can distinguish between strangers and people he knows, and he will show a tendency to only approach those who are familiar to him. Toward the end of the first year of life, wariness of strangers has erupted into full-blooded fear. It is likely that these early feelings and behaviors become, later in life, the emotional paradigm for political beliefs: the early attachment to parents provides the emotional basis for later adult loyalty to leaders; early fear and dislike of strangers provides the psychic paradigm of later adult hostility to a perceived enemy.

We are left to conclude, then, that there will always be an enemy. It is too deeply embedded within us to be otherwise. And, if there is no enemy in actuality, an enemy will be conjured; if there is no enemy who is a stranger, we will find an enemy in our midst, among us, a former friend even. From an evolutionary point of view, it is likely that our protohominid hunting ancestors found that cooperation within groups helped with defense, hunting and attack with the main threat of their day, animal predators such as lions, tigers, and leopards. But the development of early weapons minimized the danger of predatory animals, and the major source of threat was transferred over to other hominid groups who competed for the same resources. Man, then, became his own enemy. And it is, of course, a short jump to the enemy residing with you, beside you—your friend, your neighbor, even your own family.

In the mid-1970s, researcher P.D. MacLean outlined the essential neural make-up of the brain. He was able to demonstrate that the human brain is a developmental modification of older mammalian and reptilian brains. These older brains which operate from instinctive reactions are still intact and operational within us while simultaneously the newer brain, the neo-cortex, operates from reason.

MacLean's research demonstrates the biological and neurological validity of Freud's idea that aggression is innate. We can't get away from war and its derivatives, because war and its derivatives are us.

MacLean's research leads to one other compelling conclusion pertinent to love and aggression. It is from within the subcortical, ancient parts of the brain that activities such as bonding, mating, dominance striving, and aggression arise. These impulses are separate, and at times, unrelated to the newer brain, the thinking brain. The fact of the neurological embedding of these instincts is why any idea that love and aggression are rational problems, susceptible to rational solutions is doomed to failure.

Contemporary psychoanalysts have learned the lesson of MacLean and other neurologists that reason is purely a cortical function and that only cortical functions are accessible to educative persuasion. Psychoanalysis has updated itself, and no longer depends on the merely educative, interpretive interventions that Freud himself used and recommended. For any therapy to work, it must access the older parts of the brain, the parts that operate purely from electrical impulses and are responsive only to drugs, surgery, hypnosis and the like, including as well emotionally laden stimuli. The system of modern psychoanalysis developed by Hyman Spotnitz and Phyllis Meadow has specialized in the study and practice of the use of "emotionally laden stimuli,"—interventions from analyst to analysand that reach the limbic, older centers of the brain.

ON OUR FUTURE

In spite of Freud's later loss of hope for humankind as evidenced in his last, dismally pessimistic work *Civilization and Its Discontents*, psychoanalysis remains essentially an optimistic philosophy. It posits that change can be made.

Pioneering psychoanalysts and recent psychoanalytic researchers have shed light on the disastrous effects of the emotional environment to the physical, as well as mental, well-being of individuals. Renee Spitz's research informed us of a disease—now called marasmus—which is a withering away of the spirit and then the body resulting from a deprivation of maternal love. As a result of this research, we have filmed documentation of the effects of inadequate mothering. Spitz observed and filmed thirty-four infants in an orphanage. These children were rarely fondled, caressed, played with, or exposed to any of the other kinds of nourishing attention that loving mothers bestow on their children. Within three months, the babies had difficulty sleeping, had shrunken, and were whimpering and trembling. Two months later, most of them had taken on the appearance of idiocy. Within a year, twenty-seven of the thirty-four infants had died.

We see the same phenomenon, the same withering away of the life spirit leading to physical debilitation and death, in adult life, as well. Recent research of the psychosomatic components of cancer shows that cancer patients report a sense of hopelessness and helplessness—a kind of emotional dead-end—that they have encountered. And, further, the research indicates that this despair has its origins in childhood. Cancer patients, more than non-cancer patients, report difficulty in their relationships with their mothers, describing their mothers as "cold" and "distant"—surely an emotional experience something like the marasmus babies must have had.

Yet, even with the extraordinary body of work that psychoanalysts have brought to the topic of the effect of early childhood experience on physical and mental health, a mere fifteen years ago, most researchers adhered to an opposing belief. Most researchers thought that by birth, the structure of the infant's brain was genetically determined and that experience had little or no influence on the development of the personality, on the strengths and weaknesses of an individual.

Contemporary research reaffirms the psychoanalytic proposition and shows that early childhood experiences are powerful determinants in how the intricate neural circuits of the brain are wired. The genes determine only the basic wiring, the heart beat, the lungs respiring. Everything else, fully half of the 80,000 different genes in each individual, are given over to the formation and running of the nervous system: the building of synaptic connections. There are simply not enough genes to do the job necessary: that leaves experience. Experience provides the organizing framework for the child.

Experience gives to an infant the emotional tonality of his world. Experience leads a child to anticipate love and acceptance, or not. We now know enough about psychophysiology to know that all feelings, positive anticipations, or the expectation of disappointment actually have neurochemical representation in the brain.

Of course, the down side of how experience influences the brain is that there is an acute susceptibility to trauma. If the child's primary emotional experience is fear, then the neurochemical responses to fear become the building blocks of the organization of that child's brain.

Contemporary research has documented a precise neurochemical explanation of Freud's concept of the repetition compulsion. Freud stated that each individual has a compulsion to repeat the past, to recreate some essential conflict that existed in childhood, and that this compulsion of repetition is stronger even than the desire for pleasure, or, "beyond the pleasure principle." In trauma, there is the felt experience, the emotions. But there is, as well, the physiology of trauma. There is an elevation of stress hormones, one of which is cortisol. High cortisol levels during the first three years of life will increase activity in the brain structure, the locus ceruleus, involved in vigilance and arousal. The brain, then, is primed to be on hair-trigger alert.

Later in life, even as late as adult life, whenever there is an experience, a memory, even a fantasy that remotely reminds the person of the trauma, this region of the brain is activated and a new surge of stress hormones is unleashed.

When the same hormone is produced over and over again, regions in the brain responsible for other hormones, and, of course, other emotions, as well, are not being stimulated. For instance, when cortisol is stimulated frequently, the region of the brain responsible for attachment will not be stimulated. Abused children have 20 to 30 percent smaller areas in the cortex and limbic systems responsible for attachment. Adults who were abused as children have a smaller hippocampus, the region of the brain responsible for memory, than non-abused adults.

The fact of the physiological embedment of emotional experience makes emotional change all the more daunting. Emotional change is never easy. And, the link between the physiology and psychology of an individual is what makes childhood experience all the more paramount as a factor in the destiny of each of us.

Since the writing of *The Dark Side of Love*, I have become more convinced than ever that the issues of aggression and love, and a constructive expression of them, lies in what it is that we are able to give and teach to our children. Since the writing of *The Dark Side of Love*, I have become a mother, and I have come to see the raising of our children as being the most important issue for us to collectively address as a nation.

What do children need in order to grow into loving, emotionally mature adults? Children need to be talked to. The journey toward language begins in the womb where the fetus is bathed in the sounds of its mother's voice. We know that a four-day-old baby can already distinguish one language from another. French babies will suck more vigorously when they hear French spoken than when they hear Russian; similarly, Russian babies are activated more by Russian than by French. The size of vocabulary of a child is correlated with how much the mother talks to the child. The complexity of sentence structure that children use is correlated with the complexity of sentence structure that the mother uses in talking to her child. Parents today use the television as a baby-sitter. But watching television does not enhance a child's linguistic ability. Only "live" language, live interaction teaches language.

Children need exposure to a wide range of feelings. Information that is embedded in an emotional context will stimulate neural activity more than information alone. Not many of us remember what we were doing on May 31, 1976. But everyone remembers what they were doing on November 22, 1963 when they first heard that John F. Kennedy had been shot. Building synaptic connections, or what researchers call stimulation, is best done, like language, in an emotional context. Peek-a-boo, in which everybody is laughing, will stimulate a child's emotional and intellectual development far better and faster than flash-cards. Similarly, a child will learn the concept of "later" when it is attached to a trip to Toys 'R' Us as opposed to a dictionary definition of the concept. Causality, a key concept in logic, is best learned through emotion: If *I eat, Mommy smiles. Mommy wants me to eat.* This cognitive connection builds synapses in the brain.

Children need to play. The nineteenth-century philosopher, Rudolf Steiner, believed that childhood was a time for fantasy and imagination. The Waldorf schools, which have developed in order to offer Steiner's program of childhood education, dim the lights in their pre-school classes in order to facilitate the child's access to her internal world. Steiner also recommended delaying teaching reading for the child, as reading organizes the brain in a structured way. This belief, of course, flies in the face of how most ambitious mothers think. Often mothers stimulate and stimulate their children more in their quest for the ever-more perfect, ever-smarter child. There is the plight of Yeou-Cheng Ma who started violin at two-and-a-half and was tutored by her father. She excelled in her craft and won competitions until her younger brother, Yo-Yo, started cello at four-and-a half and eclipsed her. Yeou-Cheng had a breakdown at the age of fifteen. She says: "The job of a child is to play. I traded my childhood for my left hand."

Children need fathers. Research shows that children whose fathers help care for them are less likely to become violent, have higher IQ's, better impulse control and better social adaptations. Interactions between fathers and infants, like those between mothers and infants, follow a pattern that transcends class and culture. Each mother has a distinctive way of holding her child. She will do it nine out of ten times. Each father, in contrast, picks up his baby in ten different ways. Mothers play with their children in distinctive ways; mothers use toys. Fathers, in contrast, use themselves. They will use their bodies as rocking horses, monkey bars. In short, fathers do not mother. They father. Fathering is different than mothering. But it seems that the mixture of the two is better than either one alone.

Children need help with separation and the aggression that underlies the desire to be separate. They need to know that when they want to move away from their parents and when their parents want to move away from them that this is not a forever-more kind of disappearing act. Such knowledge is, most of all, what children need to be reassured of—that they can *want* to kill off the other person, but that they will not succeed. Parents need to be like those bouncing figures that keep popping up no matter how many times you punch them down. When a child tells a parent to go away, or when the child herself moves away, she is verbalizing and enacting her momentary wish to kill off her parent. She wants to kill her parent, but she wants the parent to remain alive for future reference. Children are our planet's most ardent believers in resurrection.

I find it rather astonishing that that as a culture we spend as much money as we do on the intellectual development of our children, and no money on the emotional development of our children. Psychotherapy is the only system we have developed that addresses the issue of emotional education; there is no school, no class that is part of the standard educational system that one can take to learn how to become emotionally integrated. Generally, only the most disturbed of our children receive psychotherapeutic help, and often even these are neglected.

Unfortunately, by the time most people avail themselves of psychotherapy, the therapy serves as emotional reeducation rather than primary learning: bad habits need to be unlearned; it is always easier to learn first than to unlearn and relearn later.

My hope is that in understanding more about the emotional needs of children, children will no longer raise guns to their school chums; these children as they grow into husbands and wives will no longer need to injure each other through extramarital affairs; and nations will no longer become divided within themselves. I know that this is only a hope, and perhaps it is as silly a hope as the judge in *The Practice* who believed that children could not kill. Nevertheless it is, I believe, the only hope we have.

Introduction

As a psychoanalyst, I have seen near miracles occur from the heal-ing power of love. I have witnessed depressions lift and anxieties ease. I have seen joy blossom and loneliness disappear. I have heard some claim, without apology or shame, that love has rescued them from the clutches of death itself. I have had patients tell me with a fair amount of frequency that without love, life has no mean-ing and is not worth living.

And yet, for every story of love's magic, I have heard a counter-balancing story of love's destructiveness—tales of agony and loss. I have heard of rage and vindictiveness set in motion from perceived betrayal. I've heard of rejection and loss that causes a heart pain that is as scorching as a surgical incision without anesthesia. I've heard of neglect and abuse by parents whose emotional maturity is sufficient for playing with the toys of childhood but certainly not adequate for the complex demands of adult loving. Considering how strong our need for love is, and how powerful a healing force love can be, it is astonishing that we bungle it as often and in as many ways as we do.

I have written this book because I have seen—and experi-enced—that there are better ways to love. I have learned a lesson that I (and most everyone I know) failed to learn in childhood—

that we actually need to *learn* to love well. Surprisingly, the key to a stronger love lies in our use of hate. We can love better only by making it whole, by acknowledging the full range of all our feelings, both those that are sunny and those that are dark.

LOVE'S DARK SIDE

The ways in which love's shining light turns dark are many. We may feel abandoned and lost to careless forces that seem beyond our will or control, as the one we love or want to be loved by leaves us. We may feel that some essential *goodness* or even a *badness* in us is not seen by our loved one, and we have a feeling of being fundamentally not known, not perceived. We may feel unappreciated or uncared for even by those with whom we have a committed, presumably loving relationship. Or, we may feel an emptiness in our own hearts, unable to return love to those whose love for us is unassailable. We may want to give ourselves over to the healing power of love but find our hearts are too constricted to move. Or, we may find that our hearts and our heads completely contradict each other, and we remain confused about which to follow. Even the purest and most fulfilling loves have their shadowy moments, times when loving understanding and sympathetic communications seem to have taken momentary flight.

For each of these scenarios of love's vicissitudes, for each victim of love's fickleness and disappointments, there is help and hope. Simple luck—good or bad—is rarely the cause of love's success or failure. Forces beyond one's control are usually not the cause of love's disappointments, frustrations, and pains. When we are hurt or pained by love, we feel ourselves to be hapless victims of circumstances. But love's pains and hurts are much more complex than our feelings of victimization would lead us to believe. Psychoanalysts have come to understand that we make choices for ourselves, even when our decisions are bad for us, and even though we may have no awareness of having a choice. Our decisions, wishes, feelings, attitudes, and behaviors are determined by something within us, some mysterious force at work which we call the unconscious. We are more often victims of ourselves than of our circumstances.

How we love, and how we allow ourselves to be loved, are directly related to psychological patterns developed years earlier than our current woes. Our manner of loving has its origins in our first exposure to love, during those first, helpless years of life when care and soothing from our parents were all that stood between hunger and satiation, and between distress and calmness. Although it may at first seem farfetched to directly parallel those remote early years and our adult love difficulties, it is nevertheless in understanding precisely this relationship between our past and our present that love's agonies and complexities can be unraveled and eased.

The lessons that each of us learned in childhood about love are lessons that we carry with us for many years. Our parents are our most effective teachers, even when what they are teaching us is to our decided disadvantage. We may have been taught not to expect love. Such a lesson will blind us to love's presence, even when it is there in full regalia. Conversely, we may have been taught that love is a gift to which we are always entitled, and we may delude ourselves into thinking that it's there when, in fact, it is far, far away.

LOVE AND NARCISSISM

This premise of the connectedness between early patterns and later psychological ramifications is the essential formulation of psychoanalysis, beginning with Freud. Freud identified childhood as *the* critical period of life in terms of psychological development. He understood that our emotional experiences in childhood largely determine the adults we become, and recognized that childhood is a period that needs to be managed with care and nurturance. But Freud, as it turns out, was not particularly interested in that stage of development wherein lie the origins of the conflicts that summon, most painfully, the darkest sides of love. My experience with patients has led me to believe that almost all love problems that are persistent and repetitive originate with difficulties that occur during the first two years of life—the stage analysts call *narcissism*.

Narcissism is a normal stage of development, but it needs to be outgrown. Freud felt that patients who had not yet mastered the challenges of the narcissistic phase of development could not benefit from psychotherapy. Fortunately, Freud has been proven wrong in this belief. In the last fifty years, basic modifications have been made in Freud's principles, and because of the valuable contributions of Melanie Klein, Donald Winnicott, Harold Searles, and Hyman Spotnitz, psychoanalysts are now able to help patients whose love problems have these early origins. As you read this book, you will learn about the narcissistic stage of development, and you will see why I refer to flawed loving relationships as *narcissistic love*. You will also learn how to put the lessons of these psychoanalysts into words and concepts that all of us can use in our daily life.

LOVE, HURT, AND HATE

Not all of the lessons about love that we received in our childhood serve us well as adults. As part of our love training, we are taught to fear the shadows in love's dark side—the aspects of relationships that we think will impede love or destroy it altogether. We didn't learn, for instance, that with love comes hurt and rage, pain and resentment, loss and vindictiveness—all of the hateful feelings that constitute love's other side—and that this underside of love is as inevitable and as necessary for the growth of love as the setting of the sun and the dark of the night are for the growth of plants.

Of the dark feelings that love can generate, hurt is perhaps the easiest to acknowledge. Most of us have felt pain in our loves, whether it is as fleeting as the injury from a thoughtless remark, as torturous as an unrequited love, or as deep as a loss from a failed marriage. In addition to hurt, however, there is always more. Anger, hate, and the desire for revenge—all those ugly feelings that we don't want to acknowledge as our own—are always close at hand, lurking in the dark recesses of our psyches. Negative feelings—our own toward others, as well as others' toward us—are as much a part of our day-to-day living as are all the sweet, positive feelings for which we yearn.

Psychoanalyst Theodor Reik noted that one of the primary reasons people came to him for help was the enormous guilt they felt when they realized how "abnormally" much they hated those they loved. Not only do we hate those we love, but we are drawn, too, to others' hate for us. Each of the scientific disciplines that study behavior—clinical and social psychology, animal studies, child development—finds the same curious phenomenon: Animals and men and women are often attracted to those who are kindest *and* cruelest to them.

What remains most curious about this phenomenon is that in spite of its pervasiveness, almost all of us will deny its truthfulness. Consciously, we shun our own hate and we revile others' hate. In envisioning ourselves as decent, moral, loving individuals, we will declare that hate has no place in our hearts. We may, at best, admit to passing anger, even rage, at our loved ones, but we will vehemently deny the possibility that we might actually hate them even as we love them. Of all human emotions, hate seems to be the most reviled.

Yet, in spite of our immediate revulsion for the word and the concept, *hate* is nevertheless the term that I have chosen to use. This decision needs some explanation. Hate is not, in and of itself, evil. One can hate injustice, cruelty, or poverty. Hate arises from the aggressive drive—the drive that Freud said leads us to destruction and death. But Freud reminded us that the aggressive drive can have constructive purposes, as well. Without aggression, we would have no buildings built, no concerned citizens lobbying for change, and no babies made. When I refer to hate, I mean to include both the positive and negative aspects of aggression.

I also mean more. I mean to denote the emotional feeling that is embodied in aggression when it is accompanied by anger, rage, hurt, or vindictiveness. To encompass all those meanings, I felt the word hate was the most descriptive. If at times I use the word loosely and freely, it is precisely because I invite the reader to give a personal meaning to the word that best fits his or her emotional experience.

TURNING AWAY FROM HATE

It is little wonder that we declare hate to be our mortal enemy. We have been taught that this is a feeling that is abnormal and that its presence signifies that there is something wrong, or something that should be avoided. We have been inculcated with the idea that we are bad or defective if we feel hate, especially for those we love. We have become a society that hates hate.

Yet, if we look closely at our relationships, we see that a lot of what goes on in the name of love has more to do with hate, anger, and rage than with love. Sometimes hate dresses up as love—the wolf in sheep's clothing, menacing either the beloved or the self. One of my patients continues to want to reconcile with his wife, who left him for another man, but who deigns to meet him occasionally for dinner. When I ask him why he is still interested in her, he assures me it is because he loves her. But when he talks further, it becomes abundantly clear that his professed "love" for his wife has much more to do with his insecurity as a man, his fear that no other woman will want him, and his discomfort in being close to people. This so-called love of another begins to look up-close much more like hate of self. Sometimes we feel that hating ourselves is an easier choice to make than hating our loved ones.

When we do direct our rage toward others, we seldom know how to manage our feelings. Often hate and rage flare up only at intervals, signaling a momentary feeling. Sometimes our negative emotions entirely consume what began as love. There are also times when we bury our rage so deeply that we are hardly even aware of it until we find that we are depressed, or obsessed, or physically ill, or suddenly out of control (we might even say "crazy") with our behavior.

It is here, in the symptoms of suffering, that love and hate converge. When we keep hateful feelings—essential parts of who we are—hidden, stashed away in the dark, we do not succeed in protecting and preserving love. Without some open channel to the surface, hidden feelings accumulate in the dark, subterranean area of the psyche; they rumble around and toss themselves against one another like the tectonic plates in earthquakes. When the pressure becomes too much, these forces explode, terrorizing us, opposing our rational, conscious will, and wreaking havoc on the loving relationship we thought we were keeping safe.

When we try to hide from parts of ourselves, or hide parts of ourselves from others, these castaway remnants will invariably creep up on us, unannounced and unwanted. This is particularly true when our feelings contradict our most cherished beliefs—our most basic ideas of what we want, our expectations of what we deserve, or our concept of what we ought to be. When we think one way and feel another, and when we are used to giving our thoughts and our shoulds the throne of supremacy, the intrusion of unexpected feelings can startle us.

Jung talked a lot about these hidden, unconscious aspects of ourselves. To emphasize their dark nature, he even called them the *shadow* side of our psyche. But as Jung made clear, it is not the existence of the dark feelings that is destructive to love, but rather our turning away from them.

Shadows are really just the other side of light. Our goal isn't so much to live in perpetual sunniness but to illumine the shadowy feelings in our psyches and thereby weaken their destructive power. I believe that a satisfying, devoted, precious love is possible—what I call in this book *cooperative love*—and that true love is not just the imaginative ramblings of poets, idealists, and idiots. Creating cooperative love is a challenge that each of us must assume if we are not to be enveloped by the bleak darkness of unconscious love.

The dark sides of love are in us and of us. They are not just irritating anomalies to be tolerated with disdain or acquiescence. Rather, they are integral and invaluable parts of every love relationship, and when recognized and managed constructively, actually give fullness and depth to the love experience.

SEEING OURSELVES

This book is about all of us. I have chosen, throughout the book, to liberally pepper my discussions with illustrative examples, ranging from my own patients (whose names have been changed), to fictional and mythical figures, to famous individuals whom I have never met but about whom I have read. Some stories are about people who, because of their extreme, sometimes violent, method of dealing with their passions, have crossed the line of the law and become criminals. Some of you may read these stories and find them interesting but wonder about their personal relevance. Most of us ordinary folk who are living ordinary lives do not believe that we are capable of such heinous actions as bludgeoning a loved one to death, as Richard Herrin did, or of killing nine of our own babies, as Mary Beth Tinning did. I made the decision to include these stories, however, precisely because of my belief that the line that separates normal from pathological is, at times, frighteningly thin. Protectiveness can easily turn into possessiveness; concern into control; interest into obsession. Each of us has had moments of these darkest feelings; fortunately, most of us simply don't act them out in irreversibly damaging ways.

If we look deeply within ourselves, we find that our darkest thoughts are not, in fact, so different from those of the perpetrators of horrible acts. How many of us have felt wildly jealous or possessive? How many of us have been pushed past reason by a child's behavior? Although we don't commit murder, there is nonetheless murderous rage in our hearts.

MY OWN STORY

My interest in this book and the insights within it that I share have not arisen out of mere intellectual concerns. I, too, have not been immune from love's agonies, illusions, and misunderstandings. Many of the lessons I have learned have come out of observing myself in my love relationships.

It is probably fair to say that the major emotional events of my life have been heartbreaks. The first was over Frank. I was a budding thirteen-year-old, crazy with delirium for this newly discovered entity: the male sex. I fell hard for Frank, deeply and seriously, as only a first "puppy" love can feel. I was sure that Frank was the reason for the creation of the universe. The whole of the English language had new and unexpected meaning for me, with the word "frankly"—the best word of all—in it. I expected Frank to love me wildly, as I did him. Until that time, love for me had meant warm hugs from my mother and affectionate hand-holding from my father. At the burgeoning age of thirteen, I expected love to come easily and naturally, as it had with my parents. Nothing in my life had prepared me for the agonies that came with this new love. Nothing before had brought me so close to complete despair as the day I discovered that Frank was in love, not with me, but with my arch-rival, Suzanne. This was a torture that only a youthful, all-or-nothing mind could conjure.

But, as is the province of thirteen-year-olds, my youthful resiliency got the best of me and I was soon enough on to other things and other representations of the male sex. Over the years there were David, Jay, Steve, even a marriage to Bob—relationships begun, relationships ended. All brought their various aches and pains, but all these heartaches were bearable. And then, in my mid-thirties and newly divorced, I fell deeply in love again.

Richard was, like his earlier counterpart Frank, ideal in every way. The world seemed richer, more bounteous, more beautiful with him in it. Love was as sweet as it had ever been, and we lived together for a few blissful years, I loving and mothering his two girls, my heart never failing to go pitter patter at his sight, his sound, and his touch. And, seemingly, most perfect of all, never was there a fight, or an argument, or disagreement.

But, this love was not so easy. Richard, also having come out of a divorce, was not eager to resume the responsibilities and commitments of marriage. Family life remained on the level of pretend for us. We—he, his girls, and I—looked, acted, and felt like a family, but because of his ambivalence he refused to give legal name to our union. His holding back was a constant ache for me, a chronic hurt that had become as much a companion to me in those years as he himself was.

Two years into my relationship with Richard, Jean Harris was arrested for killing her lover, Herman Tarnower, at his home. The house that Richard and I shared happened to be two doors down from where the murder occurred. This crime fascinated me. Jean Harris was a spurned lover, replaced by a younger woman, and this fact had driven her over an edge of normality. I scoured the newspapers every day, starved for more information about her and the crime. What state of mind had led Jean Harris to such an act of desperation? The physical proximity of the deed matched my feeling of emotional closeness to the situation. Although my own relationship was seemingly stable—its end was still several years away—some part of me had an inkling of the ultimate outcome. I could imagine my state of mind when the inevitable conclusion would come to pass, and I knew that my feelings would not be unlike those Jean Harris had experienced as she drove the five-hour ride from Virginia to New York, gun by her side, planning to use it on herself or possibly her lover; it probably hardly mattered which at that point. I knew that in these desperate situations, reason and concern about the future are thin barriers against the avalanche of urgent impulses pressing for discharge.

During this time, my mother was diagnosed with terminal cancer. My mother and I, dating back to my childhood, had had an uncommonly close and loving relationship. In her last, essentially bedridden year, her call to me was stronger than ever. Dutifully, faithfully, and devotedly, I made frequent trips to my hometown to be with her. But always, the pull was conflictual for me: I wanted to love my mother single-mindedly through her painful end, and yet I wanted to feel the thrill of love's promise and life's beginnings with my sweetheart. For that entire year I never knew which "love" I *should* be with and which love I *wanted* to be with.

Finally, there was an abrupt end to this conflict. While my mother was on her deathbed, Richard was still belaboring the point of his ambivalence. His phone call to me that day included a cursory inquiry about my mother's state and a prolonged discourse on the question of whether or not he loved me, whether or not he trusted me, and whether or not I was worthy of his love and trust.

That day, the day my mother died, a strength that I had not known before seized me. That day, of all days, I knew I deserved to be loved. I needed a strong, sustaining love that day, and anyone who had had an ounce of regard for me would have happily given it

to me. I was finally able to see that love's seductive power had de-
ceived me during all the years Richard and I had been together.
When I had looked at this man, I had seen only beauty; when I had
listened to him speak, I had heard only gentleness and kindness;
when I had felt his touch, I had felt only sensitivity. Yet, this was
the man who, on the day of my mother's death, had not the beauty,
gentleness, kindness, or sensitivity to love me without reservation
for even that one day of mourning.

When Richard put an end to our relationship, less than a month
after my mother's death, some core within me died. Suddenly I had
lost my mother, my lover, and two children I adored (and had imagined I would see grow up). I thought I would never heal.

But heal I have, and for a variety of reasons—some that will
sound pretty and some that will sound ugly. I had the loving support of two close women friends. I had my unwavering commitment to my work. And I had a rich therapeutic experience with my
own analyst. Through analysis and lots of hard emotional work, I
gained important insights about myself and my ill-fated attraction
to this man who, in the end, gave me so little.

In my healing, I was forced to come to terms with my own hate
and anger and desire for revenge. Every ugly wish under the sun
passed through my mind. Fantasies of taking out a contract on
Richard's life seemed too kind. Then he would just be dead. I
wanted him to suffer, as I had.

I wanted him to experience all the horrible feelings that I had
when we broke up—the incredulity, the unfulfilled desire, the
memory of those ecstasies of love that we shared, now wrenched
away from me. I wanted him to feel the doubt and self-
recrimination. (What did I do? What didn't I do? What could I have
done? Where did I fail?) All this is what I wished for him. This was
more than mere anger or resentment. This I would call hate. There
was poison in those feelings and wishes. That poison was I, for a
time.

Along the way I noticed a curious phenomenon. I noticed the
emotional freedom that came with allowing myself to experience
all those poisonous thoughts and feelings. I didn't actually *do*
anything to Richard, but as I let my anger and hate and wish for

revenge fill my being, I, seemingly miraculously, began to feel better. Paradoxically, my giving the hate its full expression finally allowed the hate to release its grip on me. The more I was able to embrace my hate without shame, the freer I began to feel.

Gradually, inch by inch, the hate proceeded along its slow path toward extinction. A day would go by and I would realize that I hadn't thought about Richard at all; and then a week, and then, finally, hate made room for something else, and joy of life and a new love flourished.

THE BOOK'S FORMAT

This book is divided into three parts. In part one, "Love's Dilemmas," we will look at the illusions and unrealistic expectations we hold about love. These illusions set us up for disappointment. Usually we attribute love's failure to the other person, or to ourselves, without recognizing that it is love itself that cannot bear the weight of our expectations. Love often falls victim to its own unrealism. If we are to know love, we must know its true nature, its underside as well as its sweet, light side. If we are to know love, we must come to understand and use constructively *all* the feelings that both love's pleasures and love's disappointments arouse—not only the ecstasy, but also the hurt and pain, the anger and hate. The bitter feelings—the ones we'd rather not have and the ones we're taught to pretend aren't in us—comprise the dark side of love.

In part two, "The Chronology of Loves," I address specific kinds of love relationships. I begin where love begins: mother and infant. This, of all loves, is thought to be the most perfect. But it is fraught with danger and difficulty, as well.

Next, we will look at that time when family, the world outside of mother and self, begins to be discovered. Loving relationships with father and siblings add richness to life, but they also lead to complex and contradictory feelings that can be difficult to manage.

Finally, we will look at sexual love. Sexual love is sometimes called romance, and sometimes marriage. Both are developmental phases of the process of our loving and being loved, but each has a different meaning. Since there is a level of commitment in marriage that sets it apart from earlier loves, I talk about romantic love and marriage in separate chapters.

Parental and sexual loves actually are not as different as they might appear. There is a lot of mutual parenting that goes on in any sexual relationship, and there is a lot of sexuality in parenting. What we'll find, though, is that here, too, the parallels between the original childhood experience and adult sexuality are awfully close. Try as we might to be better than, or different from, our own parents, the degree to which our first love experience with our parents was satisfying determines in significant ways the quality of our later loves with our partners. Patients who enter psychoanalysis specifically for sexual, romantic, or marital love problems invariably end up talking about their parents. This is not because analysts have convinced their patients that they should be talking about their parents; it is because all the loves one has are indivisible; they are all connected to one another, and they all begin with that one, first love.

Part three, "Out of the Shadows and into the Light," provides a framework within which to examine how to use constructively the negative feelings that are stimulated in any intimate relationship. When we are angry, hurt, or feeling vengeful, most of us, most of the time, either pretend that we don't feel anything at all, or we act out our feelings in words or behavior. We either *repress* or *discharge*. At times, the payment for either of these psychic operations can be very severe.

When we repress, we deny an elemental aspect of ourselves. We bury a part of ourselves that is asking, even begging, to be allowed out to see the light of day. As long as we deny the existence of any of our feelings, we prevent ourselves from being able to energetically embrace the fullness of our being. Interestingly enough, in denying our dark feelings, we also lose our capacity to fully experience our loving and joyous feelings. Emotions become muted; passions flee. There is always a dullness to the person who chooses repression as a manner of dealing with love's darkness.

The penalty for discharge as a method of psychic maneuvering is equally severe. We may lash out at another, with the wish to hurt, punish, or chastise as our primary goal. We have taken it upon ourselves to enact this role of a punitive parent for a loved one who has never asked us to do so and, not surprisingly, resents our intrusion. At other times, the object of the discharge of our rage is our own selves, our bodies or minds, leading to a host of physical and psychological ailments.

The last chapter of the book, "The Reflective Light of Psychotherapy," is for those readers who wish to continue their exploration into the nature of their love difficulties through psychotherapy. Psychoanalysis, as the first form of psychotherapy, is a process that was specifically designed for this purpose and is ideally suited to accomplish this goal.

As a psychoanalyst, I hear from my patients all varieties of impulses, thoughts, and feelings that, if acted on, would lead to all kinds of trouble and destruction. It is perhaps crucial to both our personal and global survival that we are born as helpless as we are, and stay helpless as long as we do, unable to put our destructive urges into significant action. Perhaps our growing up is, as much as anything, a lesson in learning not to turn our destructive impulses into destructive acts, toward self or other. Psychotherapy is the process by which we continue to grow, filling in what we failed to learn in childhood but need to know in order to live our lives as successful adults. It has been called by psychoanalysts an *emotional re-education,* a corrective experience to heal the cumulative effect of our emotional wounds. The last chapter on psychotherapy serves as a guide for this process.

The dark side of love makes us uncomfortable. The ugly thoughts that we harbor about both ourselves and our loved ones are frightening; rage and resentment would seem to threaten the loves we hold most dear. By ignoring our discontent, we think we can make it disappear. But, in fact, it is the very act of turning away from our hate and hurt that gives the dark side of love its destructive power. Denying our hateful feelings destroys our integrity as emotionally full human beings and destroys the possibility of relationships built on a foundation of full emotional understanding.

What we will see about the dark side of love is that any part of us that remains hidden from the clear light of consciousness is more likely to be expressed destructively. That's how the unconscious works. The more we turn away from it, the louder its voice becomes.

The love stories I tell here—both the everyday ones and the tormented, dramatic ones—could have different endings from those that leave us in despair. Most love relationships, no matter the pain, can be saved and made better with honest effort and desire. Hate, rage, pain, and hurt, when acknowledged and consciously felt, become passing shadows rather than bleak, consuming darkness. As momentary feelings, they do not manifest themselves in behavior and actions that have long-term negative consequences. It is through making love whole that we can make it better, richer, and more satisfying. That's what this book is about: making love better by making it whole. It's about growing up.

PART I

LOVE'S DILEMMAS

It is easy to fly into a passion—anybody can do that. But to be angry with the right person to the right extent and at the right time and with the right object and in the right way—that is not easy, and it is not everyone who can do it.

ARISTOTLE

The Myths of Love

A kind of "love sickness" seems to be the malady of the times. In spite of our glowing expectations about love's pleasures and joys, many of us have experienced love as dark and foreboding, or perhaps merely senseless and disappointing.

We want to believe that finding and sustaining love is as easy as taking a pill to cure a physical ailment. Yet, there is no vaccination that will prevent a loving relationship from developing a passing illness or even a terminal disease. There is no magical elixir that will forever protect love from aches and pains.

Few of us are immune from love sickness in its various forms. If you have ever wanted to shut up your screaming child at all costs because of an irritation that you can't shake; if you have ever found yourself secretly wishing, to your horror, for the death of your spouse because of a smoldering hate or rage; if you have ever been unable to control your anger, lashing out hurtfully, or even sadistically, at a loved one; if you have experienced the desperation of unrequited love or the bitterness of rejection, perhaps even reaching the point where a terminal illness would be a welcome relief—then you have come face-to-face with the dark side of love.

The root of all love sickness is our failure to recognize that love can never be what we want it to be: always comforting, bright, and strong. We burden love with unrealistic expectations that ultimately are love's undoing. I call these expectations the myths of love.

Sigmund Freud convinced us that the world is not as it seems. It was natural that Alfred Hitchcock, master of illusion, would be equally fascinated by the illusory aspects of the psyche. About love, which both Freud and Hitchcock saw as the greatest of all human illusions, Hitchcock gave his views. In his classic movie *Spellbound,* the character of Dr. Peterson, a psychiatrist, is played by Ingrid Bergman. In a moment of thoughtful reflection, she muses on the paradoxes of love: "The greatest harm done to the human race has been done by the poets; they keep filling people's heads with delusions about love. They write about it as if it were a symphony orchestra, or a flight of angels." And about the most elusive and illusionary love of all—romantic love—she opines: "People fall in love because they respond to certain hair coloring or vocal tones that remind them of their parents. The point is that people read about love as one thing and experience it as another. They expect kisses to be like lyrical poems and embraces to be like Shakespearean drama."

With keen insight, Dr. Peterson's patient in the movie, played by Gregory Peck, responds to his doctor's sardonic logic: "And when they find out differently, they get sick and have to be analyzed, eh?"

Hitchcock, following Freud's lead, was right. Repairing people's love sickness is the work of most psychotherapists today. We help people to repair broken dreams and damaged hearts. We guide them through their hurts and pains, their disappointments, their rages—their loves and their hates, and all that falls in between.

Therapists aren't the only ones to address these problems. Our pain from disappointed love has been so great and has touched so many of us that we, as a culture, have become obsessed with looking for answers that will give us respite from the agony of unsatisfying love. Talk of the "cure" for our malady surrounds us and is uppermost in our minds. We are bombarded daily in magazines, television, and books about how to combat the deep pain of our sense of unfulfilled love. Our craving for help on this subject seems insatiable, yet so often no help is forthcoming. We are left with a bewildering muddle of unanswered or half-answered questions that give us little reassurance about love's future in our lives.

The questions persist. If we don't have love, we want to know how to get it. If we have it, we want to know how to keep it. If we have it and don't worry about losing it, we finally get interested in how to give it.

LOVE'S DISAPPOINTMENTS

It is true that love, when it does occur, is a high point of human existence. Love surely does make the world go round, as the songs say. Love has inspired some of our greatest poetry and art and literature. Love built the grand Cathedral at Notre Dame, and love created the exquisite sonnets of Shakespeare, and love has kissed too many bruised knees to be counted, cooked more dinners than can be imagined, and cleaned and kept an almost endless number of homes in order.

Love may make the world go round, but it seems, at times, as though the direction of movement has been backward as much as forward. As much death and destruction has taken place in the name of love as exquisite sonnets have been written to immortalize love.

Love may be what most of us live for, but it is, as well, what a lot of us die for. Love of God has created religious wars and death and destruction throughout man's history. In the domestic arena, most murders are committed against a loved one. Experts tell us that child abuse is rampant in this country. What startles us so much about this is not only that we can be so heinous to our children, but also that the perpetrators of these crimes are those upon whom the child depends, those most intimate with the child, those whom the child loves the most. They may, in fact, "love" the child in return. Bobby Sessions, who sexually molested his stepdaughter, Shelley, from the age of eight to sixteen, never stopped protesting that he did it out of love; he just couldn't stop himself from "loving" that girl.

It shouldn't come as news to any of us that love has death and destruction as its darkest side. But even if we have not been victims of love's violent potential, not one of us has been immune to its disappointments. All of us crave loving understanding; but who among us can say that as children we felt sufficiently understood by our parents? Perhaps not perfectly understood, a feat clearly unattainable, but even *reasonably* understood—enough that our emotional growth was not impeded? Rare is such a person, in my experience.

And, as we begin our entrance into adulthood, looking forward with eager anticipation to reaping the benefits of romantic love, who can say that the shimmering promise of a gleaming future is ever attained? Even those individuals who manage to fall in love and marry the person of their dreams often eventually develop a litany of complaints about this "love" relationship. If we were to eavesdrop on the thoughts of many married couples, the conversations would not sound to us very much like love. More likely we would hear the women griping about the inattentiveness, insensitivity, or selfishness of their men, and the men complaining about the possessiveness or insecurity of their women. For many couples what started as passionate love with the promise of devotion and happiness dwindles to mundane domesticity at best. Love between the sexes most often comes to feel more like an endurance test than winning the jackpot we initially imagined it would be.

And finally, in our later years, as parents, we await the day when our children will mature and be capable of repaying us for the devotion we bestowed upon them as they grew up. Yet, how many of us can say with satisfaction that our optimistic expectations have been fulfilled? It has become almost a national pastime for adult children to tell their parents all the manifold ways in which their parents have failed them, damaged them, or abused them.

Clearly, love has disappointed us. Love may make the world go round, and love may cure what ails us, but the truth is the vast majority of us have not reaped its benefits.

With as much emphasis as we have put on love, it shouldn't really surprise us that, as much as love can exalt us, it can disappoint us, drop us down as precipitously as it made us soar. And when this happens, when we come face-to-face with this other side of love, we are stunned and feel cheated. This couldn't be love, we think, because we feel so terrible. We may retreat into an inner world, devoid of hope and optimism, emotionally untouched and untouchable.

LOVE SICKNESS

No category of love is exempt from love problems. Mothers and fathers wonder whether they're loving their children correctly; single people wonder whether they'll ever find true and lasting love; married couples long to get back to the first blush of honeymoon love they used to have. In each of these categories of love—parental, romantic, and marital—the particular symptoms of love sickness may differ widely. Some victims of this malady may suffer depression, others anxiety, still others merely a vague sense of a lack of fulfillment. But what underlies each of their complaints is dissatisfaction with their love relationships.

The ways of the hurts, pains, and disappointments of love are myriad. There are times when the one we love most of all says or does something that makes us question the validity of the entire relationship. There are times when anger, hurt, and disappointment make all attempts at communication fail and a loved one feels like an enemy. Most often these are fleeting moments, and we find our way back from the precipice of doubt, rage, or hurt to the stability of devotion and commitment. But there are also times when, despite our good will and despite our efforts, we seem to be incapable of rescuing a loving relationship that has turned dark.

Many of us have been so disappointed (or disappointing) in matters of the heart that we wonder if we should even try again. Still, like the hapless salmon who keep struggling to get upstream against all odds of success, we go on, trying again, hoping again. Our need for love is that great.

We may hold onto an illusion of pure love, rejecting any unpleasantness despite all evidence that the impulse for destructiveness always accompanies love. Or we may choose one partner after another, looking for a perfect love, never knowing that the error is our own. Some of us cling to the wrong partner until grim death parts us or some other circumstance beyond our control comes between us. Some of us live with a soul-killer because we can't quite get it into our minds that the death of our spirit will kill our bodies, too.

When love disappoints us, we may try to exact revenge, letting the poison in our feelings seep into poisonous behavior. Or we may fan the flames of our rage, because in the absence of rage there is only excruciating pain. Or we may feel nothing at all, for fear of feeling too much to bear. Some of us are disappointed even without feeling the sharp pain of love gone wrong, and we may settle into a dull sameness when the once-bright light of love turns old and flickering but not altogether extinguished.

All of our love relationships—family, friends, or lovers—encompass a potentially destructive side, because within each of us lie the seeds of aggression. Whether it is directed against the self or another, aggression appears in us at such an early age that psychologists vehemently debate the question of whether the aggressive drive is learned or innate. Whichever the case may be, children are capable of vicious acts at a remarkably early age, as anyone who has spent time in a playground knows. This aggression may be directed either outwardly or inwardly. Infants have to be routinely protected from the threatening acts of their two-year-old siblings. Even a young child is already capable of sophisticated logic, enabling him to turn his aggression against himself. A three-year-old, youngest child of a patient of mine, exclaimed, "Daddy, I think having four children is too much for you. I think it would be better if I died." Already, this child is capable of the desire for self-annihilation as a "loving" gesture to his father.

LOVING FROM THE HEART OR LOVING FROM THE HEAD?

No one ever tells us that it is necessary to learn how to love. Rather, from infancy we hear stories about princes and princesses falling instantly in love and living happily ever after. When we "fall in love" ourselves, we are unprepared for the consequences of following our heart at the expense of our head.

Sara fell madly in love with Al, a married man, and conducted an exciting romance with him, fully expecting that he would leave his wife. Two years later, after endless pleading, crying, and ultimatums, Sara finally despaired of the idea that Al would ever leave his wife. Shortly after, and clearly on the rebound, Sara met Glenn and married him. Sara's marriage to Glenn has been a good, solid relationship. They have two children, are mutually supportive of each other, enjoy their social life together, and have interesting and stimulating conversations with each other. It has been a good marriage, though somewhat uneventful and lacking in passion. Sex is infrequent and holds little interest for either of them.

Sara is in a crisis at the moment because now, six years later, Al has finally left his wife. He recently contacted Sara and they had lunch. Lunch led inevitably to bed, and Sara felt her dormant body come alive for the first time since she was last with Al. The intensity of the feelings is still there for both of them. Al is asking Sara to leave her marriage to be with him.

In the years of her marriage, Sara has made herself comfortable with her life and its absence of passion. Until Al contacted her, she had no wish to change the circumstances of her life. Leaving Glenn would be disruptive to her own children and deeply hurtful to Glenn. Yet, now that her love for Al has been resurrected, she longs to have that kind of emotional richness and intensity in her life again.

Sara's dilemma—which man she should choose to be with—is a conflict between her head and her heart. Her head (her thinking capacity) tells her that staying with Glenn is absolutely the right thing to do. When she tries to set her thoughts and feelings down on paper, every rational thought, every cogent reason leads her to the conclusion that she should preserve her marriage. It may not be fireworks, but it grounds her and her children, and has given her a solid, dependable life. For that she is very grateful to Glenn. The quality of her love for Glenn has to do with this feeling of gratefulness, and a sense of security and stability, and a rational appreciation of their life together.

Sara's heart (her emotional response), however, is sending her the opposite message. Sara knows that she loves Glenn, but their love is not an easy, affectionate love; it's more practiced and devoted. When Sara talks about Al, her eyes light up. While she has to force out the words "I love you" to Glenn, to Al they come out spontaneously and naturally. While it is comfortable being with Glenn, it is exciting being with Al. She dreams about Al when they are not together and longs to be reunited with him. It is clear to Sara that all of her feelings lead her to want to be with Al. Yet, she is unsure that this is the best decision. The conflict of not knowing which decision is the right one is torturous for Sara.

If Sara were interested in our opinion, it is probably fair to say that half of us hearing this story would come down strongly on the side of passion and feeling. This half would encourage Sara to follow the dictates of her heart. We would be cheering for the triumph of true love, and we would say to her that gratitude is a poor substitute for passion. We would even rather conveniently rationalize any ill effect her leaving Glenn might have on her children by saying that they would be helped by being raised in a household where there would be real love, rather than just stability and gratitude.

But the other half of us would, just as heatedly, argue for the sanctity and integrity of family life. Passions, we would say, come and go. Commitment, loyalty, devotion, day-to-day cooperation—these are the qualities that are constant and invaluable. Following one's heart may be fine for the romantic interludes of adolescence, but the real challenges of adulthood should be met with intelligence and logic.

This half of the population would proclaim that burning romance is intoxicating, but a romance that defies all logic is destined to become a love trap rather than a liberation.

It is true that Sara "loves" Al. She also "loves" Glenn but in a totally different way. Two people can say they love each other but mean completely different things (or one person can mean different things when love is felt toward different people). Very often the dark side of love overtakes a relationship when it becomes clear that one person's loving behavior has little in common with his or her beloved's concept of love.

We can hope in our love relationships that our personal definition of love is compatible with that of our love's object—be it parent, child, friend, sibling, spouse, or sexual partner. But because that person is a unique and different human being who is separate from us, it will never be identical. That doesn't make their love wrong or inferior, just different. Nothing we can do, say, demand, or hope will change that fact. The people we love do not love us back with exactly the same love that we give to them.

Many of us share Sara's confusion. We ask ourselves what love is. Is it excitement, or is it calm satisfaction? We want to know love's nature. Is it forever, or does it end? Is love a feeling that comes effortlessly, or is it a commitment to work toward understanding and mutual respect? Is love's origin in our heart or our head? Like Sara, we remain utterly confused about love decisions.

It is not surprising that so many of us should suffer from a lack of understanding of how to make love work in our lives. Most of us have little insight, training, or information about how to sustain loving relationships under the onslaught of daily demands, worries, and irritations. We are, as they say, "winging it" most of the time. We sail through on whatever instinctive intuition we are blessed with, but often this is not enough.

THE MYTHICAL NATURE OF LOVE

The real reason for our pervasive confusion about love has to do not so much with the inadequacy of ourselves or our loved ones, but rather with the expectations we bring to bear on love itself. We expect too much of love, and so we are doomed to confusion and disappointment. Love was never meant to be, and cannot be, all of what we want it to be. In fact, love—as we have come to expect it from both ourselves and those with whom we are intimate—is a fairly recent invention, a leisure sport, if you will. Throughout most of our time on earth, survival was what counted. Family life and its loves have been more a story of vast indifference, if not actual cruelty, than a story of affection and loving kindness.

Yet, love's mythical nature persists in haunting us. We long for it to complete us, to save us from every kind of human misery. Even as we are, at this very moment, casting doubt on love's magic, countless men and women are dreaming longingly about changing their lives through love. We believe that love should be passionate and exhilarating. We long for it to be pure, untouched by any aspect of negativity. We think it should be invariable in its intensity, and that it should last forever. We assume it will descend upon us without any effort on our part. We expect it to lift us out of our every woe. All of these are the weighty expectations we bring to our love experiences. How could we be anything other than confused and disappointed when the face that love presents to us is so different from the face we want it to have.

THE MYTH OF LOVE AS PASSION

There is an expression often applied to marriage: "Flowers for a year, ashes for thirty." Naturally, no newlywed wants to hear this. Long-lasting love—cooperative love—may have its origins in passion, but passion is not equivalent to the kind of love that has staying power.

Passion is the extreme emotion in love that is exalted above all others. It is seen as a sublime gift, the topping on the cake of the delicious dessert we call love. In the throes of intense passion, it is perfectly permissible to think, feel, and act irrationally. This irrationality is even seen as a measure of the intensity of our love. The crazier we seem, the more "in love" we must be. Passion may even contradict everything we hold dear. Passion elevates irrationality at the expense of good sense.

There is a reason why we are drawn to passion even, like Sara, against our better judgment. The strength of the attraction that passion holds for us can be understood only if we look at the actual structure of the brain, for it is here, in our neurology, that passion has its origins. To rise above our passionate inclinations requires fighting our most basic instincts.

The human brain is divided into three parts, although two of them, taken together, comprise the "old brain." The oldest part, the hypothalamic, or "lizard," part, regulates hormones and reflex action. The limbic system, or the paleocortex, governs emotions and behavior that are shared only by mammals. It is also thought that these ancestral functions of the brain are situated more emphatically in the right hemisphere of the brain. These feelings, intuitive functions of the right hemisphere, are generally understood to represent "feminine" functions.

These older parts, making up two-thirds of the brain, enable animals to survive. The fight-or-flight survival instinct is situated here. Human infants share with animals this kind of reflexive survival behavior. Infants cry when they are hungry and need to be fed, or when they are cold and need to be warmed. We are closest to our ancestral origins when we are babies—and, as well, when we are in the throes of passion. When we are in love, we return to functioning on this instinctual level. When we operate strictly from feelings, our "old brain" governs our decisions and actions. Those of us who would have encouraged Sara to follow her heart, defying logic and reason, should realize that we were encouraging her to use only that part of her brain that is oldest, most primitive, and that has the same capacity as that of a monkey in the neighborhood zoo. Because the feeling of love shares the same part of the brain as the survival instinct, it is easy to see why matters of love often feel like life or death issues.

Eventually in our evolutionary history, our human forebears matured beyond primitive feeling states and developed another portion of the brain. This third of the brain controls our thinking processes. The neocortex is responsible for thinking, understanding, conceptualizing, and communicating. It makes human beings the smartest predator and the smartest prey of all. It also has enabled us to elevate life beyond a mere survival level. Because of the neocortex, life is more varied and more interesting than searching for food and preventing oneself from becoming someone else's food. This portion of the brain is often called the "masculine" function and is situated more emphatically in the left hemisphere of the brain. Those of us who would have encouraged Sara to follow her head should know that we were encouraging her to overpower her instincts with reason.

If we look at the various messages we receive about feeling versus thinking, it is easy to understand why we have so much difficulty finding a way to unite the two. Our entire educational system solidifies the process of separating feelings from thought. From our earliest days in school we are well trained in thinking skills on all levels and are taught to use them in constructive ways. Worse, we are taught that some of our feelings are dangerous and destructive, and that we should find ways not to have them.

It is only in understanding the neurological embedment of feelings that we can begin to understand how we come to be so confused, and so foolish, about love. Because feelings are rooted in primitive, ancestral operations of the brain, it is easy to make errors in the way we deal with our feelings. For example, at times we "love" the wrong person. No amount of will or effort or persuasive coercion can change how we feel, unless we are able to change the actual neurological patterns in our brain (a process that I talk about in the last section of the book).

In matters of love, we rely on our feelings as often as we do because feelings helped us to survive long before reason and thinking came into existence. But using passion as a guidance system, without the corrective calibration of thinking, will not lead us to love.

THE MYTH OF PURE LOVE

We like to believe that love is pure and good, unpolluted by the stench of negativity. Love, for instance, is not hate. We don't hate those we love. Or do we? Just a moment of reflection for any of us will reveal that we hate, most of all, precisely those whom we love the most. Our beloveds, wondrous and perfect as they seem at times, are also the ones who invariably stimulate the most hurt and the most anger. People we don't care about are incapable of wounding us as deeply as those we love.

Hate can't be a part of love, we believe, because hate is hateful. We think that it is better unseen and unfelt. We are taught that violence arises out of hate (which it can, but need not), just as we are taught that calm arises out of love (which it may, or may not). Hate and love have been separated, and we strive for a love that is all sugar and spice and everything nice.

Love is never all warmth and brightness and security. That's *part* of what love is, but it's not *all* of what love is. Love is, among other things, a full understanding and acceptance of the complexities and contradictions of the beloved. Since we all have a dark side to our personalities, a loving relationship necessarily encompasses these complexities and contradictions.

THE MYTH OF CONSTANT LOVE

We may wonder whether or not we love our beloved if we do not always feel love. We imagine love to be constant and unrelenting, never diminishing in intensity, as though it were of one color and one fabric. In truth, we may find ourselves bored with our beloved, or longing for the company of a new sexual partner, or we may be angry enough at our beloved that we want nothing more than to flee from his or her presence. We wonder, when we are prone to such unloving feelings, if we truly love our beloved.

Fickleness is as much a part of love's nature as it is our own. Love is impermanent because feelings are always transitory. It is not our loving feelings that bind us to one another; it is rather the commitment we make to honor that love. When we demand of ourselves that love be constant and unswerving, we are giving ourselves a prescription for disaster.

THE MYTH OF UNCHANGING LOVE

Love and commitment are not the same. Commitment is a devotion to a principle of action. Commitment can be unswerving for a lifetime. Love is a feeling, and like all feelings it comes and goes. It is by nature whimsical. Love may be stronger in the morning, when one is alert and energetic, ready to meet the day, than it is in the evening, when the best thought is to take off one's shoes and belt.

As individuals, we are static only when we refuse to allow ourselves to move or be moved. Normally, we are in a process of continual change and growth. Our bodies produce new cells all the time, and if we allow our minds to roam freely, as they should, they will produce new thoughts and feelings. With all this healthy growth in an individual, how could a relationship hope to survive if it insists on remaining static? We forget that as we change, our relationships need to evolve in order to accommodate our new selves.

Love is not an absolute. It is not something that one either has or doesn't have. Love is a process, and it needs room to find its own path. The love that a mother has for her infant will not be the same love that she has when the infant becomes a teenager. The thrilling love that newlyweds feel is not the same love that a settled-in couple feels. To try to force one set of rules on a love merely because that was the original set of rules is stultifying to the deeper feelings.

THE MYTH OF ETERNAL LOVE

Just as we expect love to be forever the same, even though we ourselves are changing, we also believe that once we grasp love, it is ours forever. But where is it written that love never dies? Without nurturing and sustenance, love may well wither and fade. It *can* last forever, if we monitor its health and take prescriptive measures as needed. Left alone, however, there is no guarantee that love will prosper indefinitely.

THE MYTH OF EFFORTLESS LOVE

We want love to flow naturally and effortlessly, like a river down its bed. We hold onto this expectation as though love, and the happiness we suppose it will bring us, is a birthright, something to which we are simply entitled and for which we do not have to work. Yet, who among us would expect, at first sitting, to compose a beautiful melody or construct a lyrical poem? Just so is the burden we place on love: that it will be simple and sweet and effortless, and that we'll get it right the first time around.

The truth is, no matter our innate talents, our inherited strengths, or our acquired wealths, loving well, with a full range of emotional tonality, is a skill to be learned and a technique to be rehearsed. Its spontaneity of feeling is only the beginning.

Learning to love is a developmental task. While the *need* to love and to be loved may be instinctual, the *ability* to love is not. If our capacity to love is not developed within a certain time period early in life, we will carry a diminished capacity for love into adulthood. Our loving skills are taught to us primarily by our childhood caregivers. When the mothering we receive adequately meets our needs, we will adapt well to the world around us. Although there may be moments of frustration or fear, these feelings will not overwhelm us, nor will they become the defining attribute of our psychological stance in the world. They pass easily and quickly, and we return to the basic foundation of love in both action and feeling with which our good mothering provided us.

When there has been an inadequate match, however, between our infantile needs and the mothering we receive—for example due to our mother's diminished capacity for love—psychoanalysis shows that we are left with an abiding sense of fear, impermanence, or insecurity. These are feelings that persist throughout our lives. Although in states of love we may momentarily escape them, these painful feelings live just below the surface of consciousness and will almost always find times to erupt. Usually they announce themselves when the first blush of new love has worn off and the disappointment over the loss of idealized love has begun to set in.

THE MYTH OF LOVE AS A PANACEA

We believe that love not only feels good but also is good for us. We believe that it will rescue us from depression, from feeling unloved and lonely, and from just about every kind of human misery one can imagine. We long for love to sweep us off our feet and transport us to a new place, a better place, a place we have never known before. And, indeed, in the beginning of love it often seems as though our dream has come true. Love *does* bring us to new heights of feeling, new awarenesses, sensations, and sensitivities.

But, as we all find out sooner or later, love takes us away from our selves and our worries and unhappinesses only momentarily. It may give us a much valued reprieve from what ails us, but ultimately we end up coming back to the same old lives, the same old selves with the same old disappointments and frustrations that we had before love cast its sweet scent in our direction.

THE MYTH OF UNCONDITIONAL LOVE

More than anything, we want to be loved for exactly who we are. We want this absolute love even when we behave unlovably, when we feel to others like a porcupine with his quills raised. We want to be loved, not for what we *do* but for what we *are*, as though deeds were peripheral to who we are.

Only infants can get away with being adored while doing nothing for the other person. We feed infants, bathe them, clothe them, comfort them, and in return we get a smile or two and the satisfaction of having a clean, full, clothed, comfortable baby. We forgive such a one-sided relationship because we know neediness is in the nature of infants and we recognize that they aren't able to give back very much. We do all this giving, knowing that it is not endless, and that one day the infant will mature into a loving adult.

In our growing-up process, we must learn to move beyond the infantile position of expecting to be adored for no reason. One popular but unconstructive game couples like to play with each other is "You give to me and I'll give to you—but you go first." One cannot be on the receiving end of love forever without doing something for the beloved. A lopsided love is not what I would call mature cooperative love.

THE MYTH OF SPONTANEOUS LOVE

We think of love as something that comes to us new and fresh, unrelated to past experience. Part of its thrill lies precisely in its novelty. Love is most exciting and most fulfilling, we think, when it breaks from any past experience we have had of unhappy love. Romantic love is experienced as the one true love that will repair the damage incurred from an unhappy childhood.

We like to think that we have chosen our beloveds based on their unique qualities. We see a special "something" in them that makes them stand out from all the others.

Our choices of our loves are not as free and spontaneous as we like to think. Preferences for people are as much a learned skill as are preferences for books or music. We may have acquired good judgment or bad, depending on the quality of help we had in our formative years, when we first learned that choices were possible. We may choose beloveds who are as good for us as crunchy vegetables and whole grains, or as bad for us as sugar and lard.

Most of all, we choose what is familiar to us. In love, the acorn never falls far from the tree. We pick someone who embodies the best or the worst qualities of our original beloveds, our parents. People often describe their initial attraction to their beloved as being a sensation that is oddly familiar to them but which they can't quite place. Sometimes they may finally have a revelatory memory that this beloved behaves in a manner "just like my dad (or mom) used to."

In parenting, too, we expect that our love will flow toward our children freely and spontaneously, no matter the quality of our own childrearing experiences. New mothers and fathers silently pledge that they will do better than their own parents did. Yet, how we parent always will be determined, in part, by how we were parented. Even with our good intentions, we are likely to repeat the same mistakes our parents made. Spontaneity actually appears in little measure, even though we may be hard-pressed to identify the forces guiding our behavior.

LOVE AS A NEW INVENTION

Love has become so much a part of our culture that we assume that it has always been with us. However, most of civilization has lived without much love. Like all other advances in civilization, love had its own set of preconditions before it could flourish. When survival is all that matters (as has been the case for most of the time that we have been on this planet), when life is filled from sunrise to sunset with the activities of ensuring that you'll be there to see the next sunrise, there is little room for love. Love and affection were traditionally a barely glimpsed luxury. For most of the aeons that have passed since the primeval mother of humanity first stretched up on her hind legs, "loving," whether between children and parents or between sexual partners, resembled something closer to instinctual bonding than what we have come to think of as love.

The history of humanity and of our prehistoric ancestors reveals that hate has been as much a part of our cultural evolution as love, and has been, as often as not, the cornerstone of our cultures. The earliest known picture depicts men killing one another. As well, our ancestors who wrote the Old Testament trace our lineage back to Cain, the founder of civilization, the man who built the first city and invented agriculture; Cain, the murderer, who killed his own brother.

Marital love, like all loves, is a relatively new invention. Adam and Eve, who could be considered to represent the first prototype of marital love in Western civilization, must have had a difficult marriage. For their discovery of sex, they were banished from the Garden of Eden. Since then, their sex life and the sex lives of all their descendants have been infused with guilt and anger. And, too, one of their sons murdered the other. Not a happy home life.

Ancient Greece, the culture to which we feel the most indebted, can be described more accurately as a hate culture than a love culture. The aspect of sexual love that we know the most about (from Plato) was homosexual. Though homosexuality was freely practiced at that time, it was in quite a different form from what we see today. Homosexual love was limited to the love of an older man for a younger, prepubescent boy. Only the older man could initiate the sex act (which was limited to thrusting his penis between the legs of the boy), and the boy was cast aside after he passed puberty. Thus, in this supposed "love" relationship, we see those of higher status pursuing and discarding those of a lower status.

In the historical past women were rarely treated to adult love.

Women had to marry in order to exist, and marriage had nothing to do with love. Women were imprisoned, literally and psychically, within their marriages for the entirety of their lives. It was, as well, commonly believed that if a flame of love between the sexes should briefly flicker, the penalty for this stolen pleasure would be high. (For example, look at Romeo and Juliet or Tristan and Isolde. Those fictional prototypes of love could hardly be said to have fared well!) If love did flourish, it was usually in an adulterous relationship because it rarely existed within the marriage; the automatic penalty for adulterous indiscretion was death. Even in the courtly love of the Middle Ages, when women were presumably adored, there was a high price to pay for love. Women were so idealized that men routinely sought to prove their worth by galloping off to fight wars, effectively abandoning their cherished women.

Because women traditionally knew nothing of loving or being loved, the abuse of children was inevitable and socially acceptable. Throughout history children were objectified; they were seen as mere possessions not worth much more than newborn animals. In some cultures it was taken for granted that parents had the right to use, abuse, or kill their offspring, either whimsically or for practical reasons. Such abuse of children is documented in the world's great literature, from the ancient story of Oedipus, who was cast out by his parents to die, to the novels of Charles Dickens, documenting the rampant abuse of children in nineteenth-century England.

The reality of love is that we're still practicing how to do this recent cultural innovation, and we're not, for the most part, very good at it yet. Mostly what we're not good at is managing all the bitterness and disappointment and pain that love brings.

Love is a feeling, but it is a commitment to behavior, as well. It is neither pure, nor effortless, nor constant and unchanging. It may heal us and assuage our wounds, but it is not a panacea. It is eternal only if we take care of it and don't change our minds about it. It is unconditional only if we're lucky, and then only when we're infants. And while it may feel new and thrilling and unlike anything we have ever experienced, we unknowingly reach for the familiar. Most challenging of all, love cannot exist without hate.

Love cannot be separated from its dark side. Hurt, and the hate that underlies every hurt, accompanies every love experience. If we are going to get better at loving, we first need to get better at managing all the painful, bitter feelings that we experience as anathema to love but which, no matter how hard we try, just won't go away.

The dark side of love that we call hate exists whether we want to know about it or not. Hate is the feeling that causes us the most trouble. Hate is perhaps the hardest of all for us to acknowledge as a part of who we are. But what we will discover about this so-called "negative" feeling is that it is not just the inevitable burden or price we pay for joy and comfort; rather this dark side of love—acknowledged, understood, and used properly—is an integral, invaluable, inevitable, and absolutely necessary part of loving and being loved.

Make no mistake. Hate is strong medicine. It is every bit as powerful as love, but most of us simply don't know how to use it or what to do with it. I am going to propose the startling idea that hate—when understood and managed properly—can be a powerful healing force. If love can hurt, as we all know it can, hate can heal.

CHAPTER 2

Loving Love
and Hating Hate

We are a culture in love with love. We know that love feels good, that it comforts us in both good times and bad. It feels too exquisite and promises too much for us not to want it. And so we search for it, connive for it, and sometimes pursue it with an insatiable hunger. Some of us want love so badly that it becomes the cornerstone of our lives. It is, presumably, the only "real" reason for the major decision of our lives, the choice of a spouse.

Research confirms the importance of love. Our modern interest in the power of love began with Freud, who was the first scientist to take love as a theme of serious concern and investigation. In 1909, Freud proposed to the mental health community that an Academy of Love be created to study this mysterious force. Freud had become convinced, after much exploration and experimentation, that the urge to love and be loved is a powerful biological force. Love, he maintained, is not a luxury but a drive as innate as the need for food, air, and water. Freud felt that if we understood more about love, we would take steps to alleviate some of the human misery and suffering that comes from the absence of love.

It wasn't until the end of Freud's life that the real difficulty in achieving love became apparent to him. In his last treatise, *Civilization and Its Discontents*, Freud made an admission, with much sadness and resignation, that arose out of his having witnessed in his lifetime unparalleled forces of destruction. One World War and the Nazi brutality as the harbinger of yet a Second World War had taken their toll on Freud's earlier optimism. His final belief about man's future was that hate and rage and their destructive potential are as powerful a force as love and love's healing potential. Love and hate cannot be separated, because they are both in us in equal measure.

WHAT LOVE IS AND WHAT HATE ISN'T

Popular notions about love come not only from our experience of love but from what we hear about love. We hear about it in songs, books, movies, and from our parents reminiscing about their blissful romance. The problem with all these popular notions is that love is idealized, and its essential ambivalence is ignored.

In recollecting love, we all too easily leave out the frustrations, anger, hurt, and fear that are inevitable accompaniments to the good feelings. Our ability to "forgive and forget" is one of the skills that enables us to sustain a resilient love. But this ability is, as well, one of the greatest dangers of love. When we are in love, or remembering love, we are inclined to deny hostile feelings that are present and that need to be acknowledged.

Just as we maintain that love is pure and good, we hold onto, just as ferociously, the idea that hate is bad. But hate, like love, is just a feeling. It is, like love, an emotional lens through which we see the world and filter our experience.

Hate is neither evil nor malignant, nor even necessarily dangerous, as we are wont to believe. It is only when hate is translated into destructive action that it becomes evil. Hate, as a feeling, is part of our human condition. It is part of the very fabric of our emotional makeup. It is absolutely inescapable. Yet, few of us have had any training or any experience in the constructive management of our feelings of hate. The ability to recognize hate—to feel it as well as detect it—is an essential ingredient in the building of what I call a strong *psychological immune system*. This system of immunity, discussed later, is a valuable protector against both psychological and physical illnesses.

THE NECESSITY OF LOVE

In 1945, with the world still reeling from the global hate expressed in the massive destruction of two World Wars, the charter of the United Nations was signed. It was an organization whose express purpose was based on precisely the same principle as psychoanalysis: the idea that talking is a more constructive channel for the communication of differences and hostilities than action.

In 1950, a group of psychoanalysts was commissioned by the United Nations to study the importance of maternal love. Psychoanalysts John Bowlby and Rene Spitz took hold of Freud's vision that love needed to be studied scientifically, and as a result of their research gave us precise information on the positive power of love and the disastrous effects of its absence.

Spitz's research informed us of a disease that had not yet been given a diagnostic label. The disease—now called marasmus—seemed to be a kind of love sickness, a withering away of the spirit and then the body from a deprivation of maternal love. As a result of this research, we have filmed documentation of the effects of inadequate mothering. Spitz observed and filmed thirty-four infants in an orphanage. Although their physical needs were adequately attended to, these children were rarely fondled, caressed, played with, or exposed to any of the other kinds of nourishing attention that loving mothers bestow on their infants. Within three months, the babies had difficulty sleeping, had shrunken, and were whimpering and trembling. Two months later, most of them had taken on the appearance of idiocy. Within a year, twenty-seven of the thirty-four infants had died.

Infants are not the only ones to die for lack of love. It is a well-observed phenomenon in older couples as well. Two lives joined together for many years may feel very much like an inseparable whole. So when the bond of love between the two is broken by death, the remaining partner has indeed lost a part of his or her own life. It is not uncommon for this person to die shortly after. Most of us know personally of such cases.

In my own life, I remember a most startling example in a very dear eighty-eight-year-old friend. Before the death of his wife, Tony was in robust health and walked a hilly one-mile path every day. Three months after her death, he, too, died. Doctors could find no specific cause for his decline and death. But I know that after sixty-four years of living with and depending upon his wife, he died of love sickness.

We now recognize the loveless origins of those in our society who are the most psychically damaged, and who, in return, damage us back. Psychopaths are people who were raised without love and who feel that the emotional climate of the world is that every man is out for himself. They learn to manipulate others for their own needs. Sometimes they strike out from that internal void that is caused by love's absence. When they do, the act is an effort to remove whatever impediment stands in the way of their getting exactly what they want; unfortunately, that impediment is often a human life.

In a similar vein, studies on physical abuse reveal that the abused in our society become abusers. Mothers who abuse their children, husbands who abuse their wives, children who abuse their pets are themselves the products of love deprivation. And so we all, as a society, pay a high price for lack of love.

It is no wonder that we have become interested in—one might even say obsessed with—loving love. Its absence kills.

LESSONS IN HATING OUR HATE

As in love as we are with love, so strongly are we in hate with hate. Each of the variations of hate, and there are many, is considered a "bad" emotion.

We are taught from an early age that hate is destructive and that the feeling of hate is to be avoided at all costs. We learn that it is an emotion that doesn't really have a place in our hearts if we want to be emotionally healthy or spiritually attuned. We have been led to believe that hate is the progenitor of evil, destruction, and devastation. We have learned this lesson from our parents, who threatened to punish us if we showed too much hate (especially toward them), and from our spiritual leaders, who have warned us that hate will morally poison the hater. Even philosophers and psychoanalysts are not immune to thinking ill of hate. Rebecca West agrees with Freud that "hatred necessarily precedes love in human experience," but then assumes that hate is "an early error of the mind, which becomes a confirmed habit before reason can disperse it."

The pervasiveness of the misguided lessons we receive about hate is well illustrated in a television editorial by a popular New York newscaster. On April 7, 1990, a verdict was reached in the Robert Golub/Kelly Ann Tinyes murder trial. A teenage boy was convicted of brutally sexually assaulting and then murdering his pretty and, by all accounts, innocently sweet fourteen-year-old neighbor.

The verdict of second-degree murder had varying effects: It horrified the boy's family, who believed firmly in his innocence, and outraged the parents of the murdered girl, who felt the verdict to be insultingly lenient. Both families, in furies of rage and hatred, screamed harsh words of vengeance at each other in the courtroom after the announcement of the verdict. Newscaster Rolland Smith responded in his editorial:

> ". . . hate will not bring back Kelly Ann Tinyes, nor will it help Robert Golub live with the terrible thing he's convicted of doing, nor will it validate the family's claim that he is innocent.
>
> "Hate is a dangerous emotion. When directed at another, it has just the opposite effect. It does nothing to the intended recipient, but it destroys the hater from inside. It's addictive, cancerous and infectious. The great teachers throughout the ages caution us about the power of hate. It's as strong in its ability to hold pain as the power of love is in releasing it."

Rolland Smith's words are eloquent, and I will admit that I was moved when I first heard his editorial on TV. But Smith's lesson to us about hate fails to make an important point. It is true, as Smith said, that hate does possess tremendous destructive power. But it is also true, and he does not say this, that hate possesses tremendous constructive power. Hate can be a force for change, even a force for life.

Rolland Smith's lesson about hate undoubtedly fell on at least a few deaf ears that day. For the two families who were victimized by this senseless crime, hate, outrage, and fury were the only feelings possible at that moment. To advise them to cast aside their hate, to set aside their outrage, was the equivalent of telling them not to acknowledge the only part of them that was alive. Their idea of revenge—whether it be the wholly inadequate form of publicly screaming, or praying for justice in another world—may have been all that stood between them and utter despair. Their anger and desire for punishment might have been, ugly as it was to see, the only fuel they had to keep themselves emotionally alive. Hate gave them life.

Most of us learned lessons about hate from our parents, whose value systems we are most likely to imitate and to pass on to our own children. One family, whose home I visited, seemed like a normal, well-adjusted family with three children who were sweet and gracious. One of the children, the oldest, generously offered to bake a cake to celebrate my visit, and enlisted the help of her ten-year-old sister. As she was separating the egg yolk from the white, some of the yolk accidentally slipped into the mixing bowl, and with irritation in her voice she complained, "Oh, I *hate* it when that happens!" The ten-year-old promptly chastised her sister, reminding her that she shouldn't have used a four-letter-word. Puzzled, I asked what she meant. With all the fervor of a religious fanatic, she answered that the four-letter word was "hate." Apparently, the rules and values of this family were such that hate was a feeling that was not even allowed verbal articulation. As the simple cake-baking exercise showed, hate is going to be present whether it is permitted or not.

As a culture, we have come to believe that hate and all of its manifestations aren't lovable and that we won't be lovable if we allow them expression. We have been taught to hate our hate.

THE MYTHS OF HATE

Just as we have preconceptions about love, so, too, do we have preconceptions about hate that have led to our summary dismissal of
hate. The myths of hate are as misleading and as destructive to mature love as the myths of love.

We believe that hate is destructive—that it will destroy both the
person who hates and the person who is hated, much as Rolland
Smith warned us. In this belief we fail to make the distinction between the *feeling* of hate and the *use* of the feeling. Hate is destructive only when it is translated into destructive behavior.
Destructiveness can arise from hate, but it is not an inevitability.

We believe that hate cannot be contained—that once we set a
match to our hateful feelings the resulting flames will rage out of
control. In fact, just the opposite occurs. It is precisely when we
don't allow ourselves to acknowledge our hateful feelings that they
gather ever more destructive potential.

We believe, too, that hate can be banished, that we can wish or
will it away. We feel that it is a failing on our part if we cannot find
the means to eliminate it from our psyches. Yet hate, like all other
feelings, has its roots in both our ancestral origins and in our childhood experiences. It cannot be banished, nor should it. The aggressive drive, of which hate is a component, protects us from our
enemies.

We believe that hate is a regression to an infantile or animalistic
mode. We don't accept that hate exists in mature adults, for it is a
feeling, so we say, that is reserved for either the children or the
bestial. We reassure ourselves that certain acts—for example, the
Nazi slaughter of millions—are inhuman aberrations. Yet psychoanalysts who have studied human behavior in its most extreme
manifestations of abuse invariably conclude the absolute humanness of these acts. In referring to the Nazi tragedy, psychoanalyst
Heniz Kohut says:

> But the truth is—it must be admitted with sadness—that such
> events are not bestial, in the primary sense of the word, but that
> they are decidedly human. They are an intrinsic part of the

human condition, a strand in the web of the complex pattern which makes up the human situation. So long as we turn away from these phenomena in terror and disgust and indignantly declare them to be a reversal to barbarism, a regression to the primitive and animallike, so long do we deprive ourselves of the chance of increasing our understanding of human aggressivity and of our mastery over it.

Hate is, as Kohut says, decidedly human and decidedly adult.

We believe, finally, that hate is contrary to divine will, that it represents the evil part of ourselves, and that when we hate we become evil and capable of doing evil things. In believing this, though, we do not become more human; we become *less* human. Hate is a human emotion of which every man, woman, and child is capable. It was Jesus' insight into the inevitability of this feeling in each of us that led him to utter these words in Luke 14:26:

> If any man come to me, and hate not his father, and mother, and wife, and children, and brethren, and sisters, yea, and his own life also, he cannot be my disciple.

HEALTHY HATE

Hating our hate has profound negative consequences. Hating our hate is hating a part of ourselves, a part that gives us valuable information about who we are, the world around us, and the intersection between the two.

As much as we like to malign hate, we have to admit it has its advantages. If we didn't hate pain, how would we learn to keep our fingers out of the alluring fire? If we didn't hate injustice and inequality, how could we be motivated to correct it? If we didn't hate being treated unfairly or being abused, how would we defend ourselves? Recognized and used correctly, hate can be healthy.

In fact, there is as much scientific research documenting the damaging effects of too little hate as there is evidence of the harmful consequences of too little love. A host of physical conditions, including ulcers, headaches, backaches, colitis, allergies, and even cancer have been shown to be—on occasion or in part—related to a suppression of "negative" feelings. The *Pathological Niceness Syndrome*—a pattern of promiscuous, indiscriminate niceness at all costs, even to the point of sacrificing one's own emotional integrity—has been well documented in its link to individuals with cancer, as well as a host of psychosomatic conditions. People suffering from this syndrome have as their paramount goal the avoidance of anger and of being disliked. They strive not to feel anger, and they strive even more strenuously not to have others feel angry toward them. They repress all feelings of hostility, envy, competitiveness, jealousy, and resentment. Yet, without these "negative" feelings, a person becomes compliant, passive, selfless, and overly anxious to please—in short, a miserable shadow of a person.

Most of us, at some point in our lives, wish that someone we love would die. Married couples think this about each other; children think it about parents; parents think it about their children. When these thoughts enter our minds, we recoil in horror, hating our own thoughts and ourselves for having them.

One of my patients, Emily, finds herself frequently wishing her son would die. Her son had childhood leukemia two years ago, and though he is robust and healthy today, she is nevertheless plagued with the uncertainty of his life. She feels guilty when she leaves him home with the baby-sitter; she represses any anger she feels toward him when he acts uncooperatively. The uncertainty of his life has made her own life almost unbearably difficult. She told me that being in the house with her son is like "holding my head underwater, and I only come up for air when I go to work." Emily imagines that the only way she can find her way back to her own life, to her own sense of herself as a separate individual, is through her son's death.

Hate, sometimes manifested as the desire for the death of a loved one, is often the only means we have of separating ourselves from others. Fantasies of a loved one's death serve as compensation for a relationship in which the lives and minds of two people are too closely intertwined. Hate is a sign that there is a striving toward individual development. It is a natural by-product of a healthy process.

Hate also sustains us when the pain of loss is too great to tolerate. It intervenes until another feeling can take its place. The widow of southern black activist Medgar Evers gives a compelling account about the usefulness of her own hate in dealing with the brutal slaying of her husband in the 1960s:

> The sounds of Dixie being played on the radio raised all kinds of feelings of hatred. The voice of all kinds of elected officials, particularly the governor, made this heat from the pit of my stomach rise from my chest to my throat and spew out . . . All I could see was the color of skin and I hated everyone at that time who was white. Hatred was such a strong force. I'm not sure that I would have existed without that hatred. It gave me a fire and a fuel to keep going. That's a part of what hatred does. If I had not had that strong hatred at that moment, I would have collapsed.

WHY HATE IS HERE TO STAY

Although it is true that love can be tender, warm, cozy, nurturing, and supportive, its fulfillment also demands aggression—a determined pursuit to possess something special, to be near someone, to share interests and lives, and to attain security and comfort. If we are consistently gratified and obtain all the things we seek in a love relationship, there is no frustration. But how realistic is that? What if we are thwarted in our campaign to have everything our way? What if our parents persist in treating us as incapable children or our own children defy our wishes? What if our siblings invade our privacy or a lover becomes emotionally distant? What if our spouse spends too much time away from home or reacts with insensitivity to our feelings?

In expecting more from a beloved than he or she is willing or able to give, or thinks of as a part of the "love contract," we fall victim to the unrealistic promise of love. When this happens (and it always will), hate emerges out of the darkness, and we find it in its rightful place alongside the positive forces of love. This happens to all of us; no one is immune. If we are to experience a mature, full love, then we are also going to feel hate. This hate isn't necessarily as overt as anger with a loved one; it may assume the face of disappointment, self-deprecation, or even a psychosomatic illness. But whatever the particular manifestations of disappointed love, once we recognize them we become fearful that our love has been forever lost. Since we have been taught that love is not hate, we conclude that a love infused with hate is not a true love. But trying to exorcise hate is not possible, not advisable. Hate is here to stay.

Hate, a child of the larger force of aggression, is inevitable in a loving relationship, because as soon as two people are together, somebody is going to want something from the other. One person is going to make demands on the other and vice versa. As long as they are in agreement about what they each want to give and receive, there will be no problem. But because they are separate human beings, it is not possible for that agreement between them to last indefinitely. Sooner or later the pleasant agreeableness will break down, and the aggression will have elements of anger and hate.

Hate is also unavoidable because it is in our ancestral origins. It exists in our genes and our biology. Ethologists, who study the social behavior of people from different cultures, have found hate, and its expression, to be a universal phenomenon. Throughout the world, transcending culture and geographical distance, human beings use particular behaviors to indicate hostile intent. These include snarling, fist-clenching, foot-stamping, arm-rotating, and vocalizations. Eibl-Eibesfeldt notes that these behaviors all have the effect of giving the "sensation of a mild thrill." Hate, as well as love, can feel good.

It is probable that love and hate evolved side by side. Early on, our prehuman ancestors learned that cooperation (a forerunner of love) was indispensable for survival. The search for food, the care of infants, the defending of oneself and one's group—all these activities were performed better and more easily when cooperation prevailed.

But in spite of the benefits of cooperation and harmony, peacefulness was often shattered. We couldn't, for instance, convince the lions and tigers that peacefulness was a better way to live, and so we needed to develop the ability to defend ourselves and to attack. In fact, at times we even needed to defend ourselves against our own kind. According to authority William McNeill, marauding bands of men became experts in specializing in group violence, preferring a parasitic existence off other men and claiming for themselves food and commodities that had been produced by others. To survive in an environment where acts of hate were levied against us, we needed to learn how to hate equally successfully in order to survive.

Marauding bands of men may have been the first organized form of hatred, but man has been at war with himself ever since. We have always had war. This fact alone should give us a clue as to the inevitability of our hate feelings. Norman Dixon, a scholar on the psychology of war, has proposed that peace is a state in which our warlike propensities are merely sublimated or repressed.

Hate developed side by side with love because in order to have friends, you need to have enemies. In a world devoid of most luxuries, where survival was what counted (the world of proto-hominid), friends were defined as the ones who didn't eat you or, at the least, who didn't eat what you ate (and didn't have to kill you to get your food). The only hope of survival was to pal up with people who had no interest in killing you. If you don't know who wants to help you, you won't know who wants to hurt you.

Although it may seem paradoxical, it is nevertheless true that if there is not enough hate, there is not enough love. If there is not enough hate, it must be conjured up in order to stimulate cooperation. Uniting against a common enemy is the quickest way to bring squabbling factions together.

Conjuring up hate in order to stimulate love is a trick that both contemporary politicians and psychotherapists know and use. If you want to mobilize a nation, arrange to have an enemy who threatens your survival. George Bush's popularity as President, as well as his patriotism in the country, reached an all-time high during America's war with Iraq in 1990. Similarly, psychotherapists who are successful in getting their patients' aggression directed toward the therapist (away from the loved ones) discover that, seemingly miraculously, the patient's relationships with those in his "real" life become more loving.

But these are tricks that perpetuate separating love and hate. What we need is not to stimulate wars in order to feel love, but rather to learn how to hate in peacetime and peacefully. What we need is not to conjure up enemies in order to feel love, but to know that we can love our enemies and hate our loved ones.

THINKING IN ABSOLUTES

Life is easy when those we love live close to us and those we hate live far away, or when those we love look like us and those we hate look different. Then it is clear whom to love and whom to hate.

In premodern times, the distinction between "us" and "them" was clearer than it is today. For the native tribe the Mundrucus of Brazil, the distinction between friend and foe was embedded within their language. They were able to distinguish easily between themselves, whom they referred to as people, and the rest of the population of the world, who were spoken of as the equivalent of huntable animals. Our own language, too, retains a vestige of this distinction between friend and foe, based on the idea that only strangers are enemies. The Latin origin of the word "hostility" is *hostis*, whose original meaning was "stranger." It's easy to keep track of whom you're supposed to hate if all the people who are unfamiliar to you are the enemy.

Evidence suggests that infants also think in absolutes and have not yet developed the complex psychological mechanism that permits the acceptance of love and hate existing together, or of a loved one being an enemy. Love and hate are kept separate.

As infants, we are able to separate love and hate as easily as we do because of a psychological mechanism that is imperative for our psychic survival in early infancy. But danger arises if we continue to carry this psychic operation with us even when our need for it has been outgrown. This psychic mechanism, *splitting*, was first described by Melanie Klein. It means that we, and the world around us, are seen in either-or terms. Klein called it *all-good* and *all-bad*.

Imagine a young infant's confusion over the fact that the good mother, who feeds, satisfies, and relieves the infant from distress, is the same person who fails, at times, to do all these things. Inconsistent behavior is hard for us to fathom at any age, but it is particularly threatening to an infant, who is totally dependent on good mothering. In order to preserve the integrity of the good-mother image, the infant perceives the good mother and bad mother as separate mothers. Good and bad are split from each other. The loved "good" mother is, then, effectively protected from the hate of the infant.

This clear distinction between good and bad continues throughout infancy. By the end of the first six months, the child can distinguish between strangers and people he knows. It is surely not coincidental that the first signs of anger are manifested within this same time frame. The infant shows a marked preference for those he knows and a wariness for those unfamiliar to him. This uncertainty develops into a full-blooded fear around the end of the first year, and no matter how much reassurance the mother gives that "the nice lady [who is a stranger] means no harm," the infant refuses to be reassured. Fear may be a part of what the infant experiences, but there is anger and hate in those wails, as well. Paralleling the primitive mind of native tribes like the Mundrucus, the infant knows that it is an "us" and "them" kind of world.

Psychoanalyst Bruno Bettelheim shows how fairy tales reveal to us the true concerns in a child's unconscious. One of the most prevalent themes dealt with in fairy tales is the split between the good and the bad mother. Story after story tells of a cruel mother (or stepmother) and the opposing good fairy godmother, who rescues the poor beleaguered child and transforms her into a princess or gives her her knight. In writing about this seemingly magical process of transformation, Bettelheim refers to how Little Red Riding Hood's grandmother suddenly turns into a wolf wearing the kindly old lady's clothes:

> How silly a transformation when viewed objectively, and how frightening. . . . But when viewed in terms of a child's ways of experiencing, is it really any more scary than the sudden transformation of his own kindly grandma into a figure who threatens his very sense of self when she humiliates him for a pants-wetting

accident? To the child, grandma is no longer the same person she was just a moment before; she has become an ogre.

For the child, knowing that the person whom he hates is the same person whom he loves is often too frightening a thought even to contemplate.

FUSING LOVE AND HATE

When we fail to recognize that people can be both bad and good at the same time, we are stuck thinking in infantile terms, unable to move beyond this good-and-bad splitting mechanism. An example of this dynamic playing itself out in adulthood can be seen in the Linn family. Laurie and Dave Linn were having serious disagreements about their teenage daughter. Dave's point of view was that Meri was an adventuresome, fiery youth, willing to spread her wings to experience life's varieties. Laurie, on the other hand, saw Meri as unruly, undisciplined, and disrespectful of the family's need for order and regularity. They never knew when Meri would be home for dinner. She always took off on the weekends with her friends, her mother suspecting that she was doing disrespectable, perhaps illegal, things, her father believing that she could and should be trusted and that Meri was just "out for a good time."

Harmony in this family was restored only after Laurie and Dave came to understand that they were both locked in an infantile manner of handling their positive and negative feelings toward their daughter. Laurie could see only all-bad; Dave could see only all-good. For resolution of this family's difficulties, good and bad had to become fused. Dave had to recognize that there was a rebellious aspect to Meri's behavior, that, in fact, Meri did derive some pleasure from being so provocative to her mother, and that she had an aggressive interest in keeping her parents apart and being Daddy's only "little darling." Laurie, on the other hand, had to come to the point of acknowledging that her daughter was not a juvenile delinquent, that she was responsible and mature in many ways. Her grades at school were good; her popularity was as much because of her sweetness and sensitivity as because of her fun-loving nature. Meri is, like all the rest of us, part good and part bad—both lovable and hateful.

It is only late in the psychological development of the individual that love and hate become fused. Life becomes infinitely more complicated when we hate those whom we also love. We need a mind capable of tolerating complexities and contradictions in order to process conflicting feelings.

In terms of the historical evolution of consciousness, it was the Greeks, in the Western world, who perfected the notion of a world cosmology based on the idea that the world is a place where conflict and contradictions exist. They developed the idea fully, and this enlarged the capacity of the human mind to tolerate contradiction, paving the way for the fusion of love and hate.

The Greeks tell a story about a time when all the men went to war. It was the thing to do in ancient Greece and Rome. Actually, those times were a lot like our own times: Men were admired for their gallantry in war, and every few years wars were fought and new heroes discovered.

This war, though, was different from all other wars. In all the other wars, including our own contemporary wars, the women cheer as the men march off to fight. Throughout the ages in wartime, socks are darned, weapons made, food grown, wounds nursed—all by the women. Women have encouraged men to go to war and have been as busy in the pursuit of war on the home front as the men are in the war zone. And when men come home from the front lines of war, the women wait with open arms and outstretched legs, to love them lots before the men march off once again to exercise their hate toward an enemy they know nothing about. Women are left with the children (and the nonvirile men, who are either too young or too old to do anything with the women other than keep them company).

During this war, though, so many years ago, the women weren't waiting with open arms and outstretched legs. During this war, the women went on strike. They said, long before we thought of it, "Make love, not war." And then they said, "No more love until there is no more war."

The story is the play *Lysistrata*, and it has a moral about love and hate. These smart women of ancient Greece understood that love and hate go together, and that it is best to resolve, first, one's hate difficulties with those one loves. The women of *Lysistrata* used their hate toward the men who were abandoning them to find their way back to love.

The Greeks used their gods, too, to illustrate basic human phenomena. The prototypical example of the fusion of love and hate was the marriage of the god Ares and the goddess Aphrodite. In Greek mythology, Ares, god of war, was not a particularly well-liked god. In the *Iliad*, Zeus says to him: "Of all the gods who live on Olympus, thou art the most odious to me; for thou enjoyest nothing but strife, war and battles." Yet, Aphrodite, goddess of love, found Ares exciting and irresistible, and consummated an adulterous relationship with Ares. From this union of love and hate three children were produced: Eros (Life), Harmonia (Peace), and Anteros (Passion). Like Ares and Aphrodite, we, too, need to both hate and love in order to pursue life with fervor and to attain inner peace and to keep our passion alive.

Despite the lessons from the Greeks, philosophers, scientists and the rest of us continue to struggle with the difficulty in accepting hate as a natural complementary force to love. We would rather believe that we can live without it—that if we just handle things correctly we can avoid the presence of hate and rage in our lives. But discoveries in virtually all of the scientific, philosophical, and psychological disciplines have led us, inescapably, to the opposite conclusion.

The Greek philosopher Empedocles saw the union of Ares and Aphrodite as the prototype for existence. He foreshadowed modern science by 2,000 years in his belief that all life is a fluctuation between the two opposing but equal forces of love and strife. Konrad Lorenz, a Nobel Prize-winning ethologist, said that love is "the most wonderful product of ten million years of evolution," and he goes on to show how love is not possible without aggression. He notes that indications of love and altruism are found only in aggressive species of animals, and asserts that while aggression can exist without love, there can be no love in a species lacking aggression.

Freud said that the human mind is torn between two forces:

love, which he called *Eros*, and hate, which he called *Thanatos*, meaning death or destruction. It is in the opposition between Eros and Thanatos that we can see the destructive power of love and its dark side most clearly. The aim of Eros is to bind together, to preserve by fusion, to establish greater unities—the best of what we expect from love. The aim of Thanatos is to disperse, to undo connections, to destroy things—the worst of love turned angry, sour, and destructive. But the distinction is merely conceptual. In actuality, all experiences are conflicts and compromises between the two. Love and all the dark aspects of ourselves that are stimulated by love—jealousy, vindictiveness, rage, hatred, possessiveness—imply one another; one can't exist without the other.

Hate and love are not really so different from each other. Indeed, they have more in common with each other than they have differences. We hate when we care and when we want; so, too, when we love. Hate is an active process that implies active involvement; so, too, is love. Hate, like love, stems from an unconscious drive related to self-preservation. Hate, constructively channeled, and love belong together.

CHILDREN AND HATE

In order for us to learn to accept our own hate feelings toward others, we need to witness others accepting their hate feelings toward us. The people who will hate us the most are the same people who will love us the most—our families. In order to get early training in the acceptability of hate, we, as children, need to feel hated by our parents but without being treated hatefully by them. As shocking as this idea sounds, there is ample evidence that children who are not exposed to constructive hate—hate that is felt but not acted upon—will be damaged in their ability to handle their own hate and the hate of others toward them.

There are many good reasons to hate children. Children are at times hateful creatures. They can be sadistic, manipulative, threatening, and destructive. The aggressive instinct in the child is closer to its raw form than it will be later in life, when the child has matured. At their worst, children kick, bite, and tease; they tear off the heads of dolls and squash bugs, draw on walls, crash tricycles.

Evidence of the destructive inclinations of children was studied by British psychoanalysts during World War II. At first, it was thought that exposure to war conditions, and the kind of wholesale destruction that typifies war, would horrify and repel children. Psychoanalysts discovered, however, that rather than turning away from acts of destruction, the children turned toward them with a primitive excitement. The childen played joyfully on bombed sites; they played with blasted bits of furniture and threw bricks from crumbled walls at each other. War merely provided another, more varied playground for the children.

The danger here was not that the child, innocently caught up in the whirlpool of war, would be damaged. Rather, as Anna Freud pointed out, the danger lies in:

> . . . the fact that the destructiveness raging in the outer world may meet the very real aggressiveness which rages in the inside of the child. Children have to be safeguarded against the primitive horrors of war, not because horrors and atrocities are so strange to them, but because we want them, at this decisive stage of development, to overcome and estrange themselves from the primitive and atrocious wishes of their infantile nature.

Children are hatable precisely because they themselves hate.

The mother who does not permit herself to hate her child is refusing to respond to the real person that child is. In such an atmosphere of denial, the child will never have the feeling that he is known, accepted, and fully loved for who he is.

During the first few years of life, children struggle with powerful wishes to do away with people of whom they are jealous, or to injure those who disappoint them. The wish to hurt others shows up early but is greatly influenced by the adults who surround the child. Parental horror of hate is actually as damaging as an acceptance of destructive behavior.

In some families, hatred is suppressed at all costs. First the child's expression of hate and rage is restricted (for example, he is punished or shamed for crying); then his hateful feelings are suppressed by commands and prohibitions ("You may not tell me that you hate me"); and finally, the child's destructive urges are completely repressed and disappear from consciousness. On the surface the adults have created the model child they wanted, but seething in the child's unconscious is all the aggression the parents sought to eliminate—and the child hasn't a clue how to manage it when it erupts. When the child is brought up in an environment devoid of hate, he will remain incapacitated to use his own hate constructively.

In other families, destructive behavior is predominant. If acting on destructive impulses is acceptable in a family, then this is the lesson the child will learn. It is enormously difficult for children to learn to control their aggression when all around them people are getting injured or hurt. In families where there is violence, emotional or physical, even when the abuse is not directed toward the children, the children will learn these destructive patterns of behavior.

Healthy psychological growth is fostered by parents helping their children to recognize and feel their destructive wishes and, at the same time, to refrain from acting on them. Constructive hating—hating without destructive action—will allow the child to be hated and to hate without being frightened of the consequences.

Psychoanalyst Donald Winnicott says: "It seems to me doubtful whether a human child, as he develops, is capable of tolerating the full extent of his own hate in a sentimental environment. He needs hate to hate." Mature love, based on the principle of individuals fully knowing one another, needs a full range of feeling. Without justified, honest hate, there can be no love.

DESTRUCTIVE HATE

Hate may be inevitable, justified, and useful, but it can also be a tool for great destructiveness. Hate is the emotion behind abuse, violence, and war.

The ancient Greeks told the story of Zeus and Prometheus to explain man's attraction to the destructive use of hate. In those days it would have been odd not to think that man would be disposed to destructiveness, since the gods themselves embodied this characteristic. Zeus, the most powerful of all the gods, had a violent father whom he fought and finally destroyed. Once established as the god of all gods, Zeus then turned his violent nature against the lesser dignitaries. Prometheus, whose constructive interest in humanity led to his desire to share with mortals his discovery of fire, particularly antagonized Zeus. Prometheus was punished in a horrible way: He was chained to a rock for eternity, having to fight off the incessant attacks of a lacerating eagle.

But even this heinous punishment was not enough to satisfy the vindictive Zeus. He needed to punish all of mankind, too, for its acceptance of Prometheus' gift of fire. And so Zeus gave to mankind our legacy of an attraction to destructiveness. Zeus roared, "I shall give men an evil as the price of fire. *They will clasp destruction with the laughter of desire.*"

When we embrace the destructive aspects of hate and give license to the destructive expression of hate, then hate loses its usefulness. It is in the management of our hate feelings that we determine whether hate becomes a positive, healing force, or a negative, destructive force in our lives.

HATE MISMANAGED

How each of us manages our hate is individual and largely dependent on what we learned in childhood. Mostly we manage our hateful feelings badly and with great difficulty.

Some of us glorify hate and use the impulses born of hate as justification for action and abuse. Nancy, for instance, makes no secret of how and why she hates her husband. Both in public and private, she criticizes, chastises, and generally threatens him as if he were a child. Nancy glorifies her hate for her husband under the mistaken belief that if he looks bad, she looks good. She complains that his behavior justifies her verbal abuse. "He deserves my criticisms. He needs to be corrected," she says. "If he didn't act so badly, I wouldn't have to keep telling him how to improve."

Others express hatred through word or deed, but then engage in brutal self-retaliatory punishment, hating themselves for their own hatefulness, and thus perpetuating their own never-ending cycle of hate. Eddie is an example of a self-retaliating hater. Eddie was raised in a family in which his parents freely expressed their rage at each other through verbal arguments. In fact, they would talk about their heated disagreements almost with a tinge of pride, attributing them to their "hot" Latino heritage. But Eddie married a woman who was raised in a family that was extremely quiet and polite, and her reaction to Eddie's rage is a fearful, tearful plea for him to stop. Only after Eddie has completed his ranting is he able to be sensitive to his wife's feelings. He then realizes that he has lost control over himself and has been verbally abusing his wife, just as he had observed his father doing with his mother. He then attacks himself for his inadequacies and slides into a remorseful depression that takes several hours to lift.

Some of us push our hateful feelings down, knowing all the time that they are there but committed intellectually or morally to another way of behaving. Bob is a good example of someone who consistently denies any expression of hate feelings. He generally knows when he is angry but has not yet found a way to constructively express his feelings, so he usually decides to simply not say or do anything at all. The inadequacy of this approach became painfully clear to him after a dinner engagement he had with his sister and brother-in-law. Bob had initiated the dinner plans because he had something very delicate and very painful to discuss with them.

Bob is a highly paid corporate attorney. He had recently discovered that he had unintentionally committed legal malpractice. No one else knew, and it was likely that if he handled the situation with artful skill no one would ever know. So long as his error remained undisclosed, no one would be injured by it. Were he to publicly acknowledge his error, though, the consequences would be enormous, and possibly involve a lawsuit on the order of ten million dollars. Bob had spent an agonizing week going over in his mind all aspects of the situation and had finally decided to ask his sister and brother-in-law for help in his decision of how to proceed.

The response of his brother-in-law, Carl, infuriated Bob. Carl responded that as far as he was concerned there really was no moral issue at all because "everyone on Wall Street is sleaze anyway."

Although Bob was enraged that his brother-in-law could so blithely dismiss a matter of such serious import, he decided not to say anything to either Carl or his sister. In deference to his sister and out of his love for her, he decided to let the matter drop. But he knew without a doubt that no matter how much he loved his sister, he absolutely detested her husband.

Bob left the dinner palpably upset. Although he felt that he had made the best choice possible in staying silent, he remained emotionally distraught for several hours after returning home from dinner, until he found himself in violent abdominal pain. He was rushed to the hospital and diagnosed with a bleeding ulcer that had chosen that precise moment to make its presence known.

There are, too, those of us who find hatred so offensive that we are not even aware of its presence. Arnie professes that he feels that his mother is a wonderful woman, and that he has no complaints about her. Yet, somehow he never finds time to visit her. He excuses himself, claiming that he simply has too much work to do, or should play with the kids, or help his wife to rearrange the furniture. When Arnie speaks to his mother he is exceedingly polite but never warm or loving. His wife has noticed that whenever Arnie and his mother are together for family events, Arnie can always be found in whatever room his mother is *not* in. Arnie remains completely unaware of his true feelings for his mother, because he was taught that respect is the *only* feeling permitted for one's parents. Arnie and his mother have never had a fight. They have also never exchanged any honest emotion, and their relationship, like their overly polite manner with each other, remains stultified and distant.

These are only some of the ways that we mismanage our hate feelings. There are almost as many forms of mismanaged hate as there are different personality types. Some hate shows up in neurotic behavior, in which the underlying hate is not immediately apparent. Neurotic haters do not overtly reveal their hate; rather what is visible are signs of psychological disturbance. But if one looks at the ultimate effect on relationships, the hate that hides behind these masks of neuroses becomes evident. These neurotic hates, described by Gerald Schoenewolf in *The Art of Hating*, are always destructive.

Obsessive-compulsive hate is an acting out of hate through extreme behavior. The behavior has the characteristics of defiance, stubbornness, stinginess, or extreme orderliness. Obsessive-compulsive rituals are subtle ways to exert domination over another person. An obsessive-compulsive woman, for instance, may be so interested in keeping her house clean that both her husband and her children feel they live in a museum rather than a home. She is getting even with her family, but in the guise of taking care of them. Obsessive-compulsives would rather be rigid than know they hate.

Passive-aggressive hate is the most subtle of all the manifestations of hate. Passive-aggressive people can't admit that they have any hate at all. A passive man, for instance, will be superficially sweet and say and do all the supposedly "right" things. But, in fact, he will be driving his wife into a rage by not giving her precisely the thing she wants most, a genuine emotional communication of love. By withholding genuine affecton, he has the satisfaction of provoking his wife without actually doing anything that is overtly objectionable.

Masochistic hate is the expression of, as psychoanalyst Theodor Reik said, a "victory through defeat." Masochistic people stay in abusive relationships, proving to others what innocent victims they are. They express their hate perversely by arranging to be hated by the other person.

Psychosomatic hate is hate turned against the body. It represents the severest form of self-hatred and is often life-threatening. Psychosomatic illnesses are likely to befall the psychosomatic hater, who would rather hate himself through the channel of his body than know that he has hate for anyone else. The psychosomatic hater is prone to express his hate through asthma attacks, ulcers, back problems, gastrointestinal disorders, skin conditions, cancer, heart disease, or any number of other physical ailments. Generally the psychosomatic hater is the nicest and most pleasant of all forms of haters, because it is only himself whom he wishes to destroy.

Schizophrenic hate is also a hate of the self, but its direction is against the mind rather than the body. The schizophrenic has retreated into a fantasy world, preferring to destroy the integrity of his mind rather than know that he holds hatred in his heart. Like psychosomatic haters, schizophrenic haters are in a convoluted way altruistic in their hate, because they destroy themselves in order to protect others from their hate.

Depressive hate, like psychosomatic and schizophrenic hate, is an expression of hate turned against the self. Depressive haters blame themselves and get themselves into a state in which they believe that nothing will turn out right for them. They tend to push people away, refusing to be helped, holding on to their unhappiness. They tend to be flooded with feelings of hopelessness, helplessness, low self-esteem, and guilt.

Each of these methods of mismanaged hate takes a precious toll. Not all the individuals who have these problems are neurotic haters, but all neurotic haters have problems, some serious, indeed. There are surely better solutions than the tortures that we are capable of putting ourselves through in not wanting to know our hate. Recognizing our hate and finding nondestructive outlets for it is the task that we must accomplish if we are to hate successfully and not be destructive to either ourselves or our loved ones.

HATE MANAGED CONSTRUCTIVELY

In spite of all the ways that we have found to hide our hate, the fact remains that hate has the potential to both heal and help, as well as harm or hurt. It is only when it is hidden that it becomes destructive.

Hate occupies a place in our psychological processes analogous to that of heat in physical processes. All mechanical friction generates heat. All emotional friction (and there is eventually friction in all human interactions) generates aggression and hate. We have learned to channel heat to make energy that makes our lives more pleasurable, more fulfilling, and more comfortable. Such is the promise of hate.

Coming to know the constructive potential of hate has been influential in my work with my patients. Catherine is a patient who, through our work together, came to understand something of the inseparability of love and hate and the constructive value of coming to know her own hate feelings. She came into treatment because she felt she had fallen out of love with her husband. She described her marriage as solid and good but no longer as passionate and exciting as it once had been. She missed passion in her life and had come to wonder, as many of us do at some point in our lives, "Is this all there is?"

After only a few weeks in therapy, Catherine surprised us both by falling, quite unexpectedly, in love with her physician and beginning an affair with him. In her relationship with him she found passion and what she felt was a long-lost dream: in-loveness rekindled. She felt that this man embodied all of what her husband lacked: He could maturely acknowledge her as a woman; their communication was intense, filled with long and serious conversations about life, love, religion, politics—all the questions that stimulated them intellectually and spiritually. The affair continued for some months, and Catherine painfully tried to sort out in therapy her feelings and priorities. Should she leave her husband? This man was offering her marriage, and it would be, she thought, a marriage more exciting than what she had had with her husband for the last seven years.

Catherine spent the next several months in treatment, agonizing over what her decision should be. She talked glowingly about her doctor and bitterly about her husband. What became clear, as Catherine sorted out her feelings, was that what bothered her most about her marriage was not that she had fallen out of love with her husband but that she was in a state of rage toward him. He wasn't cooperative enough; he wasn't romantic, never brought her flowers, never took her out to dinner; he was too tied to his family, whom she hated but with whom he insisted they meet for dinner once a week. What became apparent was the remarkable extent to which Catherine had been able to keep these hateful feelings out of her consciousness.

Soon Catherine became more interested in spending her therapy time railing against her husband than extolling the blisses of her affair. And the more she verbally decimated her husband, the less interest she felt in her lover.

What Catherine had to learn about herself was that she was in love with love and had not yet learned to fuse love and hate. Catherine eventually came to understand her affair as being a bit like ice cream, all sweet and sugary but without much sustenance.

As Catherine became more conscious of what she wanted from her husband, she was able to communicate with him in an effective way, and found that there was a cooperative man hiding there all the time. As he understood Catherine's desires, she found herself getting flowers and going to candlelit dinners, and her love found its way back into her marriage. For the first time in their marriage, the two of them found themselves having fights and then making up sweetly.

In deciding to stay with her husband, Catherine chose a full emotional relationship that included moments of anger and disappointment as well as moments of love and joy. She came to enjoy the sweet and the sour, and the calm and the storm that complete love brings.

MAKING LOVE WHOLE

When we don't accept hate in our love relationships, we find that it seems to have its own guidelines of behavior. If we try not to feel it, there it is, bubbling up even stronger than before. Hate never wants to go away, whether in momentary trivial experiences ("I hate it when cars splash muddy water on me") or in matters with lifelong consequences ("Why did I marry that man, anyway?"). It is, of course, long-lasting, intimate hate that gives us the most trouble. But the fact is, making hate conscious is the only way to reduce its power over us.

In our struggles to make our lives and our loves more whole, we need to look at the forces of hate and aggression that go, inevitably and inextricably, with love. We may die from a lack of loving attention, as Spitz's infants showed, but we may, as well, be fatally malnourished by a love that has no balance.

Shakespeare presents this essential dilemma of love in *The Merchant of Venice*. The fair and wise Portia is bound to take as her husband only that suitor who is able to choose the right casket from the three that are before him. The caskets are of gold, silver, and lead, and the correct one is the one that holds within it her portrait. Two suitors already have been summarily dismissed after picking the gold and silver caskets. Bassanio, the third suitor, favors the lead, and in so choosing, wins the hand of his beloved.

Bassanio's decision surprises most of us. We would have been quick to select the prettier or the more precious caskets. But Bassanio knows something about the nature of love. He knows that love can be like pure gold or silver—beautiful, gleaming, and splendid, but impractical in the quotidian world of day-to-day transactions. As desirable and as beautiful as pure gold and silver appear, they are too soft, too perfect, two precious to be useful to us. In the same way, gleaming, pure love is not enough to sustain our daily love life. When we ask love to serve human nature, we must make sure that it can withstand the wear and tear. Just as gold and silver must be mixed with less valuable metals and fired and hammered to give them the strength to be useful in the real world, so must love be tempered with hate to be whole, enduring, and strong.

CHAPTER 3

The First Face of Narcissism: The Hate That Looks Like Love

It is no accident that people attracted to each other often describe the experience as "electric" or "like being hit by a bolt of lightning." These are, in fact, accurate metaphors. The transmission of electricity between two poles is very much like the transmission of feelings between two people.

For the flow of electrical energy to be complete, there needs to be two poles, a receptor and a sender. If for any reason one of the poles is eliminated, the flow of energy will cease. So, too, it is with people. For feelings to be exchanged between individuals, there needs to be a sender and a receiver. In a mutually loving relationship, both people perform both functions. If for any reason one pole drops out of the circuit, the flow of feelings is interrupted and emotional contact is lost. There are times when feelings are directed toward another, but these feelings are simply not received. ("I love him but he doesn't even know I exist.") Conversely, there may be a receptor for feelings but no sender. ("I want so much to be loved. Why can't I find someone to love me?") Both of these dynamics are essentially one-sided—that is, narcissistic.

Narcissists can function only in one direction. Unlike people who are more emotionally balanced, narcissists cannot both give and receive love. Either they focus solely on their own needs or they focus solely on the other person at the expense of their own needs. Narcissistic people who form relationships based on either of these principles are engaged in what I call *narcissistic love:* a love that never completes its path from pole to pole and thus never matures into a communicative, mutually giving and receiving cooperative love.

THE STORY OF NARCISSUS

A long, long time ago, according to legend, there was a man who seemed to fall in love with his own reflection. His name was Narcissus, and it is his story that has spawned the diagnostic category for neurotic illness that is among the most prevalent and well recognized today (and from which we derive the term "narcissism"). His story illustrates the tragedy of unbridled self-preoccupation in its extreme form.

Narcissus is an astonishingly attractive guy. He is just the kind of man whom many women find most appealing and fall instantly in love with. He is deliciously handsome, exquisitely confident, maddeningly "in love" with himself. But alas, as all of us know who have been involved with a narcissist, he is, as well, just the kind of man whom women know, in their own best interests, to stay as far away from as possible. His good looks, his confidence, and his apparent love for himself hide a painful secret. It is a secret of hate, and any woman who comes close to this kind of man is going to feel the scorching heat of this hate. This is the kind of man who breaks women's hearts.

Narcissus, like any proud, vain, and ambitious man, spends many years searching high and low for a mate. He has a great many admirers. He considers all possibilities—both male and female—but finds none suitable. All have some defect that makes them not up to his level of expectation of the right person on whom he would deign to bestow his love and attention.

After years of fruitless yearning for a beloved as perfect and as beautiful as himself, at last Narcissus finds his match. In stooping down to satisfy his thirst in a reflective pool of water, so the tale goes, there in the clarity of the water does he find his beloved: his own image staring back at him. So entranced is he in his beauty, so engrossed in his love for his own image that he fails to recognize that it is he himself who is the object of his love. In this delusional state, Narcissus decides from that moment on to stay by the spring. There he spends the rest of his days, gazing longingly at his own image.

THE NARCISSISTIC WORLD OF SELF

The story of Narcissus is a useful metaphor with which to understand how and why we love badly and destructively, because it illustrates the basic principles that underlie pathological narcissism. When we make unwise choices in whom we love, or when love feels more painful than pleasurable, then we are experiencing patterns of thoughts, feelings, and behaviors that were laid down in the narcissistic period of development—the first few years of life. In a state of narcissism we may, like Narcissus, fall in love with a beloved whom we can never truly know, who is not interested in ever truly knowing us, who will never truly love us or whom we can never truly love. In these situations our love will have become like the incomplete electric circuit: no contact. This is an isolating, incomplete love more than it is a togetherness love. This is a "love" whose goal is separation and isolation.

Narcissus' self-admiration and preoccupation with himself remind us of many self-absorbed people with whom we are acquainted in our lives. One of my patients, Amy, would appear to be very much in love with herself, judging by the amount of time she spends preening. She admitted that since she was a little girl she has spent an inordinate amount of time looking in the mirror. After she started therapy, I became a substitute mirror for her. She asked me incessantly about every aspect of her physical appearance, from the new color of her hair to which dress would give which "look" (she needs a new "look" each week). When she talks about others, it is only in relation to herself: "It's not that I have little use for people. It's just that I really like being involved with myself. I've always found that it's better to let people come to me, to try to understand me, rather than to try to understand them. It takes so much of my time and energy to get outside myself."

Amy's excessive preoccupation with herself is not a healthy pastime, but it has its origins in a perfectly normal process. Narcissism, meaning self-preoccupation, is, in fact, a normal developmental stage of infancy and childhood. But it is, as well, a term used to describe a mental disturbance. The two are not unrelated. As a stage in development, the newborn *is* not and *should* not be aware of much beyond his own needs. Survival for the infant depends on the fulfillment of his needs: "I need to be fed." "I need to be warm." "I need to be comforted." The infant recognizes the existence of others only insofar as they fulfill his needs and relieve him of tension when these needs are pressing. This self-absorption is, for the infant, life-preserving.

In this narcissistic state, the infant does not yet have true feelings toward others. He is not yet even aware of the existence of others except insofar as their behavior affects him directly. In this state he is aware of sensations and impressions. He is comfortable or uncomfortable, hot or cold; he is being touched gently or violently.

THE RETURN TO THE PAST IN NARCISSISTIC RELATIONSHIPS

The psychological development of the child centers around his increasing awareness of the fact that he is not the center of the universe. The child comes to learn that the people who love him have their own separate thoughts and feelings and needs that are only at times related to him.

Childhood narcissism goes through a process of gradual diminution as interest in the surrounding world increases. The child is able to forgo the immediate gratification of his own desires as his interest in others becomes more highly charged. But this process of leaving one's infantile narcissism behind does not occur smoothly or steadily. At any given time, a child, adolescent, or adult can revert back to a prior level of narcissism that has not been completely outgrown. Some of us are more successful at leaving narcissism behind than others. A vestige of our infantile narcissism remains with us throughout our lives.

Our psychological processes are buffeted by the conflicting forces of progressive forces (those that engender maturity) and regressive forces (those that lead us backward). Progressive forces impel us toward the mature, productive, responsible, interdependent efforts of making a happy family and a happy society. These are working against the regressive forces that urge us to relinquish such productive, creative, working effort and return to the more passive-receptive-dependent state of fetal life, infancy, and childhood.

Narcissistic relationships are those in which the conflicts that are manifested have their origins in the narcissistic phase of development, the first few years of life, which represent the psychological birth of the individual. Unlike biological birth, which is a dramatic, observable, and well-circumscribed event, psychological birth is a slowly unfolding intrapsychic process that can be broken down into three phases.

First the child experiences oneness—*symbiotic fusion*—with Mother and the world around him. This is the "oceanic" feeling that Freud refers to, the paradise of total care and comfort to which we each yearn to return.

Next, the infant comes to acquire a sense of separateness. Margaret Mahler, a psychoanalyst who has done extensive research on this phase of development, refers to this period as the *separation-individuation* phase.

Later, when the infant has acquired locomotion, he becomes interested in the experience of being away from Mother, developing his own stable sense of identity as a separate individual, while simultaneously wanting the option of returning to Mother at his whim. Mahler calls this phase *rapprochement.*

These three stages of development are normal and necessary for psychological maturity to take place. However, when the tasks of any of these infantile stages are not mastered the individual will continue to struggle with the challenges of those tasks. Movement to the next developmental challenge cannot take place, and the individual continues to function on an early emotional level. Such an individual may proudly display the body of an adult, but the body houses the psyche of a child.

NARCISSISTIC LOVE

As the infant develops both cognitively and emotionally, his ability to feel becomes more developed and more specific. Instead of being aware only of his own needs, he begins to experience himself as a separate entity, a distinct individual with a complex set of both needs and feelings. Further, he begins to be able to direct his feelings *toward others.*

It is through our exposure to the people around us the most, our parents and siblings, that we learn our first lessons about relationships. It is here, in our first family, that we develop sensitivity about the qualities in people that attract us. Within the family are our first "loves." These first loves lay down the basis for our later loves.

As a child, we find that when someone speaks to us lovingly, it feels good. When our father takes pleasure in throwing a baseball with us, or our mother listens raptly to our piano playing, we are drawn closer to them. In these states of pleasure, children will hug and kiss their parents and say, "I love you," and do all kinds of things that look like love. But what infants and children feel cannot really be called love, or at least not mature love. They experience a feeling that is based on the fulfillment of their needs only. It is a feeling that is in large part gratitude for our ministering to them. And, most of all, it is a feeling that arises out of an idealistic attribution of extraordinary powers. A child "loves" anyone who has the capacity to take the terror out of the dark, to supply answers to every curiosity, and to fulfill every whim. The love of a child is not based on a realistic assessment of another person. This idealized child-love, based on belief in the omniscience and omnipotence of the other person, is the immature love that I call *narcissistic love*. It is appropriate for young children, but creates misery for adults.

NARCISSISTIC HATE

It is also in this early stage of development that we learn about hate and rage. We all learn soon enough that the world is not always a cozy place to be. For some of us this lesson is particularly bitter, and the world is a place where there is as much frustration as there is gratification. Our caregiver may respond too slowly, or not at all, to our needs, and we are left in discomfort—too hot, too cold, wet, or hungry—for an unduly long period of time. From this frustration, tensions develop that need to be discharged.

How we discharge our displeasure in infancy will determine how we hate in later life and whether we will have learned to use hate destructively or constructively. Hate and rage are inevitable consequences of frustration. As infants, we are either helped or hindered in relieving ourselves of these tensions through constructive communication. If, as infants, we are uncomfortable for any reason, we cry. Crying is a signal of distress and it is the primary means of communication that the infant has available. At first the crying is merely communicative. A responsive parent or caregiver will welcome this communication as an opportunity to understand the needs of the infant better and to relieve him of discomfort.

But if this attempt at communication is not welcomed or goes unheeded, the crying becomes a wail, more of a complaint than a communication. There is frustration and aggression in this wail, and if it continues it will likely reach a pitch of unadulterated rage. Even with this amount of rage, the infant is still pleading for a relationship. The hate is still communicative, and resolution of the cause of the distress will lead to a feeling of gratitude and love.

The more distress we feel as infants, and the less successfully it is relieved, the more hate will continue to be the defining psychological characteristic of our lives. Our infantile frustration will reappear as rage or depression (rage turned against the self) in most intimate relationships. As in narcissistic love, though, this hate is not based on a realistic appraisal of the relationship. Rather, this is a historical hate from which we have not been able to free ourselves. This child-hate I call *narcissistic hate*. Like narcissistic love, it is always destructive to cooperative, mutually enriching relationships.

COOPERATIVE LOVE

Cooperative loving requires a full appreciation of the separateness of self so that feelings can be directed toward a beloved. Cooperative love is reasonable and rooted in a genuine understanding of the other person. Cooperative love means the renunciation of the dreams of omniscience and omnipotence that one has as a child.

Only relatively well-developed personalities are capable of a mature, cooperative love. Developing an integrated personality, in which love and hate are both allowed expression, is an on-going task of life. We all achieve some level of success in this endeavor, but we usually do better with a deeper understanding of ourselves and our feelings. People with integrated personalities have a definite sense of self, which brings with it the ability to recognize and acknowledge the differences between oneself and others. When we have a sense of self that is strong enough to accept these differences, we flourish and are able to savor love, because we realize that relationships involve another person who, no matter how carefully selected, is still, inescapably, a person with different wishes, purposes, temperament, preferences, and rhythms. This mature love involves cooperation—two selves joining for the common purpose of creating a cooperative love relationship.

When we truly love, we cannot, like Narcissus, expect to embrace clones of ourselves. Others are not precise mirror reflections of ourselves; they invariably will do things that arouse anger, disappointment, rage, jealousy, and despair. When we are emotionally able to deal with this, our relationships can grow and thrive and even be strengthened by their inevitable dark moments. However, if we are not emotionally able to accept separation, and stay stuck in the narcissistic phase of development, we refuse to allow for differences between people and our relationships will either wither from neglect or explode from unbridled intensity.

COOPERATIVE HATE: THE LOVE THAT LOOKS LIKE HATE

Narcissistic love is rooted in the blissful dreams of omniscience and omnipotence that all children have during infancy, and which narcissistic individuals continue to carry with them throughout their lives. Narcissistic hate is rooted in the nightmares of abandonment, loss, and fear that all children have on occasion, but which narcissistic individuals have in excess and which they never outgrow.

Hate, however, is not always related to painful, unresolved issues from one's childhood. Mature hate, like mature love, can be a reasonable response based on a realistic appraisal of another person. There are many objective, wholly warranted reasons to hate. Mothers, for instance, are justified in feeling enraged with their infants. Husbands and wives, too, often resent each other. These feelings of rage and resentment are not, of themselves, something to fear.

Any relationship involving two separate people is going to be fraught with legitimate, compelling reasons why one person should harbor negative feelings toward the other. Mature cooperative hate, like mature cooperative love, is justified by the other person's own hateful aspects. Cooperative hate is necessary in every parent/child relationship, and in every romantic/marital relationship. Cooperative hate is a realistic response based on a recognition and acceptance of the hateful (or annoying, or infuriating) aspects of the other person. Cooperative hate is, in fact, loving.

OVER-GRATIFICATION AS A CAUSE OF NARCISSISM

Whether or not we learn to grow out of the stage of normal, infantile narcissistic love depends largely on the love training we get from our parents. At some point in our growing-up experience, it is proper for our parents to expect that we will begin to give back love and cooperation. Such a demand is essential to help the child grow out of his self-centered world.

When these expectations are communicated to the child with sensitivity to the feelings of the child, such progress occurs without undue difficulty. A mother may say, for instance, "Jimmy, I know you want to go out and play ball, but you must take a few minutes first to clean your room." Such a communication conveys the message that in order to get what you want, you may have to tolerate a little frustration and give somebody else what he or she wants. A healthy balance between frustration and gratification is thus achieved. Or, the message may be a pure request for affection: "Give Daddy a kiss." The child learns that Daddy has needs, too. These communications are gentle reminders that love is a two-way street.

However, in those cases in which childhood needs have been overly gratified, the child never learns to feel comfortable with his feelings of frustration. He does not grow out of the "I"-centered child's world and will always want love relationships that gratify every whim and fulfill every need. As the narcissistic adults they become, these people strongly resist the idea that love cannot always be good and warm and wonderful. They deny the natural and inevitable dark side of love and respond to its presence either by running away from potentially workable relationships as soon as they become demanding, or by destroying the relationship through their own incessant demands.

More than 200 years ago, French philosopher Jean-Jacques Rousseau saw the danger in this kind of permissive upbringing:

> Do you know the surest way to make a child unhappy? You must accustom him to being given everything. For his demands grow increasingly. Sooner or later your inability will force you to refuse him something, and this unaccustomed refusal will be a far greater torment to him than the lack of the thing he demands.

Rousseau cautioned against any extreme form of upbringing. As we will see in the next chapter, under-gratification as a means of raising a child is just as damaging, though in a different way, as over-gratification. If these two were the only choices available to us, we would be raising half the population to be dictators and the other half to be their compliant servants.

THE HATE IN NARCISSISTIC LOVE

For twenty years I have been observing the development of the son of friends. I first met the boy when he was four. I was staying at his parents' home for the weekend. That weekend the entire household was subjugated to the tyranny of this four-year-old dictator. The parents did nothing to thwart a single wish of his, from deciding what we would eat to which channel we would watch on television. I felt strongly that this boy, never learning how to deal with frustration, would have a difficult time when he learned that the rest of the world was not as willing to gratify his every whim as his parents were. Now, at the age of twenty-four, this young man has repeatedly been suspended from a variety of schools; he has acquired a string of traffic tickets, including several for driving while intoxicated; and he has had a series of unfulfilling relationships with young women, three of whom when they became pregnant had abortions at his insistence. His parents, with whom he is barely on speaking terms, wonder what went wrong.

This young man was trained by his parents from an early age to become a classic self-aggrandizing, grandiose narcissist. He was never required nor expected to have an ounce of regard or sensitivity for the needs or wishes of others. His emotional posture in the world is, as an adult, the same as it was when he was a child: "I come first."

Expecting the world to bend to our every need and want invariably leads to tremendous frustration and rage. Every event that is beyond this young man's control, from getting a traffic ticket to getting a woman pregnant, only further convinces him of the unworthiness and hatefulness of the world. What went wrong is that this man was brought up to be a dictator, but he can't find enough people who want to be dictated to by him. He may one day find a woman who will, like his parents, subjugate herself to his commands, but this will not be a marriage made in heaven. It will be a narcissistic marriage held together more by hate than by love.

When we meet dictatorial narcissists, at first we are taken in by their supreme air of confidence. We envy them, wishing that we could think as highly of ourselves as they apparently do of themselves. Women are attracted to the macho man, for example, who struts around expecting all the girls to fall in love with him. In fact, many do. Men are attracted to the perfectly dressed, perfectly mannered, perfectly poised woman who exudes the feeling that she knows she is the best. But anyone who has loved a self-loving narcissist knows that their self-love has gone to such great lengths that, like Narcissus, there is no room for a love of anyone else. In fact, their self-love is just an elaborate masquerade for the hatred toward the world that they really feel. In keeping their gaze fixed exclusively on themselves, they reject others.

NARCISSISTIC PROJECTIONS

Narcissistic love originates in the self. The narcissist who is "in love" lives in a world of illusion, ascribing attributes to the beloved that are, in reality, creations of the mind of the narcissist. We call these false attributions *projections*, and they may comprise parts of ourselves that we cherish and embrace, or parts of ourselves that we disavow and hate. Children, for instance, need the world to feel safe and secure (unpredictable as it is, from the child's point of view), and so will attribute to adults the power to slay dragons and eliminate all scary things. A woman who must see herself as a kind, loving person will not want to know when she is enraged with her husband and will attribute to him all the hate and rage in their relationship: She will say it is *his* anger that leads to their fights; it is *his* dissatisfaction with her, rather than hers with him, that leads to their unhappiness with each other.

Projections exist in every narcissistic love relationship. In the beginning stages, projections may all be positive: The beloved may be seen to embody all of the narcissist's ideals—good qualities the narcissist possesses or may wish for—and commonalities between self and other are glorified. We assure the solidity of the relationship by proclaiming how alike we and our loved one are. "We have so much in common," we announce. "We think and feel the same about so many things," we boast. And proudly we declare, "We barely have to speak to each other to know what the other is thinking." One might ask, however: If that's the case, how interested *are* we in our beloved?

At the same time, in a narcissistic relationship we tend to gloss over the differences that we don't want to be there. We minimize them, or ignore them, or tell ourselves they don't matter. We want so badly to have our beloved be the "right" person to love that we fashion him (or her) in our minds into what we want him (or her) to be. We become a Pygmalion, carving another self out of the raw clay of our own projections.

The effort to mold a loved one into a likeness of ourselves is ultimately destructive to mature love. If everyone we love were a mirror for our positive ideas, needs, sensitivities, and actions, our world would feel like a warm bath—a cozy and comfortable place where we would exist without experiencing any shocks to our systems. We and the world would be in such perfect harmony that the split between us would be barely noticeable. We call someone with these expectations a Pollyanna, someone who denies any dark aspects to the world.

If, on the other hand, the world consisted of all of our negative projections and hated parts of ourselves, then we would feel ourselves to be in a perpetual nightmare of grotesque proportions. This is surely what the world feels like to schizophrenics, who live in the shadow of all their worst thoughts and feelings and then project them out, ascribing them to the world instead of to their own psyches.

Most of us, of course, fall somewhere in between these two extremes. Most of us project onto others some of our positive and some of our negative attributes.

THE NARCISSISM OF FEAR

Twenty-seven-year-old Marcie is a good example of someone who, even in her adult life, continues to live out painful memories from the earliest narcissistic phase of development. Marcie came to me because of a desperate loneliness. She had had a succession of short-term relationships and seemed unable to determine why none of them had worked out. After being in treatment briefly, she met Rick, and after dating for a year they became engaged to be married. Marcie was happier than she had ever been, but as we look at her words we can see that this "love" that she has for Rick has a peculiar quality to it. Marcie would say, "I absolutely hate living alone. I hate everything about it. I hate it when it's dark and I have to go turn all the lights out; I hate being in my bed alone; I hate feeling that there is no one next to me, no one to make sure that nothing bad happens to me. It'll be wonderful after we get married and Rick will be there every night. I won't feel afraid and I'll never feel lonely."

Note that there is no mention of Rick other than in relation to Marcie. She is preoccupied with what Rick will do for her; there is no mention of what she is going to give Rick. We don't even get a sense of who it is that she is marrying—what his temperament is, his likes and dislikes, his moods, or even his feelings for her—other than that he is apparently willing to marry her.

Marcie's assumption that loved ones take on the role of protector, guardian, and savior is not an unusual belief. Greeting cards and songs gush with sentiments that say, in effect, "I need you to silence the things that go bump in the night." Women with these needs look for a man who will guard, shelter, save, and champion them. Similarly, men look for women to nurture, care for, and "mother" them. If, as in Marcie's case, these are the only criteria used to define love, then these people don't really want to be "in love," they want only to be "out of fear." As we'll see, relationships that are judged solely by how safe and secure they make the individuals feel often crumble in the absence of mutual giving and taking.

The clinging need that Marcie shows has little to do with love, because her feelings toward Rick are an insignificant part of the relationship. As in all narcissistic relationships, Marcie's feelings have much more to do with her remote past—the narcissistic stage of development and its hold on her—than with any current feelings toward Rick. Throughout Marcie's life, she has been reliving some painful memories of early events that happened in a time frame outside of her conscious memory. Rick is providing a temporary respite from the feelings that these memories evoke. This safe haven, or this state of being "out of fear," is what Marcie is calling being "in love."

Fear and dread have their origins in the earliest experience of the newborn. You can imagine how terrifying it must be to be a totally helpless and confused infant, alternately comfortable and pained, soothed and distressed. Fear and dread are so pervasive in infancy that we might say they are the infant's most constant companions. Often these feelings linger, as they have with Marcie, far beyond the time when they should dissipate. In order to understand how relief from fear can be interpreted as love, let's look at the experience of the newborn and the feelings that each of us, without exception, was subject to at that early stage in our development.

Every fetus experiences profoundly the sense of being enveloped by the protective world of the uterus. So important is this period of development that the Chinese date the birthday of an infant from the time of conception, not birth. The womb of the mother is the nest for the developing fetus—cozy, warm, secure, and insulated. Every square inch of the tiny being within has the sensation of being safe in this nourishing and protected environment.

Birth, then, brings the shock of being forcibly pushed out of a secure home. From being securely fastened in place, we suddenly find ourselves without supports. Like Humpty Dumpty, we are perched precariously on the edge of a world that makes us vulnerable to falling and breaking. From being nourished fully and constantly through the umbilical cord, we become susceptible to pains of hunger. From a climate of consistently warm temperatures, we find ourselves suffering from too much heat or too much cold. From the quietude of muffled, predominately soothing sounds, we are subjected to loud and irritating noises from which there is no escape.

Birth means physical separation, and from then on finding love, closeness, security, and intimacy means finding a way to bridge that distance between self and others. From childhood to old age, we are never quite able to recapture that closeness and security so completely fulfilled in the womb.

How our parents handle our early fears determines lifelong patterns of feelings of separation and fear of abandonment. If our parents reassure us and hold us snugly, then our fear subsides. We develop the idea that fear and a sense of danger are passing emotions.

However, if our normal childhood fears are improperly handled, our sense of panic never really fades into the background and our basic stance toward life becomes one of terror. If, for instance, when we become afraid we sense that our caregiver is just as afraid, the lesson we learn is that fear and danger are always present.

For most of us, the fear and dread so vividly experienced in infancy become part of a remote past, but they are never completely erased. Under the right circumstances they will reemerge with shattering intensity. In times of emotional stress—brought on, for example, by separations, a sense of failure or inadequacy, or a loss—these fears return to us. These memories of fear from birth and infancy exist in each of us, whether they are deeply repressed and reveal themselves rarely or lie just below the surface, threatening to erupt at every turn.

Adult relationships are often based on an attempt to flee from terror. Often the relationship that stops the terror is mistakenly labeled "love." The legend of adult love carries with it the suggestion that it will relieve the burden of individuality, that the task of finding ourselves, with its risks and displeasures, is finally over. The bridge of separation will once again, as in the womb, be transcended as one body and one soul unite with another. Fear, isolation, and insecurity will become things of the past, because there is another human being who, like the perfect mother, the mother of the intrauterine experience, lives to fulfill our needs.

It is probable that the need to be relieved from fear is a very basic, primal craving, overriding even the need for food. In psychologist Harry Harlow's famous experiments, baby monkeys were separated from their mothers at birth and given a choice of substitute Moms. One substitute was made of soft cloth, and the monkeys were able to easily cuddle up to it. The other surrogate was made of inflexible wire but it had one great advantage—a supply of milk. Each of the infant monkeys preferred to cuddle up to the soft "Mommy," and chose to leave her only when hunger intervened. When frightened, they clung more desperately to the soft

Mommy, in spite of her lack of response and her inability to feed them.

It is not such a great leap from baby monkeys to baby humans. Infants need to cuddle close for safety and security, to cling to something warm in order to escape from the terror of being outside the womb and subject to all kinds of fear and discomforts. This need for security, however, cannot be called love, and any expectation of another person based on this need is bound to be disappointed.

It is true, as Marcie discovered, that relationships built on relief from fear can actually function quite well for a while—but only for a while. Marcie will "love" Rick as long as he is always there to fulfill her needs, protect her, and provide her with a sense of security. Similarly, some parents will "love" their grown children as long as they visit or call every day, and many grown children will "love" their parents as long as they respond without question to their every need. But eventually these relationships will topple under the weight of the need, and the hate and aggression hidden beneath the veneer of narcissistic love will emerge from the darkness. Marcie's "love" won't hold up to the stress of a baby, who will steal Rick's attention. Family tempers can ravage "love" when grown children start their own families and can't always be responsive to their parents' needs. And "love" dies amid shouts and slammed doors when parents must finally say "no" to grown children who insist that their parents "owe" them. No matter how caring two people may be, they can never live in absolute harmony, and they cannot keep the feelings of fear and dread away forever. Always they will return. Always, close at hand, are those distant memories of the distinctions between the calm of the intrauterine environment and the disruption of birth and the permanent separation that it brings. When we look to others to relieve our fears, we are in fact looking in the wrong direction.

CHILDREN AS LIVING TOYS

Even when we are called upon to be parents ourselves, we are still subject to fears and hatreds of infantile narcissism. Just as parents, husbands, wives, and lovers may serve as "need objects" for narcissists, children, too, may serve this function for their parents. They exist, in the eyes of their parents, as extensions of their parents rather than as separate, independent individuals, with their own desires, preferences, and concerns. They become, for their parents, living toys, objects to be played with or shown off rather than distinct personalities to be nurtured into being most fully their own person.

Narcissistic parenting includes psychological abuse much more often than physical abuse. Indeed, narcissistic parents may look like model parents, and the effects of their narcissism may be difficult to discern. Beneath narcissistic parenting, however, the needs of the parent are always paramount, while the needs of the child matter little.

Bonnie, for instance, is an exceptionally beautiful woman, and quite successful in her career as an advertising executive. At the age of thirty-eight, Bonnie found herself still childless and mateless. She was not particularly concerned, however, because she knew this situation could easily be rectified. Bonnie had her pick of lovers and it wasn't hard for her to pick the one most suitable to sire her child. So, baby Evan was born in the expectation that he would complete Bonnie's life plan. Today, Evan is Bonnie's pride: He is a child any woman would be proud of. He is bright, as would be expected of a child of Bonnie's, and is quite musical, also a requirement for any child of Bonnie's. Bonnie proudly displays Evan to all who will look, because Evan is one more thing that makes Bonnie look good.

Evan is a trophy kid. Bonnie's narcissism has prevented her from being concerned about Evan's own needs and desires. She has molded him to develop in the way that suits her. This narcissism is destructive to the child that Evan would be under more sensitive guidance, the child that he really *is,* rather than the child that his mother *wants him to be.* Bonnie is giving Evan a lifelong legacy of feeling a painful conflict between his true self and the self that he knows will please his mother.

Annie May was another proud mother who loved to show off her little Mamie. Though she was only a sixteen-year-old mother and lived in a slum tenement, Annie May showed an industriousness rare for someone so young, poor, and burdened with mothering responsibilities. She paid for Mamie's clothes, food, and medical bills with money she earned as a teacher's aid in a child-care center. But Annie May had her own unmet childhood needs, and when little Mamie took sick one day, Annie May lost her mothering capacity. Three days later, Mamie's body was found, badly charred, in the incinerator of her building. Annie May was charged with the murder of her one-year-old daughter.

Evan and Mamie, worlds apart in privilege, are not so far apart in their origins. Both their mothers used them as playthings to satisfy their own needs. Annie May loved to "play" with Mamie just as she had loved to play with her dolls not so many years earlier. A child loves a doll when she feels the urge; there are no other requirements for that love. When the doll is put away, it is forgotten. But, as Annie May discovered, using a child as a living toy is enjoyable only as long as the child cooperates. If the "living toy" asks for more than the mother wants to give, the pleasure of play may turn into a real-life horror. When the cuddly doll turns into a real live infant who cries from a sickly fever (as Mamie did), or becomes a stubborn, contrary boy who wants to play baseball rather than practice his piano (as Evan is now insisting), mothers of dolls can't stand the assertion of needs that are independent of their own. When the child no longer serves as a source of gratification, these mothers become, in one way or another, hostile to their children. Their abuse runs the gamut from persistent ridicule to severe authoritarian control; from emotional deprivation to physical battering and sometimes (as in Annie May's case) to outright murder—all inflicted by "loving" parents who come to hate their children for failing to meet their expectations, and to despise themselves for failing as mothers.

We have all heard stories of men who were pushed by their fathers to become doctors or lawyers and who, suddenly, at mid-life undergo a "crisis" or a realization that it was never what they wanted for themselves. Some, such as one of my patients who gave up his dental practice to open up a business selling art, actually do manage to succeed in transforming their lives and in making a final psychological separation from a narcissistic parent who never encouraged the child to find his own individuality. For others, the narcissistic influence of the parent remains too strong for successful separation to take place.

For Ben, a distant relative of mine, it was never an issue which profession he would choose. His brother, two uncles, and father were attorneys, and the family had its own law firm. Ben was, in fact, much loved by his clients and, after twenty years of practicing law, was making more money than he could ever spend in one lifetime. But Ben remained as unhappy in his decision to be a lawyer as he had been when he had entered law school. After several years of contemplating his move and discussing it with his wife, Ben finally took the plunge and gave up his practice. He used his money to pursue a lifelong dream of starting his own investment firm. Three years later, Ben was still floundering in his dream, having lost all the money his friends and clients had entrusted with him. But Ben had inherited from his parents more than their desire for him to be an attorney. They had also ingrained in him a surfeit of the need to be successful. While Ben's savings could well have covered the losses, his shame at failure was too great for him to stand. He began to gamble heavily, seriously depleting his financial reserves, went into manic frenzies of buying, and began to talk about suicide. Less than a year later, Ben swerved his car into an embankment and was killed instantly.

Narcissistic parents are themselves children. Because their own needs were met inadequately in their own childhood, they remain, even as adults, compelled to relate to their loved ones from their unmet childhood needs. Although these parents may be quick to proclaim that they love their children dearly and would do anything for them, their narcissistic love is not a true love at all. It is a love based on who they are and what they want, rather than a love based on who the child is and what the child wants. In denying the authenticity of the child, this love is a hateful love. If you spend all day and night trying to train your cat to think and act like a dog, we would have to conclude that you don't really like cats. If parents spend their parenting years molding their children into their own image, we would have to conclude that they don't really love their children as they are.

COOPERATIVE LOVE EMERGING

Most of us live some percentage of our day-to-day lives in a partially narcissistic state. It is even possible to live reasonably happily, for a while, in a state that fluctuates between self-involvement and true perception of and feelings toward another person.

Marty and Alicia are a couple I've treated for a few years. When they began treatment they were both still highly narcissistic, but they are now beginning to be able to acknowledge their self-preoccupations. They've been together for six years, married for the last four. They don't strike anyone who knows them (or themselves, for that matter) as dramatically unhappy or unsuccessful; there is much about their lives that they enjoy and feel positive about. Neither would say that their relationship is in any kind of crisis.

To hear them talk, one might initially conclude that their relationship is stable and pleasurable to them both. Marty, for instance, never stops extolling Alicia's virtues: He proclaims her to be the best chef this side of the Mississippi; since he likes good food, he's happy about her talent in cooking. He describes her as ambitious and successful; since he likes to live well, her income is a perk in his marriage to her. He boasts about her body, that it's trim and sexy and that she has enough stamina to keep up with him on his runs; since he's devoted to keeping in shape, Alicia's shared interest gives them more recreational time together.

Alicia, similarly, has many good things to say about Marty: She never worries about his chasing other women; he's appreciative of her cooking, which she takes great pride in; he doesn't force her to spend too much time with his parents, a task she doesn't particularly enjoy.

Though each has complaints about the other, none seems particularly unusual or relationship-threatening. Marty complains that Alicia doesn't read enough, so he can't talk to her about all kinds of subjects he's interested in. Alicia complains that Marty gets too involved with his work and doesn't spend enough time with her.

What becomes apparent, though, as we analyze how they express themselves, is the utter self-absorption of both of these decent, not unloving, and by no means unusually neurotic people. Neither ever refers to anything about the other except in relation to himself or herself. Compliments and complaints are equally self-absorbed. The only mention Alicia makes of Marty's work is that it distracts him from her. And his reference to her cooking is all about how pleasant it is that she does it for him.

Marty and Alicia would both be hurt to hear it suggested, but what we are seeing here is a noticeably underdeveloped capacity for being in touch with the existence of another person. Much of the time their relating to each other has little to do with the other's inner life. Their relationship would not be described as bad, but rather as unfulfilling. Each of them has a sense that this is true, but only a vague understanding of why.

The hate behind the narcissistic love that is being expressed here is not overt. It is not outright abuse, which we would clearly and quickly recognize as hateful. Rather, what is hateful in their relationship is that neither is giving full recognition to the other. How can they *love* each other if they don't even *know* each other? This refusal (or inability) to come to terms with the fullness of the other person's existence is not deliberately mean, nor consciously hateful. But anyone who has experienced narcissistic love, with its predilection for projections, knows that this is not a loving love.

There are many psychological and sociological forces that worked to pair up these two people and that continue to support their relationship. But the dark side of their love that comes in the narcissistic way they relate to each other is evident, and as we listen to them it gives us a sense of foreboding about their relationship, a sense that without some changes in each of them their relationship is not going to get any better, and in times of stress might well get a lot worse. The dark side is visible in the fact that each has some degree of awareness of the other's lack of real engagement. Both express a sense of not being known, not being understood, not being truly cared for. Though there is no deep, scorching pain here, there is a seriously destructive emptiness at the center of this relationship—a vacuum into which much goodwill may disappear.

These feelings of not being known by another, and of not know-

ing another, are the feelings that define any narcissistic relationship. These are feelings that will continue to grow unless they are
addressed curatively. Imagining the other in resemblance to the
self is but the first step in developing love, and any relationship
stuck in this early stage is characterized by only a rudimentary
kind of love, narcissistic love.

Two years after beginning treatment, Marty began to move from
his narcissistic way of relating to a loved one to a fuller recognition
of the "otherness" of another. Alicia had given birth to their first
child, and both initially related to the whole experience as though
it would make no difference in the habits and customs of their life-
style. They were sure it was going to be fun to have a child, but it
didn't seem too difficult to imagine the child fitting easily into their
household without too many adjustments. Alicia would stop work
for six months, and then they would hire an au pair to take over the
lion's share of childkeeping duties during the day, when Alicia was
back at work. In Marty's own words, we can see the process of
moving from narcissistic preoccupation to a genuine awareness of
the reality of another person, in this case, his child:

> I had this really sort of bizarre experience the other night. Until
> just a few days before Chris was born, we were still using her
> room as storage. And even after she was born, we'd gotten the
> room itself ready for her, but the closet in there still held boxes
> that weren't all emptied out right away. So, one night I was in
> there to get a carton out of the closet. I didn't flip the light on be-
> cause I didn't want to disturb the baby. So there I was, in the mid-
> dle of this dark room. Chris was sleeping soundly, not a stir from
> her. And suddenly, it came over me, and it was like the floor had
> dropped six inches under me: There's a person in this room; I'm
> not by myself in a storeroom, there is a person in the crib. *Chrissy
> is a person.* It was actually scary—like in a scary movie, when a
> hand comes out of the darkness and touches the guy on the
> shoulder—but thrilling, too, and exciting.
>
> So, you know what I did next? The very next day I cleared out
> the whole closet. I didn't want Chris' closet being a storeroom. I
> wanted her to have her own domain. I know that there's no
> chance on earth that Chris knows on any level that the closet

exists, so it probably wasn't even really for her. It was because I wanted to keep the idea alive in my mind that Chris is a person, a separate and unique person. I mean, it's great that she's all the things she is to me, but she's also something beyond all that; something of her own, not someone purely in relation to me.

Marty's emergence out of his narcissism came in relation to his daughter, Chrissy; but once the process began, it extended to all his other relationships, as well:

Since that day, I've been thinking about the same thing in relation to all the people I know. I think about my father-in-law-who-drinks-too-much-for-me-to-be-comfortable-with, or Arnie-who-I-talk-to-about-the-Giants. And, of course, Alicia. Most of the time I just think about her as a wife to me—sometimes a wonderful wife, sometimes a terrible wife—"the person who does this for me" or "the person who doesn't appreciate me." But whether I'm liking her or hating her, it's still always in terms of her function in my life rather than Alicia as a separate self, a self apart from me and different from me.

Hurts by the thousands might be produced by the charge that's generated when two selves come near each other. But the alternative is far worse: a center of emotional isolation that characterizes the pain of narcissism.

Whether we are the victims of narcissistic love or narcissistic hate, what all narcissists have in common is their failure to recognize the separate, real existence of others. An infant may cry and cry and cry, oblivious to the effect it is having on the other person. Such is the normal narcissistic nature of infants. But older children come to know of their effects on others and learn to modify their behavior and the expression of their feelings and needs to accommodate others. Adults are presumably the most sophisticated of all in evaluating their relation to the world, in judging their effect on those around them, and in making decisions about their own feelings and their own behavior in order to accomplish their desired goals. Narcissists never learn enough about themselves or others to negotiate relationships that take into account all of these factors.

Narcissistic love is always dark, but as long as each of us harbors even a small seed of awareness, there is always the potential for satisfying and cooperative love. Still, there are many obstacles in trying to reach that goal. The first challenge of narcissism is developing the ability to separate oneself from others. But once we have done that, we then need to cope with the full range of feelings that we are going to have toward those separate entities that are other people. In the next chapter we will see the enormous difficulty of this challenge and the various ways in which we both succeed and fail.

CHAPTER 4

The Second Face
of Narcissism:
Destruction of the Self

You may be wondering, at this point, what happened to our friend Narcissus, who was last seen gazing longingly at himself in his pond. You may wonder whether or not his finding his true love, at last, made him happy, and whether or not this love fulfilled the fantasy that had spurred his long, long search.

In fact, Narcissus never did find happiness in his love. His choice of a beloved was not a very wise one, since there was no real other to love or to be loved by. His beloved was an ephemeral illusion.

Narcissus, though, never recognized the source of his suffering. He kept hoping that one day his beloved would respond to him lovingly, and in this vain hope he remained at his pond, hopelessly yearning for the satisfaction of a love that could never be.

Narcissus' plight is familiar to any of us who have had the experience of falling in love with a person who is, for one reason or another, unavailable. Perhaps our beloved is married, or emotionally distant, or ambivalent about commitment (unavailability can take on myriad forms). Still, we continue to "love" this elusive partner with all our heart, as Narcissus pined for his own image.

THE HIDDEN MEANING OF THE
NARCISSUS STORY

It is tempting to regard Narcissus' brand of passion for himself as self-love. His self-preoccupation certainly has the appearance of self-love. If we continue to follow the story, however, we will see that there is a hidden meaning to Narcissus' plight.

If we look carefully at this long-ago scenario of Narcissus idling by his pool of water, waiting for love's satisfactions, we begin to notice that things are not entirely as they seem. For instance, it doesn't look as though Narcissus is having a very good time with his "love." It may begin to occur to us that the story's point is not that Narcissus is "in love," but rather that he is rapt—caught. He can't take his eyes off that image in the pool, can't leave it. And, while at first we envisioned, as the myth describes, a lovely, tranquil day— we are told the pool is one of purity, perfectly clear and unpolluted by any animals or birds or even falling branches—gradually and then stunningly, as we continue our imaginative venture, we begin to realize that *there is something wrong.* The picture of Narcissus and his love is not just still—it is eerily still; there is no movement at all.

Narcissus has become so immersed in his own image that the outside world, and his relation to it, have been obliterated. Even physical needs have been forgotten. It is in this state of yearning that Narcissus meets his tragic fate. Staring at himself, wasting away through self-neglect, Narcissus finally starves to death.

This behavior cannot by any definition be called self-love. Pleasure is no part of this picture; hate and pain (and eventual suicide) are much stronger components. Behind the outward appearance of self-love is the bitter kernel of self-neglect and self-hatred. For Narcissus to have cared so little about his own needs that he succeeded in killing himself he must have had a great reservoir of self-loathing.

This, then, is the underlying meaning of the story of Narcissus. In narcissism there is tremendous rage and hatred turned against the self. The narcissist, who turns his gaze toward himself exclusively, as Narcissus did, isn't just turning away from the world;

he is obliterating his role in it. The key to unraveling the mystery of narcissism, then, is in unmasking the self-hatred that lies below the surface of self-love. This is a self-hate that looks like love.

The self-hatred of narcissism lies deeply buried behind the glittering image of self-love. Narcissists are focused only on the glittering image—the surface reflection of the mirror. They have never truly loved themselves because they have never become interested enough in who they are, beyond the glittering surface, to find out their true thoughts and feelings.

With this new perspective, self-love begins to take on a different cast. Isn't it true that if Amy, the perpetual preener, were more confident of herself she would not be spending every dime she earns on improving her looks? Couldn't we surmise that the self-absorbed heartbreakers—male or female—wouldn't need others to worship them quite so much if they admired themselves only a little more? Although we might initially be taken in by these postures of "self-love," we conclude that the outward conceit is merely a self-congratulatory mask covering a deep insecurity and feelings of worthlessness and self-hatred.

NARCISSUS AND HIS MOTHER

There are other, little-known facts about Narcissus that help explain the terrible plight he found himself in. Narcissus was conceived in rape and was brought up in a single-parent home. Narcissus' mother, Liriope, was imprisoned in the waters of the river god Cephissus, unable to escape his advances. It was only through her imprisonment that Cephissus was able to subjugate her and forcefully have sex with her.

These two critical facts of Narcissus' origins—that he was a child of rape and that he was the product of a single-parent home—had important implications for his upbringing and the kind of man he became.

The fact that Narcissus was conceived from rape means that he was a child born of destructive hate. The fact that Narcissus was not a wanted pregnancy would have affected how his mother felt toward him. From the moment of his conception, it was preordained that Narcissus' unconscious would fashion for him a life drama in which hate and rage would play a pivotal role.

The fact that Narcissus never knew his father (and apparently had no siblings) must have placed an extraordinary demand on the relationship between him and his mother. She was, in effect, all he had. Whatever feelings Narcissus developed—love, hate, disappointment, curiosity—all had only one person toward whom they could be directed: his mother. The fear of losing his one source of emotional nourishment (no matter how bad a mother Liriope may have proved to be) must have been enormous.

In becoming fixated on his own reflection, Narcissus was actually returning to a basic activity of infancy: mirroring. Psychoanalyst D. W. Winnicott discusses the image of the mother gazing at the baby in her arms, and the baby gazing at his mother's face and finding himself therein. The mother mirrors for the baby who he is, and thus aids the baby in the long procession of events that occur, culminating in the formation of a stable self-identity. But this process works only if the mother is looking at the baby as he truly is—a small, helpless creature needing her love and protection. If she does otherwise, she is projecting onto the baby her own identity, her own fears, expectations, and plans for the child. In this case, as Alice Miller has said, ". . . the child would not find himself in his mother's face but rather the mother's own predicaments. This child would remain without a mirror, and for the rest of his life would be seeking this mirror in vain." Narcissus, evidently failing to find this mirror early in life, finally managed to fulfill his childhood need late in life—but with disastrous consequences.

In finding his love in a mirror, isn't Narcissus revealing to us that he had "unfinished business" from his infancy that he needed to address? For each of us who searches and searches for a beloved and never seems to be satisfied, aren't we, too, looking more for a return to infantile ways of relating and for the mother of our infantile narcissism than for a beloved with whom we can share a mature love?

WHEN LOVE BECOMES TOO PRECIOUS: THE NARCISSISTIC DEFENSE

Whatever lack of satisfaction that Narcissus may have received in his upbringing, the fact remained that Liriope was all he had. As his only source of emotional nourishment, his mother must have seemed awfully precious to him. It is easy to understand why he would have had difficulty in feeling any anger toward her, in spite of the fact that he clearly had some very compelling reasons to be angry.

Many of us feel, as Narcissus did, that it is neither safe nor proper to hate those we love. When we have received enough love to crave it but not enough to make us feel secure in its continuance, we are faced with a dilemma. We become afraid to risk losing any love by showing any unpleasantness. One of my friends told me that she never got angry at her husband until after they were married. Some would consider even this brave. In her mind, showing anger meant risking the end of the relationship.

Gratification is, then, a precious commodity—in fact, too precious. Hence the dilemma: As the infant matures into his own separate person, gaining access to language and complex behavior that can be directed outwardly toward a loved "other," there is the ever-increasing danger that his destructive impulses may be turned against those upon whom he depends for this precious bounty.

It is in the narcissistic phase of development, when the definition of self begins to emerge, that this conflict is most highly charged. For the movement from symbiosis to separation to be mastered, the infant must know that the mother will survive the discharge of his aggressive impulses toward her. He needs to learn that expressing his rage does not actually hurt his beloved parent. In Winnicott's words, the child must know: "I can destroy the object and it can survive." The child who does not receive this message will forever believe that his own rage is destructive to others. He will stay stuck in the narcissistic phase, never able adequately to make the separation between self and other. Such narcissistic people will not have learned how to hate constructively, and they

will be placed at a disadvantage in their loving relationships until
they learn to do so.

When we choose to shield our beloveds from our anger, we believe that our rage has the power to destroy them or to destroy the
love that they give us. Out of love, and out of concern to protect
our love, we direct our destructive impulses elsewhere. How this is
done is the unique talent of the narcissist. Rather than destroy his
beloved, he cunningly turns the destructive aggression against
himself. Because it is not safe to consciously feel rage or hate, the
narcissist simply puts the feelings into his unconscious. Psychoanalyst Hyman Spotnitz calls this defensive operation the *narcissistic defense.* All the tricks that we unconsciously use to deal with our
unrecognized feelings are the myriad manifestations of narcissistic love and the narcissistic defense against our rage.

In spite of our unwillingness to hate, the destructive impulse
still needs an outlet. The need for discharge of the aggressive drive
is an essential aspect of the health of any living organism. If a situation does not exist that allows for appropriate discharge, then we
unconsciously devise a misdirected means of discharge.

The innate need for the release of aggression explains why children who are not permitted to hate their parents will find some
other object on which to release their anger. Children who are prevented from hating their parents will often hate themselves instead. Hate does not merely cease to exist just because it is not
allowed to be felt. It will always seek a victim. When it cannot be
directed elsewhere, the self becomes its prey.

The narcissist, then, suffers from internal rage that is seeking an
outlet. Herein lies the danger. Murder is in his heart, but the
murder he would want if he could allow himself to know his true
feelings would destroy the very person upon whom he depends
and whom he loves. It has become too dangerous even to feel. By
killing his angry feelings toward his beloved, the narcissist is able
to "rescue" his beloved. Psychological suicide has replaced the
urge to murder the beloved. As one self-hating narcissist said,
"Instead of knowing you want to harm someone else, you wipe
yourself out." However, as Spotnitz has said, knocking out the
potentially destructive self to forestall dangerous action against

others is equivalent to smashing a gun to bits in order to prevent oneself from pulling the trigger.

The origin of the self-preoccupation that is observed in narcissism becomes clear from this perspective. By focusing exclusively on their own wishes and needs, narcissists can successfully turn a blind eye to the hateful feelings they would rather not have. This self-preoccupation is an elaborate masquerade, one of the narcissist's tricks of the mind that successfully enable him to avoid confrontation with his destructive wishes.

CHILDHOOD LESSONS IN NOT HATING

People who engage in narcissistic defense—the redirecting of one's rage into the unconscious—have in common a particular kind of parenting. The common thread in the parental training of people who engage in narcissistic defense is that they did not get adequate help in learning how to deal with their destructive impulses. The basic message given to them as children, which they then carry into adulthood, is: "It is better to feel bad about yourself—" i.e., to feel hopeless, or worthless, or inadequate, or to believe that you are overly dependent, or not pretty or smart enough, or to think that you will be loved only if you sacrifice yourself "—than to feel bad about your mother or father." Low self-esteem is most often a by-product of unconscious rage against a parent.

Lessons about the acceptability or unacceptability of hate and lessons about love are learned simultaneously. As infants, we experienced our earliest hate feelings—we hated being hungry, cold, or lonely—but our way of dealing with our anger was limited. We could cry or yell, and if our caregiver had the sensitivity, time, and inclination to attend to us, our anguish would be relieved. But a mother who has not yet grown into the mature role of motherhood will respond to the hate of her infant with destructive hate. She may yell at the baby to stop screaming; she may ignore the baby, either leaving it alone (one of my patients said that her mother thought that when babies cried it meant they "wanted to be alone") or always giving it to an alternate caregiver; or she may turn her hateful feelings against herself, becoming depressed and feeling inadequate as a mother. Each of these reactions is a powerful communication to the infant that if he wants mother's love, he is not to be angry or dissatisfied.

I saw an event in the playground that illustrates how this message is conveyed to children by even the best of parents. A neighbor of mine, a kind, devoted father, was playing with his daughter on the swings. A friend of his walked up to him and he momentarily diverted his attention away from his child. She kept swinging and then, without any particular fanfare, proceeded to fall right out of the swing onto the ground. He swept her up even before she had a chance to utter a cry, comforting her as any loving father would do. Assessing that there was no damage, he said, "Now, April, look what you went and did to yourself." It was only at that point that April started crying. How many times does April need to hear that she has done something wrong (when in fact it was she who should have been angry with her father for not paying sufficient attention to her) before she will feel that there is something wrong *with her*? This man is, in many respects, a good father—as good as I've seen, in fact. But it's so much easier for all of us to blame the other person—especially someone less powerful than us—when something has gone wrong than it is to assume our own fault and accept the ensuing anger toward us that would accompany our acceptance of blame.

As children, self-hating narcissistic individuals were not allowed to hate their parents. Not only were they prohibited from *saying* that they had negative feelings about their parents, but to be good children they were not allowed even to *think* or *feel* these emotions. They, in effect, buy love by being the good children their parents want them to be. They become so successful at hiding their hate that they themselves become unaware of its presence.

The efforts we make in our attempts to hide our hate are legion. John Bowlby studied the effects of separating infants from their mothers and found that childhood hating, and the avenue it takes toward destruction of the self, progresses in stages.

Separation from mother is possibly the most painful and frightening experience a child can have. It arouses more rage and protestation in the child than even hunger. Initially the act of separation results in the expected cries of protest. If the mother quickly returns, the infant will regain his sense of comfort and interest in the world. Or, if the mother is predictable about her return—for example, she behaves consistently—the infant learns that people come and go and he accepts this with less and less fear.

The infant who is not consistently reassured and who is often left in a state of terror when young can still be coaxed, when the effort is made, to be interested in the world. He can forge loving relationships later in life. But always throughout this individual's life there will remain a deep sense of distrust and foreboding that has its origins in this painful period of his life.

When separation is unduly long, more hate and rage is stimulated than the infant has the ability to tolerate. After crying and crying, the infant eventually will quiet. Rather than continuing to express the rage, he will become silent, eerily calm (much like the atmosphere surrounding Narcissus and his pond). He appears to be calm only because he has stopped making demands on the people around him. In fact, he is in a state of deep mourning. His sense of detachment is profound, and, like Narcissus, he has lost interest in the world.

When this happens repeatedly, he will become permanently remote. Even any renewed attempts at caregiving at this point will fail to arouse him. The infant has withdrawn from a world that has withdrawn from him.

In order for the infant to have reached this degree of withdrawal, he has to have reached a point where he has lost all hope. Too defeated, too helpless and hopeless to try again, he has shut off all feelings of rage toward his caregivers. A psychological death has occurred; the infant has succeeded in killing the feeling function of his psyche.

This state of withdrawal and detachment is the state that Spitz discovered was inevitable when infants in the foundling hospital received no maternal attention. This apathy, one of the steps that the infants took as they began their descent into idiocy and eventual death, is the real enemy of love. This apathy—not hate—is the opposite of love. It is this apathy that leads first to the death of the psyche, and in its extreme form to the death of the body.

UNDER-GRATIFICATION AS A CAUSE OF NARCISSISM

Many self-hating narcissists have childhood histories of having their needs rarely gratified. They have learned the bitter lesson that love is not for them; they feel destined to have painful and disappointing love relationships. These are the children whose experience of parenting was a perpetual "No." If they wanted it, almost by definition they couldn't have it. This lesson, carried into adulthood, becomes an expectation that is self-fulfilling. Self-sacrifice becomes the mode of relating; pain and hurt are embraced.

Rachel is this kind of self-sacrificing narcissist. Although she works long hours and her long-distance boyfriend doesn't work at all, it is she who makes the four-hour trek in the car to spend the weekend with him. It is she who does all the cooking and food shopping for the two of them. The fact that this is hardly fair doesn't occur to her. She is used to being the one who makes sacrifices, and she merely assumes it is the way of relationships.

Narcissistic self-sacrifice takes a variety of forms. It is found in depression, in codependent relationships, in addiction, anorexia, and even psychosomatic conditions. Its origin is always narcissistic hate that is turned against the self. The self-sacrificing narcissist idealizes his beloved and believes it is only himself who deserves contempt or hatred. The idealized beloved is completely insulated from the narcissist's rage.

When the psychic self—from whence come thoughts and feelings, impulses, wishes, and desires—is sacrificed, the mind is virtually anesthetized and thoughts and feelings are blocked from consciousness. The narcissistic defense has the advantage of protecting any loved others from the rage, but it has the terrible disadvantage of making a sacrificial lamb out of the psyche of the protector.

NARCISSISTS IN LOVE

Research indicates that people tend to choose partners who are on the same basic level of mental maturity. It is likely, then, that narcissists will be involved with other narcissists (narcissistic women will find narcissistic men, and vice versa). Most often, then, narcissistic love relationships involve a collusion between two people who are unconsciously committed to perpetuating destructiveness in the relationship. The same narcissistic pairing can also be present in relationships between siblings, friends, or between parents and children.

The Narcissus story is instructive in this regard, as well. It turns out that Narcissus actually does have a rather long-term relationship with one woman before he settles on himself. Her name is Echo, and by the time their relationship ends, they have made each other exceedingly unhappy. But their story starts off quite romantically.

Echo falls instantly in love with Narcissus as she watches him wandering around the countryside, searching for his true love. He, of course, is oblivious to her, as he has been to all previous admirers. Nevertheless, Echo is persistent in her pursuit, waiting patiently for the day when she might be able to make her presence known to him. Then finally one day Narcissus, feeling a bit adventuresome, wanders off from his buddies and, finding himself alone, calls out: "Is there anybody here?" Echo is listening and wants badly to call out to him in return. But Echo has suffered a painful and damaging past and has an affliction that makes conversation with other people extremely difficult. Echo can only repeat the sounds she hears. Echo's answer to Narcissus is: "Here." Each time Narcissus speaks, Echo faithfully answers back, repeating his last word.

Echo is relatively easy for Narcissus to tolerate. As long as Narcissus perceives that Echo is making no demands on him, he continues trying to talk to her, believing that what he is hearing is the voice of another. But this "other" is in fact simply a projection of himself. In fact, there is no "other" at all in Echo. She has no self; she exists only as a reflection of Narcissus. Neither Echo nor Narcissus is capable of any true emotional exchange, because neither has a highly enough developed self to have a separate identity.

We are tempted to conclude that Echo must have loved Narcissus a whole lot for her to tolerate this painful situation of loving him when he clearly did not love her in return. He was, at best, only tolerating her. He never complimented her, nor told her that she brought pleasure into his life. In fact, most of his communications to her expressed dissatisfaction, his impatience with not being able to find her.

Echo is not, however, a hero of love; she is, simply, like her beloved, a narcissist. She is able to tolerate the pain of a one-sided relationship with Narcissus not because she loves him so much, but rather because she hates herself so much. Echo makes the same fatal choice in choosing Narcissus as a beloved that Narcissus later makes in choosing himself. Although they both appear to be "in love," Echo, in her vain pursuit of Narcissus, and Narcissus, in his hopeless pursuit of his reflection, are in fact both directing murderous hate against themselves. Both Echo and Narcissus attempt to obliterate themselves by choosing to be involved with a person incapable of fulfilling a single desire or need of theirs. Yet, as Echo stays with Narcissus, continuing to pursue him, and permitting herself only to mirror him, so, too, does Narcissus stay with his reflection in the pond.

What kind of person is able to tolerate such a frustrating and destructive relationship? Someone who, like Narcissus and Echo, enters into the relationship already damaged. Someone who is totally self-absorbed—a narcissist (whether in the guise of grandiosity, as Narcissus personifies, or self-deprecation, as Echo personifies)—would find such one-way interaction fairly familiar and comfortable. The main attraction of this kind of doomed love relationship is that it provides the narcissist with an opportunity for self-destruction.

The particular kind of narcissistic pairing that Narcissus and Echo had is not unusual and is always destructive. When a self-sacrificing narcissist falls in love with a self-aggrandizing narcissist, their neuroses mesh perfectly—and both people end up unhappy.

Soon enough the destructiveness sets in. The self-aggrandizing narcissist becomes more and more dissatisfied with his mate, because his needs are insatiable. He may even resort to abuse. The more abuse that is heaped on the self-sacrificing narcissist, the more apologetic and submissive she becomes. She tries everything in her power to please her mate, but all attempts fail. She knows it's her fault (nothing, after all is *his* fault) and her self-hatred becomes all the more intense. Usually, as in the case of Narcissus, the self-aggrandizing narcissist will leave his mate in her misery, in search of a more perfect beloved.

Such narcissistic love pairings are doomed to failure because neither individual is capable of knowing or loving the other. Echo, without a true self, represents the self-sacrificing narcissist, who is too damaged to want or expect anything for herself. Narcissus, obsessed with his own image, represents the self-aggrandizing, grandiose narcissist, who thinks only about his own needs. In the end these two narcissists, like Narcissus and Echo, will be alone, their self-inflicted misery being their only companion.

THE NARCISSISM OF DEPRESSION

Narcissus, as we have seen, was extremely agile in getting other people depressed. He left Echo in a shambles; another admirer, Amenias, killed himself. Narcissus' secret to doing this was quite simple.

In fact, one of the easiest things to do is to get another person depressed. All you need to do is tell someone something that will provoke hostility, and then seal off any outlet for their discharging of their aggression. It is a technique that is used routinely by parents on their children, and when these children grow up they use it on their spouses and their own children.

For instance, Andy begs his mother to let him try out for the football team. She says maybe, she'll discuss it with his father. He asks the next day. She says they're thinking about it. The boy explains that all his friends are trying out, it's really important to him, he really wants to do this. She says, "Maybe, we'll see." The boy knows it's not a sure thing, but she hasn't said no, so he keeps hoping. He asks again the next day and this time she says, "No. It's too dangerous." Andy is crestfallen. He imagines lonely afternoons, walking home alone after school while all his chums are staying for football practice. He imagines the closeness his buddies will feel while he is left out. He feels terrible. Then he realizes that his mother is the only mother in the neighborhood who has said no. It seems unreasonable. Why is she being so mean and unreasonable? he wonders. It's not fair.

In his anger, Andy starts to protest: "But, Mom, all the other kids' mothers are—" She interrupts him: "That's enough, Andy. I don't want to hear any more about it." "But Mom—" "That's it. Subject closed. We've made our decisions." Andy skulks away, feeling dejected and upset, and goes to his room to listen to his records. Then he thinks that he could go over to his buddy Tom's house and at least get a little sympathy from Tom about his mother's unfairness. He starts to leave the house and his mother asks him where he is going. He says, in a barely audible tone, with his head down, not meeting his mother's eyes, "Tom's house." She responds, "Oh, Andy, are you still upset about that football thing? Come on over here, let me give you a hug. You know I love you. I just don't want you to get hurt." Andy passively lets his mother hug him, and goes deeper into his depression, not quite knowing why, since his mother obviously loves him.

This kind of scenario, replayed over and over again between Andy and his mother, will leave Andy permanently scarred. It is not that Andy's mother doesn't love him; she does. She may even have a reasonable point about not wanting him to get hurt. But it doesn't *feel* that way to Andy. The situation frustrates Andy and makes him angry. While Andy's mother may love Andy, she does not help him find a way to express his frustration and anger. Instead, Andy learns the lesson that the only proper thing to do when he's angry is to get depressed. So, as the pattern becomes ingrained, throughout his life whenever he is in a situation in which his hostility is aroused, he will get depressed. Andy's depression will have destructive consequences, not against those who arouse it but against himself.

THE NARCISSISM OF CODEPENDENCE

Mara and Jay have a codependent relationship not unlike that of Echo and Narcissus. Mara was a twenty-year-old college student when she fell in love with her drama instructor. As captain of the tennis team, an officer of the student government, and homecoming queen, Mara had her pick of dates, but she was drawn to Jay because she knew he needed her. Jay was a thirty-nine-year-old, twice-divorced alcoholic. On stage he used his melancholic and brooding personality to dramatize the brilliance and passion of classic theater. His students were a captivated and enthralled audience. After each class he and Mara would linger to further discuss the class. Often Jay took Mara into the city to teach her more about drama, art, and music. He opened her eyes to the beauty of the fine arts and he opened his suffering soul to her willing sympathies.

Mara's family history gave her experience in dealing with Jay's torment, which was familiar and even comfortable to her. Her father was emotionally distant and her mother was an alcoholic. She knew Jay's pain. He hurt, she reasoned, because he was so alone. And he drank to drown that misery. She knew she could save him from self-destruction.

To do this, Mara turned down the advice of her family and friends and married Jay. Then she dropped out of school and went to work full-time so that Jay could go back to graduate school for his doctoral degree. Although Jay was still drinking heavily and was staying out until all hours of the night, Mara continued to struggle and sacrifice for his sake; she quietly bore her own pain and unhappiness because she knew in her heart that eventually she would make Jay happy and he would be forever grateful and loving.

Jay and Mara live in a codependent relationship, because Jay is as dependent on Mara as she is on him. This is actually quite common between narcissists. Those, like Jay, who are absorbed in their own needs and desires to the exclusion of anyone else's can relate only to partners who are able to put aside all their own needs and wants and cater exclusively to them. And those narcissists, like Mara, who are absorbed in their own worthlessness, can relate only to partners who perpetuate their feelings of self-loathing. Each one, deprived of mature personality development, enables the other to wallow forever is his or her own concerns. Neither one can truly love; they both feel only needs. Each depends on the other to fill those needs.

THE NARCISSISM OF SELF-SACRIFICE

Cathy, a patient of mine, is a self-sacrificing narcissist who is repeating in her adult life a frustrating and painful past. Cathy has been living with Neil for four years. During most of this time Neil has jockeyed for the upper hand. To keep her in her place he has, in subtle but persistent ways, criticized, denigrated, and ridiculed her daily. Cathy (like Echo) reacts by simply mirroring what he says about her and blames herself for his unhappiness. We might say, as has Robin Norwood in her popular book *Women Who Love Too Much,* that Cathy "loves" Neil too much, since she is willing to put up with all kinds of emotional abuse. In fact, a closer approximation to the truth would be that Cathy hates herself too much.

A typical illustration of the imbalance in their relationship came up recently in a conversation about her tennis game. "I've started taking lessons," she said, "and my coach says I'm really doing great. Neil loves tennis and I had hoped it was something we could enjoy together. But I guess I was naive to think that. He's been playing for ten years and is really very good. I shouldn't have been disappointed when he said that I wasn't good enough to play with him. He's right; I should be better than I am by now. Maybe if I concentrated more and tried harder, I'd be good enough so that he wouldn't feel it to be burdensome to hit a few balls with me."

It's not surprising that Cathy had a domineering father to whom she (and her mother) submitted, and that Neil, too, had a domineering father whom he imitated. In Cathy's household, women were "loved" and protected only as long as they played by the father's rules. If Cathy's upbringing had been different, she might not be so quick to take all the blame and criticism in the hope of hanging onto the affection of her lover. At this point in her life, it is still impossible for her to say, "Of course we're on different levels of play; how about helping me to improve by hitting me some balls?"

The dynamic between Cathy and Neil replays itself in many ways throughout each day. Neil tells Cathy she's inadequate, and rather than risk a confrontation that might shake the fragile peace, Cathy internalizes and believes his pronouncements. In her mind, her own needs have ceased to matter; only his count.

The phrase "loving too much" conjures up an image of someone who gives, nurtures, and sacrifices, and then gives some more. People who "love too much" get little satisfaction out of the relationship and yet will do anything to keep it intact. Parents, for example, who are repeatedly subjected to the cruel and insensitive actions of their grown children and yet still bail them out of one jam after another could be accused of loving too much. Lovers and spouses, too, can get caught in loving-too-much relationships, in which one partner scurries to make everything just right, tries to meet all the needs of the other person, and takes full responsibility for everything that goes wrong. As Robin Norwood says: ". . . they measure the degree of their love by the depth of their torment." The more frantically they "love" their partner, the more completely they obliterate their own personalities and desires. This is why "loving too much" is a powerful form of psychic suicide.

THE NARCISSISM OF ADDICTION

It's also possible to anesthetize the mind by means of various addictions. Substance abuse is the most obvious mind-numbing device, but sometimes narcissists get addicted to another person, rather than to a substance. In these cases, the person to whom the addict is attached serves the same mind-anesthetizing function as an addictive substance. The "enabler," the person who is depended on, needs to have someone to depend on him. Both addict and enabler play a hating game with each other and with themselves, the addict expressing self-hate by becoming totally dependent, and the enabler by choosing to live his life with a person who cannot exchange true feelings.

Maggie, another patient of mine, is what we would call a "love addict." She uses love as she would any addictive substance or behavior—purely for need gratification; it helps her avoid facing her own fear, pain, and rage. Maggie always had a boyfriend and would do whatever she felt she had to do to keep him or to find a new lover quickly.

Because Maggie married Paul only eight weeks after they met,

Paul had no way of knowing the depths of Maggie's needs. Yes, he had wanted her to love him, but he didn't understand that this love would be so overwhelming and demanding that he would soon need to pull away from its grip. Paul actually was not interested in being an enabler, but he found himself married to a woman who could not tolerate any separation from him, physical or mental.

For about a month after the wedding Maggie functioned quite normally and all seemed well. The first signs of Maggie's addiction appeared when Paul had to work late or take a client to dinner. Maggie would panic and assume this meant that Paul no longer loved her and was trying to avoid her. In Paul's absence, Maggie's self-loathing would surface. She would pace the floors, unable to concentrate on anything until Paul returned to hold her close and give her a "fix" of reassurance.

Although Paul's promises of love calmed her down temporarily, in truth no amount of reassurances could calm Maggie's feelings of insecurity and self-hatred. Maggie felt she needed more and more time with Paul, and soon dedicated her life to avoiding the fact that Paul might have needs different from her own. Maggie dropped all her own interests and clung to his. She canceled her membership at the gym because Paul wasn't interested in working out; she stopped socializing with her friends because Paul was more of a loner than she and she knew that he preferred quiet times at home to social nights out. She put away her palette because Paul didn't seem interested in her talent. Maggie's new hobby became Paul.

It didn't surprise me when Maggie started talking about the fact that she drinks wine most nights. Alcohol is often an accomplice in the destructive pattern that obliterates the self. When we talk about her drinking, Maggie says, "It helps ease my fear of being alone. I know if I ever really have to face my feelings, I'd probably want to kill myself. Drinking calms me down. When I've had a drink, I don't hurt so much."

Maggie may have found a way to ease the pain of her self-hatred, but she's paying a high price for "love." She is in the classic double bind of the narcissist: On the one hand, she is giving up her identity, yet on the other, her own cravings are so overwhelming that she is unable to focus on her beloved. Love-addicted narcissists are driven by their own need for constant attention, depending upon their lovers to fulfill their insatiable needs.

As with all love addicts, it looks as though Maggie craves love. But more love will not solve her problem. Because she has not matured past the stage where need gratification comes first, Maggie can't yet give or receive mature love.

NACISSISM OF THE BODY

The narcissist, unable to tolerate consciously the dangerous rage that he (or she) feels, may turn his destructive aggression against either the mind or the body. The child who learns to discharge frustration/aggression against his body becomes a likely candidate for psychosomatic illness later in life. Rather than being depressed, anxious, or love-addicted, he may instead be physically ill. One of my patients, who suffered from stomach ulcers when he started seeing me, told me he was plagued with stomachaches every summer between the ages of ten and thirteen. He remembered those summers as being times when his father had to travel abroad. They were also the summers when he was playing Little League. Only years later was he able to feel conscious rage at his father for not being around during those months. As a child, the idea of hating his father was too threatening to tolerate, so his anger redirected itself against his own body. Those stomachaches were a forerunner for his later bout with ulcers.

Physicians have known for centuries that there is an intimate connection between the mind and body. Such is the premise of the field of discipline called psychosomatic medicine. It has been only within the last fifty years, however, that we have been able scientifically to document the link between destructive aggression turned against the self and physical illness. A wealth of experimental and clinical research indicates that psychosomatic conditions are experienced primarily by narcissistic individuals who find their propensity for destructive aggression so frightening that they paralyze their potential for destructive action by turning their aggression against their own bodies.

Sherry is such an individual. She was thrilled with her upcoming marriage to Les, but anxious at the same time:

> He's so perfect. Everything I've always wanted in a man. I can't believe he's going to marry me. I've never had good luck like this in the past. Something's got to go wrong.

Sherry was right. Something was bound to go wrong, and something did. Two weeks before her marriage she developed ulcerative colitis, a painful inflammatory condition in the colon. But it wasn't bad luck that brought on this condition. In elevating Les, Sherry was denigrating herself. Whatever aggressive feelings she may have been having toward Les—the perfect fiancé—were now being redirected against her body. Although her words suggested an unconscious dissatisfaction with Les, she seemed intent on not allowing herself to recognize or experience these feelings:

> I want to redecorate the house. I was really hoping to get that done before we moved in. But Les thought that that was a bad idea. We would have had to cover the cost of two apartments while the work was being done. We can afford it, but I guess it really is a bad idea. It's ok. He's usually got better sense about these kinds of things than I do. It's just that it'll be more inconvenient to do it when we're living there—you know with all that sawdust and paint. Really, though, I don't mind. I shouldn't even be thinking about the inconvenience. What's important is that we'll be married and together.

As the immortal words of Macbeth suggest, perhaps the lady does protest too much. While assuring herself that she's fine, Les is fine, and their love is fine, Sherry can't help but reveal her repressed anger. Even more of her repressed rage filters through to her body.

Sherry had some painful reckoning to do in order to clear up her colitis. Only after she accepted her rage toward Les for always insisting that they do things *his* way and rendering her a virtual slave to his decisions did Sherry begin to recover.

FATAL NARCISSISTIC ATTRACTIONS

Not all narcissistic individuals who resort to turning their aggression against their bodies have Sherry's resiliency. Some are unable to reverse this self-destructive pattern and have a lifetime of illnesses. Some die of their ailments.

Years ago I began to notice in my practice a particular kind of narcissistic love relationship that led invariably to the death of one of the partners. This observation came out of my work with cancer patients. I wondered, as have many of my colleagues, why some patients with medically hopeless conditions survive against all odds, while others with far less threatening cancers succumb to the disease.

The answer seemed to lie, in part, in the kinds of relationships each attracted. My patients who never managed to triumph over their disease, despite favorable odds medically, seemed to have in common a particular form of narcissistic love relationship.

When a self-sacrificing narcissist who turns aggression against the body is bonded to an overly gratified narcissist, the self-destructive urge of the self-sacrificing member of the partnership is particularly strong. At the same time, the sole goal of the partner who has a history of excessive gratification is to bend the other to his will.

Vera and Gregg were such a couple. When Vera came to me, she had been diagnosed with early breast cancer. She talked about the period of time just preceding the diagnosis:

> The best thing that ever happened to me was when I got my job at NBC. They recognized what I had to contribute. I knew that if I brought Gregg into the job it would prove to be disastrous to me. At first I resisted. He kept hounding me and hounding me; he was unemployed and he needed the work. He kept telling me how selfish I was, and that he wouldn't treat me that way in the same position. So finally I relented. It took about all of two weeks before he had completely taken over. He got the director to start taking orders from him; he changed the script. Every idea I had was thrown out the window, without even a discussion. I moved from being an up-and-coming star to being his little lackey, and

he had everyone believing that this was what was best for the project—the project they had hired me to do.

I started getting sick right after the project was over. Gregg made me feel like he would just as soon have me dead. He talked about our financial situation, and how difficult it would be if I got too sick to work. He was talking about me as though I were already dead.

I wanted to leave him but I had wrapped up all my money with him. I had no money of my own. We actually separated for a month. During that time my son acted out continuously; he had terrible fights with me; he started not going to school. When I went back to Gregg his acting out was instantly over. I decided to stay with Gregg for my son's sake.

At some point, I just know that my fight left me. My aggression was always a little like white bread to begin with—so refined it was valueless. But with this situation, I couldn't even argue anymore; I couldn't fight Gregg or try to persuade him to see how destructive he was being. I felt like I was a sponge and he was squeezing my life's waters out of me. If he doesn't stop, it all is going to kill me.

Vera died of cancer six months later. Gregg remarried three months after her death.

The kind of narcissistic pairing that Vera and Gregg demonstrate has actually been studied in Germany. Researchers distinguished individuals who were psychologically homicidal from those who were psychologically suicidal. Then they correlated these two types of psychological patterns with physical diseases and found that cancer patients are characteristically blocked by others (i.e., are suicidal), while cardiovascular, diabetic, and gastric ulcer patients chronically try to block others (i.e., are homicidal). It is easy to understand how a homicidal/suicidal pact between two narcissistic people—one who can't love himself or herself and the other who can't love another—can lead to the death of the suicidal member of the dyad.

THE BEAST OF NARCISSISTIC LOVE

What each of these psychological maneuvers—attacking either the mind or the body—has in common is the obliteration of the feeling portion of the psyche. This is, as I have said, an act of psychological suicide.

The devotion and self-sacrifice that characterize many narcissistic relationships may at first look like love. However, love has nothing to do with the psychological dynamic that is being played out. Self-sacrificing narcissists try to improve their relationships by obliterating themselves. They "love" so much that they willingly incinerate their own needs on the altar of self-hate.

There is a short story by Henry James, "The Beast in the Jungle," that depicts a fatal narcissistic love relationship. The protagonist in James' story is in love with a charming and devoted woman, to whom he has no difficulty declaring his love and his intent to marry after a suitable courtship. But he arrives one day on his customary visit to her with dire news. In a flash of inexorable uncertainty, it has come to him that he is doomed to some terrible fate that, like a beast in the jungle, will leap upon him without warning and utterly destroy him. Though he has little understanding of the origin of his feeling, he has no doubt as to its authenticity. He cannot, then, in all decency, thrust his imminent and tragic fate upon one whom he holds so dear, and insists on relaxing his claim on her. In vain she protests that their love binds them to share his fate. Yet despite her fighting for the preservation of their relationship, he is adamant.

Months go by, and the two never marry. The man is willing to continue seeing his lady love, whiling away his time, waiting for his fate to befall him. He begins to enjoy his nocturnal discourses with her, speculating endlessly about how and when his fate will arrive. While he seems to thrive on the anticipation, quite enjoying the role of a tragic figure, she does not. She loses weight and vitality, becomes sickly, and eventually dies. He is appropriately grief-stricken and somewhat puzzled by the fact that her family does not include him among the chief mourners. He has, after all, been loyal in his visits to her and honorable in freeing her from his still-awaited fate.

In spite of her family's shunning him, he continues with his devotion to her—now his memory of her. He makes it his practice to visit the cemetery regularly and lay a little flower offering on her grave as a memorial. One day, as he enters the cemetery to perform his customary ritual, he finds himself face-to-face with a man just turning away from a newly dug grave. The man's expression is one of such raw, stark, tragic loss that our hitherto complacent hero suddenly knows that the beast has sprung. He realizes that he has never allowed himself to love anyone enough to suffer the pain of tragic loss. He has been, in fact, a selfish receptacle for feelings, but has lacked the ability to send feelings out. She was a self-sacrificing sender of feelings, tolerating a relationship in which none came toward her. The beast was not in the jungle but within themselves—the beast of narcissistic love.

THE FINAL LESSON OF THE NARCISSUS STORY

According to legend, after starving to death from self-neglect, Narcissus takes root in the banks of the river and is transformed into the poisonous flower that bears his name, and which ever since blooms in splendor but destroys those who try to consume it. The narcissistic love of all those—parents and lovers alike—whose "love" is a thin disguise for hate carries the same destiny.

PART II

THE CHRONOLOGY OF LOVES

Immature love says "I love you because I need you."
Mature love says "I need you because I love you."

ERICH FROMM

CHAPTER 5

The Dark Side of Mother Love: Mother's Kisses and Dangerous Feelings

It seems fitting to continue our journey into the myriad ways that love can turn dark by going to the source—that illustrious blueprint of other forms of love: mother love. The relationship between mother and infant is the most sacrosanct love relationship we have. It is a love that is not supposed to be open to ambivalence or error. It is a love that is expected to be unconditional and unswerving. Babies are, after all, loved for who they are, not for what they do.

Similarly, mother love is presumably born out of the wellsprings of our deepest emotions. In a world where it has become acceptable to trade in spouses, change jobs, and abandon friends, mothers are expected to love and care for their children forever, no matter what kind of parenting skills they have and no matter what kind of children they produce. Mothers of doctors and lawyers, rapists and psychopaths—all mothers are supposed to love their offspring. All of this is not to say that fathers don't love their children deeply (of course they do) or that fathers aren't important (of course they are), but mother love seems to have greater burdens placed upon it than any other type of love.

No mother can live up to our idealization of mother love. Motherhood is fraught with as many negative feelings and as many dangers as any other kind of love, and for many good reasons. For example, mothers of young children have less freedom, less sex, less time, and less money for themselves than women without children.

Mothers turn their dreams of motherhood into nightmares when they are unprepared for the feelings of resentment and rage that inevitably accompany the restraints and sacrifices that motherhood demands. The hate in mother love can turn destructive when the mother is unable to balance her needs with her child's needs. If she holds the child accountable for her problems, or projects her own conflicts onto her child, she has made the child a victim of her own neuroses. The child is in effect punished for sins that are unrelated to him or her.

Mothers need to find the place between love and hate where they can give themselves permission to feel hatred toward their children and actually use that emotion to nurture a secure and healthy bond of love. Denying this hatred does not have the intended effect. Instead of strengthening the mother/child bond, focusing exclusively on warmth, affection, and joy has the effect of driving resentment and anger into the unconscious, where it seethes until an explosive opportunity presents itself (and one always will).

MOTHER LOVE

Whether in spite of or because of the expectations we place on mother love, the love a mother has for her child does seem to be different from any other form of love. I have asked countless mothers to describe the difference between the love they feel for their husbands and the love they feel for their children. Without exception each one of them declared that, without hesitation, she would give up her life to save her child. Only a few women professed a willingness to do the same for their husbands.

Mother love, in fact, assures the survival of the species. Humans need to be caring to their offspring. Many authorities believe that the human infant is born with only half of its gestation period completed. This first half of gestation occurs within the womb, and the second half begins with birth and lasts until the beginning of crawling—about ten months. During this extended extrauterine gestation, the infant is entirely at the mercy of her (or his) caregiver. If no one feeds her, she will starve; if no one warms her and protects her, she will die.

Mother love, the active concern for the well-being of the child, is the first love each of us knows and our life literally depends upon the strength of that bond. This, then, is another reason why later in life we feel that love is a matter of life and death—that we will "die" if our beloved doesn't love us back, or that our beloved is "killing" us with inattention or brutal attention.

All of the needs that the infant has for its mother create a parallel need in the mother. A mother's emotional need for her infant is often as strong as the infant's need for her. Through these interchanges of needs, the mother/child bond is forged.

The sacrifices mothers are willing to make for their children are illustrated every day in great and small ways. As researcher K. Robson has suggested: "The human mother is subject to an extended, exceedingly trying and often unrewarding period of caring for her infant." But the rewards apparently make the sacrifices worthwhile.

Primary among the rewards that the mother receives is the responsiveness of the infant. When an infant recognizes her mother and establishes eye contact or smiles, the mother experiences extremely positive feelings. Robson points out the benefit of these intimate exchanges: ". . . nature has been wise in making both eye-to-eye contact, and the social smile . . . behaviors that . . . generally foster positive maternal feelings and a sense of payment for 'services rendered.' "

Fortunately, the rewards for the fierce devotion, loyalty, and sacrifice that accompany motherhood continue as the child develops. Although the length of the bond may stretch, it still remains, tying mother and child irrevocably together. Every achievement the child accomplishes fills a loving mother with pride. A sweet embrace by a loving child can warm even the stoniest of hearts. Pains of the child are felt by the mother as though they are her own. For the biological mother, the memory of the oneness that once existed between mother and fetus is never very far from consciousness. This maternal ability to bond with an infant is apparently instinctual enough in some women that even though they cannot bear children they attain the same level of sacrifice and commitment to an adopted child.

MOTHER'S SECRET

Everyone loves a baby. Hardly any of us can resist the chubby cheeks and soft, supple skin of a newborn. But there is a secret about this, a truth that all mothers know. Everyone loves a baby except, sometimes, its own mother.

Ambivalence to one's own child, or even downright aversion, can begin with pregnancy. Until recently it was assumed that "normal" mothers-to-be would naturally rejoice at the prospect of mother-hood. Should the expected feelings of joy not appear, the mother-to-be had the glorious choice between feeling guilty or feeling that there was something "wrong" with her.

As any expectant mother knows, however, ambivalence and fearfulness are part of pregnancy—even a planned, much-desired pregnancy. All mothers-to-be wonder what effect their unborn will have on their life plans, their marriage, and their figures. Pregnancy itself can bring aches, pains, inconveniences, and even life-threatening complications. The fetus demands more than he gives (he gives, mostly, just a promise), and the mother can come to resent the one-sidedness of this relationship. Along with love and happy anticipation, hatred of this parasite who is sapping her energy is also a natural response by the mother-to-be. This "beloved" creature, no matter how wanted he is and who only *this* woman can give life to, is just as likely to be experienced as a vulture than as an angel.

Ambivalence about pregnancy can be manifested in a variety of ways other than mere alternation of good and bad feelings. Some of my patients respond to pregnancy with illogical feelings of resentment or betrayal, as though they were not willing participants in the event. Sometimes a woman may feel that the pregnancy is being forced upon her, and she may resent her husband and blame him for the circumstances. She may fear the loss of love of her husband and anticipate, with her ever-expanding body, that he will find her repulsive.

Pregnancy, as well, stimulates feelings that are related to our own mothering. Each of us carries within us the baby each of us was and is no longer. How we relate to our children—born and unborn—is in part determined by how our mothers related to us. If our own mothering was imbued with destructive hate, we may identify with this hateful mother and fear that we will damage the child.

It is common folklore to reassure fearful and ambivalent mothers that their negative feelings will instantly and magically disappear upon the arrival of the baby. This does not always happen.

Sheila was a patient of mine who suffered from what is commonly called postpartum depression. She had Zachary when she was twenty-five. Shortly before his birth she began to suffer from vague feelings of imminent doom. Both she and her husband assumed it had to do with the natural fears of giving birth. Neither was unduly concerned at that point.

But Sheila's anxiety about her own state of mind rose precipitously when Zach was first brought to her to nurse. She looked at the child—her child—and felt no sense of recognition, no sense of: "Oh—so this is you—the you I've felt inside me—kicking and bulging—letting me know all the time about your presence—the you who's finally come out to meet me and whom I'm eager to know and love." There was, instead, only a vast gulf between them, mother, ultimately, feeling as helpless and blind and in as unfamiliar a place as baby.

None of this was made any better by the blue flowers and baby birds that seemed to fill every empty space: the books demanding baby's picture and baby's thumb, and the stuffed animals waiting to be squeezed and honked and held onto. And it wasn't made any better by the instant love that any passing stranger seemed to be able to confer quite naturally and spontaneously upon baby Zach, which his own mother did not feel.

Sheila was operating on a misconception. Had she known more about the true nature of mother love, she might have saved herself a lot of tears or a lot of fitful nights brooding over her failure as a mother.

Mother love, like all other loves, does not necessarily come easily or even spontaneously. We can accept this in our adult relationships much more readily than we can in mother/child relationships. New mothers who do not instantly love their child feel they are defective. In her book *My Mother, My Self,* Nancy Friday refers to the mother/infant ideal and postpartum depression: "I suspect that when postpartum depression enters, it begins in the silence she must maintain if her child does not fulfill her fantasy of perfect maternal bliss."

Sheila knew that her baby was a precious, tiny angel. But during those first few days he was, to her, anything but. He was a rapacious mouth, a great giant insisting on satisfaction, encouragement, and understanding; insisting on all kinds of things that Sheila herself had gotten only intermittently and certainly not enough so that she felt capable of giving them back. Because of her own experience of maternal deprivation, Sheila was unprepared to be the generous, all-giving mother that motherhood demands for infants. She was ill equipped to manage the host of complex and contradictory feelings, sensations, and urges, both her own and her infant's. She wanted more than anything to love her baby. She hated herself for the jealousy she felt toward the baby for the showering of affection he was receiving. She hated the baby for his apparent displeasure with her discomfort with him. All of these were normal, inevitable feelings for Sheila to be having, given her own history of maternal deprivation. But Sheila, like so many mothers, had bought a picture-perfect version of motherhood and remained convinced that her negative feelings for her child were a signal that she was failing in this monumental task of motherhood.

The impossibility of this mothering ideal is conveyed by a little-known legal tradition, still in existence, in England. For a year and a day after childbirth, a woman may not be judged criminally liable for killing her child. The law has determined that during this time frame, the woman may not have made the necessary separation from her child to enable her to be completely rational in her attitude toward her infant. She may, rather, see the child as still a part of herself, and in killing the child in a fit of rage or despair, she may be symbolically killing a part of herself. In the case of Mary Beth Tinning, convicted (American) killer of nine of her children, eight of them were killed within six months of her having given birth. The only exception, the ninth, was killed when he was two and a half. He was also the only child of Mary Beth's who was adopted.

Sometimes the disillusionment, instead of becoming apparent shortly after the child's birth, comes later in the evolving relationship between mother and child. Mothers and babies have their own psychic paces; some do better with one stage than another. Some mothers adore the symbiosis of early infancy, but when the child begins the process of separation, unresolved conflicts from the mother's own childhood are reactivated and she begins to fear abandonment and rejection. She may cling to her child unduly, hoping to ward off the demons of her vision of a lonely future; or, she may push the child away, rejecting him before he has a chance to reject her.

Other mothers can't tolerate the demands of the early dependence and eagerly await the day when the child is more self-sufficient. The child then receives the message that dependency needs are not good to have, and that only independence is cherished. Some mothers have the most interest in their child when the child learns to talk; others when the child can't talk. Each of these phases of the child's development will reawaken in the mother her own experience in her own developmental history. The success of her relationship with her own child through these phases will have a lot to do with the success her own mother had with her through the same developmental phases.

In addition, there are the experiences that are related strictly to the individual personality of the child. Tracy and Mike, for instance, had no difficulty with the pregnancy or the first few days after birth. Little Joey seemed to be the perfect child, and they were looking forward to bringing him home from the hospital with unbridled glee. They were both professional people in their thirties who had worked hard to build a savings that would allow Tracy to be a stay-at-home mom. They had planned that after Joey's birth, Tracy would settle peacefully and contentedly into the state of motherhood. However, what Tracy and Mike had yet to learn was that their little Joey was going to develop a personality that would make peace and contentment a thing of the past in his new home.

Once home from the hospital, Mike and Tracy quickly found that if Joey was not "in motion," he was screaming. To their dismay, they found the only way to quiet their infant was to give him rides in the car, the carriage, or in their arms as they paced the floor. Mike and Tracy tried everything they could think of to quiet their child without having to physically carry him around. But the rocking chair, the mechanical swing, and even a seat on top of the vibrating washing machine could not calm him.

At Joey's three-month checkup, his pediatrician announced with satisfaction that he was in perfect health. Tracy could no longer contain her frustration and burst into tears. "Please find something wrong with him so I can understand why he cries all day and all night," she pleaded. "You've got to either fix him or keep him. I can't take this child home as he is."

The pediatrician tried to comfort and reassure Tracy. He believed that Joey was what he called a "difficult" child. "These kinds of children are very demanding," continued the doctor. "But most often they grow out of this period of crying and constant irritation when they reach six months of age and are better able to manipulate their world. Give him, and yourself, some time."

Tracy left the office feeling neither comforted nor assured; instead she was completely worn and defeated. She walked out into the day, knowing that until Mike came home to begin his shift, she would do nothing more than bend to the demands of this twelve-pound dictator. For the rest of that day Tracy cried as often and as loudly as her son. She asked herself over and over how this long-awaited miracle of love could cause her to suffer exhaustion, frustration, anger, and even hatred. How could she love her son so dearly and yet feel so estranged from him?

Tracy had reached the point where she was at the limit of her motherly generosity. She did manage, however, to find a solution that offered her temporary reprieve. Late in the afternoon she dressed Joey in the warmest clothes she could find, covering him from top to bottom. She put him in his stroller, lay three blankets on top of him, and on the coldest day of the year, she placed him in his stroller on the back porch. She closed the sliding glass doors, and proceeded about her business of cleaning house, with earphones on her head, oblivious to any sounds that might be emanating from Joey's mouth.

When Tracy's husband arrived home, he was shocked and enraged to find Joey out in the frigid weather. He thought that Tracy had lost her mind. He accused her of child abuse and ordered her to see a therapist immediately. Tracy found her earlier conviction that her decision had represented the only course possible to her other than outright violence suddenly dwindling under the force of Mike's argument. Perhaps Mike is right, she thought. Perhaps I *have* gone off the deep end. Now panicked, Tracy called the same physician she had seen earlier and asked if she might have harmed her child. The doctor replied that if the baby had stayed warm (he had), and had spent at least some of the time resting peacefully (he did), no lasting physical damage would have been done.

Tracy's solution to Joey's incessant demands was not the best solution, but it was a first step in her ability to acknowledge that she could not live up to her own expectations of motherhood. Although there were doubtless better solutions, still the act of temporarily removing her child from her field of awareness had allowed Tracy a necessary part of the day in which she was able to shore up her reserves in order to meet the continuing demands of the days after. Even mother love has its limits.

Mother love, like all other forms of love, is infused with a great deal of hate, anger, and resentment. These feelings are normal and inevitable. No matter how desired and how intensely loved, children are not always bundles of joy. Infants do a lot of defecating, urinating, spitting up, crying, and whimpering for attention. They demand constant supervision, cannot feed or clean themselves, and can only minimally entertain themselves. As they grow, children become more emotionally gratifying in a wider range of ways, but also more verbally demanding and destructive. They interrupt conversations, throw food on the floor, knock over vases, and track mud through the house. When they are finally old enough to take some responsibility for themselves, they can become insolent, arrogant, and challenging. Through all this, "good" parents are supposed to maintain an even temper and loving behavior. Of course, this doesn't happen, and every woman who has been a mother knows it, as does every father who has, even for a short period of time, served as the exclusive caregiver.

MOTHERS IMPRISONED

J. B. Watson, founder of behaviorism, was interested in how mother and child influence each other negatively. He sought to find the stimulus that caused the first provocation of anger in the mother. He identified restraint of movement as the main instigating factor.

Even with today's jet-age travel, children bind their mothers to home. Working mothers rush home to spend their precious little time with baby. Women who worked long hours at the office or who traveled prior to motherhood generally either feel too guilty or miss the baby too much to continue this life-style, and will suspend their ascent up the working hierarchy to spend more time at home. Even a trip to the supermarket with the baby means juggling concerns that leaves mothers exhausted at the end. It is no wonder that the site of the most frequent child abuse in the country is probably your neighborhood supermarket. It is a place where I never fail to see mothers screaming at, threatening, or hitting their children.

Barbara, mother of two teenage children, found herself unexpectedly pregnant at the age of forty-four. She and her husband agonized over the decision of whether or not to have this child. They finally decided not to, because the child would have threatened their long-awaited plans for when the kids would be independent and they could spend each summer traveling. Their upcoming trip to Europe, the first of a long list of destinations they had longed to see, would have to be canceled. I do not mean to indicate that Barbara and her husband were cavalier about this. But both felt deeply that they had already made many sacrifices in their parenting roles. It was time, they felt, at last, to give to themselves.

Most often it is not just physical space that is yearned for but also psychic space, although the two are related. In the case of Barbara, the desire to travel may simply be an unconscious transformation of the unacknowledged need for emotional distance—distance from the child, distance from the role of parenting, and, most of all, distance from the unrealistic expectations that she herself carries about her responsibilities and commitments.

For Ronnie, many factors converged in making her a mother imprisoned by her own sense of good mothering. Her original role model for mothering—her own mother—presented a picture of a self-sacrificing mother whose primary emotional stance was the-world-is-an-unsafe-place-for-children. As a child, Ronnie learned her lesson well and, as an adult, remained painfully shy and fearful. She chose a profession that allowed her to work at home, and a husband who found endless rationalizations to support her retreat from the world and her emotional isolation from everyone except him. Just at the point where therapy had helped Ronnie to begin to free herself from these chains, she got pregnant with Chloe. Throughout the pregnancy Ronnie remained deeply ambivalent, and fearful of losing whatever ground she had gained in her search for her own identity as a woman in the world, separate from her mother and her husband.

When Chloe finally arrived, she was born with a birth defect that threatened her fragile existence for her first few weeks. No wonder Chloe's parents felt protective toward her; no wonder Ronnie easily regressed back to her old pattern of emotional withdrawal. For the first year of Chloe's life, one of her parents was with her at all times; Ronnie and Jeff wanted to make sure that their baby would experience no undue anxiety, fear, or sense of being unloved. It was important to both Ronnie and Jeff that Chloe be in their sole protective custody. This was fine with Jeff as long as it was Ronnie who was doing the caregiving. No matter that eventually Ronnie felt like a prisoner, chained irrevocably to her infant, alternately loving her life as an all-giving nurturer, source of food and comfort and unparalleled sensitivity, and hating her state of isolation and lack of intellectual and social stimulation.

After six months of exclusive mothering, Ronnie finally decided that she needed some time to herself, so one afternoon she left

Chloe with Jeff. It was only then that this baby's father came to know firsthand the torment of motherhood. By the time Ronnie arrived back home, Chloe had been screaming nonstop for over two hours; Jeff was exhausted, defeated, and in a rage. It was not his fault, he reasoned, that he and Chloe had come to such a hateful place in their relationship; it was an anatomical fact of the human male that had made them suffer. Chloe needed her mother's breast. The milk from the bottle wasn't good enough; neither was his comforting, his warmth, and his sensitivity, nor even his desperate efforts to merely entertain and distract her. Jeff was convinced that only mother's breast would do.

Ronnie, who had lived daily through many such hours of inconsolability, knew that her breast might solve the problem, but then again, it might not. Babies' needs are ever changing, ever unpredictable, and at times ever so difficult to read. It is perfectly natural to become furious with someone who consistently deprives you of your right to a peaceful existence, but when that someone is your own child, you must juggle your feelings of maternal affection with pangs of anger and guilt. Mothers who have exclusive care of their infants despair over this inescapable antagonism every day of their lives. Thus begins the balancing act that mother love demands.

SLEEPING ANGELS

Given the fact that crying is one of the loudest sounds a human can make, it is not surprising that mothers often reach their limits of constructive mothering by the end of the day. Crying promotes the physical stress signals of a quickened heartbeat, pounding headache, and rapid, shallow breathing. It is also no wonder excessive crying is the trigger that sparks infant battering in 80 percent of the reported abuse cases of children under one year of age. Mothers who have not yet learned that "it's okay to hate this baby" are even less equipped to handle incessant crying than mothers who can freely acknowledge that babies can drive you nuts. Mothers need a space in time when they can be alone without the demands of a helpless child. Often this space is found by putting the baby to sleep; hence the generations of mothers who have bundled up their screaming children in the middle of the night, strapped them in the car or carriage and rode them into silence. It is, of course, just this dichotomy of love and hate that is the theme of our most famous lullaby:

> *Rock-a-bye-baby on the tree top,*
> *When the wind blows the cradle will rock,*
> *When the bough breaks the cradle will fall,*
> *And down will come baby, cradle and all.*

It is no accident that this lullaby is, as are many others and nursery rhymes as well, a death threat wrapped in melodic refrain. In fact, it contains the only two stimuli that J. B. Watson asserts are innately feared by infants: a loud noise and loss of support. Such are the complexities, contradictions, ambiguities, and subtleties of mother love.

On closer examination, we can see that most nursery rhymes are attempts to aid both mother and child in tolerating the murderous feelings children induce in their parents. Their lilting melodies and their charming language are good protective covers for the underlying meaning. It is precisely the nursery rhyme's ability to make us forget the content of the tale told that is the success of the method. Murderous rage toward the child is, generally, an unacceptable impulse to mother, who feels it; to baby, who is victim to it; and to father, who observes it. It is sometimes only in the veil of a loving, sweet-pitched voice of refrains repeated mindlessly from generation to generation that such feelings can even begin to be approached and tolerated.

Fairy tales appeal to children who are older. Like nursery rhymes, many are freely given and passively received. No mother need feel guilty about the implicit meaning of a fairy tale because the attractive gift-wrapping of the moral satisfies her concern that the story be wholesome. It is, after all, just a story that countless generations of mothers have read to their children—and children need not feel threatened by the story, because, after all, it's not "real." The child's innocence, the fact that he could not at this age comprehend the extent of the hostile impulses toward him, is often his best protection. If the child were to become too quickly conscious of the battle lines drawn between himself and mother, he might try to defend himself, thereby starting a war he cannot win.

Bettelheim made the important point that fairy tales are preparation for life. The fact that the theme of getting rid of children through either abandonment or killing (or the symbolic equivalent, putting them to sleep) is the most prevalent theme in fairy tales means that the most important preparation a child needs is in withstanding the murderous rage that his own beloved parents are going to feel toward him. Fairy tales, more than anything else, may be a warning delivered by adults to children.

Take the story of the Pied Piper of Hamelin. The rats are drowned and the children are taken away. Both rats and children share a common fate. In Cinderella, the stepmother abuses the child; in Snow White, the stepmother tries to poison her child. The use of the stepmother as the murderous villain is not because there were so many divorces and remarriages in those days (there weren't). Attributing the murderous intent to a stepmother (or a wicked witch, another common character in fairy tales) is merely a clever ploy. A mother who wants to do away with her own child is too disturbing an image. Taking these urges away from the real mother is simply an additional disguise of the infanticidal impulses out of which these tales arose, and which continue to have meaning to the unconscious minds of mothers and children in all cultures.

As our lullabies and nursery rhymes and our own mothering experience tells us, all parents on some occasions want to rid themselves of their children. The craving for a time when there is no crying and no demands may last only for a moment, but it happens without exception. If the mother doesn't have the ingenuity to deal artfully with this desperate need, or if she can't maintain a sense of protectiveness toward her infant in spite of her rage, a constructive solution may not be found.

In his story "Sleepyhead," Anton Chekhov illustrates the desperation of a child's caregiver who has been deprived of her sleep. In the story, a young nursemaid is instructed to help her infant charge to fall asleep. As she watches the infant and rocks the cradle, she is filled with an overwhelming need for her own sleep. She longs for sleep with the same fervor that a starving man yearns for food. But the infant won't cooperate and despite her attempts to comfort, the child will not stop crying. Finally, she kills the child. The story ends: ". . . and having smothered the child, she drops to the floor and laughing with joy at the thought that she can sleep, in a moment sleeps as soundly as the dead child."

We know, of course, that such events are not purely fictional. Mary Beth Tinning said of her four-month-old, whom she smothered with a pillow, "She was always crying and I couldn't do anything right."

On the level of the unconscious, sleep and death are the same. The child's sleep represents that lapse in time, a psychic space of aloneness that is essential if the mother is to regenerate herself. For the mother, the child's sleep represents a reprieve, a temporary elimination of baby without her having to be the eliminator.

It is important that mothers recognize their need for some quiet "alone" time and see this need as legitimate and understandable. If this desire to escape the demands of the child causes the parent to feel guilty, a destructive cycle begins that may eventually give destructive impulses free rein. Maternal guilt leads to feelings of anger toward the baby. These feelings can grow to hate, which leads back to guilt. Guilt leads to resentment, which leads back to hate, and the cycle continues with increased momentum. How many times would you guess this can happen before the parent is whipped into a frenzy and the child becomes the target of impulsive, murderous discharge?

MOTHERS DEPRIVED

The first line in *Hansel and Gretel* gives us another reason why parents might want to do away with their children. The story opens: "Hard by a great forest dwelt a poor woodcutter with his wife and his children." We are told, significantly, this family is victimized by poverty. "What is to become of us? How are we to feed our poor children, when we no longer have anything for ourselves?" Food is a problem; parents and children are in competition for whatever scarce resources are available. Although most parents would gladly give their last morsel of food to their child, you can imagine that on some level they would resent having to starve themselves to feed another.

Sometimes parents feel as helpless in coping with the vicissitudes of the world as the child really is. As one psychiatrist has said, "Love is like a bag of jelly beans." When you're near the bottom of the barrel, the mother is just as threatened by the scarcity as the baby.

There are many things that can create a situation where mothers feel that their jelly bean bag is depleted. On the emotional level, mother herself may not have had the kind of mothering that prepared her for this new role in life. Or, father may be making the same demands on her that he always did, without realizing that after tending to baby she has little energy left over for him. Father himself may feel abandoned by mother's attention to the child, and he may regress to an infantile level of neediness in order to try to reclaim his wife. Most husbands will complain that with the birth of their first child, they traded in a wife for a mother.

Economic concerns, too, may give the parents the feeling that the baby is a drain that they can ill afford. In the barrios of Argentina, for example, it is standard for the seventh or eighth child to die. The youngest girl child is picked, and through deliberate starvation and neglect, the mother's burden is eased. In the United States, in poverty-stricken urban areas, corpses of newborns turn up in sewers and garbage cans with some frequency.

The all-powerful maternal instinct, with its potential for determining how we manage all our later loves, is no more able to flourish without the right environment than is any other form of love. There are times when we move perilously close to our animal ancestors. When our own survival is at stake, and competition for scarce goods is fierce, love becomes a distant luxury.

There are, as well, basic antagonisms between the needs of the mother and the needs of the child. The basic relation of parent to child is one of self-sacrifice. Of course, there are rich and meaningful compensations for this sacrifice; but that does not change the fact that children add to the weight of their parents' struggle for existence. At times, the sacrifice the parent is called to make feels too great to the parent, and the child may then become the victim of the parent's rage and frustration.

The caveat of motherhood is in the discrepancy between the extraordinary lengths we go to in our care for our offspring and our inability to escape feeling hatred toward them. This is why parents have such difficulty accepting that the way they have been *told* they should love their children is often quite different from the way they *do* love them.

MOTHERS WITHOUT SEX

The most frequent complaint I hear in my practice from married couples is that there has been a loss of sexuality in the marriage. This complaint comes from couples who, in the past, enjoyed frequent and pleasurable sex, and from couples whose relationship is positive in many other respects. The one change that seems most frequently to accompany the decrease in sexual interest of husband and wife in each other is the addition of children to family life. And so, we come to yet another reason why parents may hate their children. Pregnancy and children interfere with sex.

As we unravel the reasons for the incompatibility of parenting and sex, we must remember one crucially important fact. The initial experience we have all had in family life was that we weren't supposed to experience sexual feelings toward our family members. In creating our new family, our family of choice, all of a sudden the rules have changed. First there is a sexual object—our spouse—who is there precisely because of our sexual desire. This transition—from being a member of a family in which our own sexuality with family members was discouraged, to being a member of a family in which our sexuality is almost required—is a major leap in role adjustment. And no matter how in love we feel at the time of our marriage, eventually married life begins to feel like our other family. Spouses can feel more like brothers or sisters or parents than objects of great sexual passion. Then this situation is further complicated by the arrival of children.

In studying the relationship between motherhood and sexuality, Charles Darwin found that motherliness and pregnancy are almost universally regarded as deficits to sexual attractiveness, even in cultures where fertility is highly valued. Every woman runs the risk of losing her husband's interest when she becomes a mother. Within every husband are the residues of the incest taboo with respect to his own mother. Often, the wife stepping into the mother role will reawaken these old conflicts in him. Indeed, research indicates that sexual waywardness in the husband is most frequent when the wife is pregnant. Stories of husbands having affairs while their wives are simultaneously suffering through childbirth can begin to make sense.

Vladimir Nabokov's imaginary Lolita was irresistibly attractive precisely because she was so far removed, in both physical appearance and age, from motherhood. So was Marilyn Monroe. We often see women attempting to be attractive and elicit love from a man in a role that is far away from her eventual role as a mother. Women make themselves helpless, like children; they speak in childish tones; and they accentuate their babyish traits of the face: with makeup, cheeks are colored, lips are shaped into a mouth pursed for sucking, and the eyes are enlarged. If not consciously, unconsciously women feel that the peak of their sexual attractiveness will be over by the time they are mothers.

As a result, mothers may feel hatred toward their children because of the fear of losing their husbands. Fathers, too, are not immune from these feelings. The Punch-and-Judy puppet show, which remained a favorite throughout Europe for several centuries, had as its main theme the notion that children interfere with the sexual life of the parents, and that husbands may go elsewhere to gratify their urges. The hatred toward the child, and the barely disguised wish to do away with the child who interferes with the free expression of Punch's sexuality, was characteristically a part of each show.

Whatever rage the wife may feel toward the husband for his lack of attentiveness is often directed toward the child. It's safer. As far as men are concerned, mothers aren't supposed to have sexual needs anyway, and it may not matter whether the mother is their own or the mother of their children.

There's also a much more mundane reason why parents don't often have sex. They may be simply too tired. If one parent—almost always the mother—is too exhausted from the toils of child-rearing to even move her body in other than essential ways, the other parent may resent this fatigue and the children who caused it. The children, as before, know nothing of this problem, but they may still be on the receiving end of a lot of parental hostility. Although nothing is said directly, the message is conveyed to the child that the mother doesn't have time or energy for him. Such a message is an indirect, hostile way of blaming the child for the parents' difficulties.

THE UNLIVED LIFE OF THE MOTHER

Because of the original symbiotic relationship between mother and child, the child is particularly sensitive to the unconscious or unspoken wishes, fears, and feelings of the mother. Jung commented that nothing influences children more than the "silent facts" of the homelife, or the "whispering of the walls"—what is palpable but remains unarticulated in the lives of the parents. More than anything, this whispering is found in the parts of the mother's life that prevent her from being satisfied or from pursuing her own fulfillment—her unlived life, as Jung refers to it. The child, sensing the unhappiness of the mother, desperately wanting to right things and unaware that he doesn't possess such power, will go to extraordinary lengths to please the mother.

A sensitive child who is able to read the unconscious of his mother will try to fulfill her unconscious wishes. It is out of his love for her and his wish to be loved that he will try to find a way to rescue his mother.

Rescuing another from his or her own misery is, of course, not a task that one human being can fulfill for another, but it is a particularly burdensome task for a child, who is still subject to the magical thoughts of childhood that delude him into thinking that he may actually succeed. The child, then, has taken on the shadowy aspects of the mother's unconscious, unaware that the life he is living is not, in a sense, his own but his mother's.

D. H. Lawrence's story "The Rocking Horse Winner" illustrates beautifully this subtle wounding of the child. A mother is described who can't find joy in life or in her children. When she is with her children, she feels the center of her heart go hard. Though all her neighbors and friends speak admiringly of her mothering, she and her children know otherwise. They read it in one another's eyes.

One wish obsesses this woman. She thinks that if she had more money she would be happy. The house comes to be haunted by the unspoken phrase, the whispering of the walls: There must be more money. There must be more money. The children hear this refrain all the time, though it is never spoken.

Paul, one of her sons, thinks that if he can only get enough money, she will be happy and free to love him. Paul, with the help of the gardener, begins to make money by betting on horses. He discovers that he has a magical talent: He can ride his rocking horse until the name of the winning horse comes to him. He rides and rides, working himself into frenzied states, and makes lots of money. Paul gives the money to his uncle, who passes it on anonymously to the mother. But no matter how much money Paul makes for his mother, it is never enough to make her happy or to free her to love him. Paul exhausts himself riding the horse, gets sick, and dies.

Children are often willing to sacrifice themselves to the needs of their parents, and parents are often willing, even desirous, of the sacrifice. Whatever the whisper may be in the home, it is likely to influence the child in ways of which he is not even aware. The whisper may be, "There's no one as trustworthy as our own family"; or, "You need to prove your worth by becoming successful"; or, "I sacrificed a promising career for you"; or, "You're not as smart as your sister." There are a thousand different whispers possible, each giving a powerful message to the unconscious of the child. The mother sending these messages to her child destructively (and narcissistically) spills out her unresolved conflicts onto the child.

FAMILY SECRETS

It is not only the unconscious of the parent that gives the child a legacy of the parent's own unlived life. Family secrets, too, have this effect.

Gina is a patient of mine whose public persona was created by what was unsaid in her family. Gina is a successful professional in her early forties, with an engaging and friendly personality; yet, there was always a feeling of secrecy about her. She talked easily, with much sensitivity and intelligence about other people's lives. She rarely revealed anything about herself and didn't give any information about her history. Only her best friend knew that she lived a secret life. Although she was divorced, she did not want her son to know about her sexual liaison with a man. She continued this affair all through her son's childhood and adolescence. She rationalized that a man's presence in her son's life would interfere with their close relationship.

After several years in therapy Gina's mysterious, secretive quality was explained. Gina's father had died when she was twenty. Shortly after his death Gina's mother discovered that he had been having an affair all through their marriage. He owned a bar and used to explain that since he closed so late it was easier just to sleep in the bar. In fact, he had been living with another woman during the week, returning to his family only on weekends. He had a child with this other woman, as well.

When Gina finally did start talking about her father, she did it lovingly and with much compassion. Though she did not consciously know about the affair when she was growing up, she was aware of the silent suffering of her mother. She asked me, "What could I have said to him? 'Where are you? Why don't you come home like other fathers? Aren't you aware of how you're hurting Mother?'" Gina's questions were the questions her mother didn't ask. Her mother's silence taught Gina the lesson that the feelings of rage and hurt were to be tolerated in silence. From childhood, the strongest element in Gina's personality was what was hidden rather than what was visible. She had raised her son under the same premise.

We do not practice good motherhood when we keep essential information from our children. Most of the time they sense it anyway, and the secrets breed distrust. As well, we deprive them of their feelings. Children need to experience feelings of sadness, loss, anger, and frustration. But when the parents themselves hide from their own suffering, the children will never come to understand the relationship between what they feel and why they feel it.

Jung says that neurosis is the avoidance of legitimate suffering. Bettelheim laments that children are not being allowed conscious suffering. Had the whispers in Paul's family been verbalized and dealt with appropriately, Paul would not have had to resort to an obsessional struggle to the death in order to please his mother. Had the whispers in Gina's family been brought clearly into communication, she would not have had to develop such a strong shell of protection around her. As Suzanne Short has said: "To undo the damage that such murmurings can cause, we need to make real whatever is the message of the family."

MOTHER THE ABUSER

The most vulnerable members of our society are targeted most for the destructive expression of rage and hate. These are, of course, the children. Children are injured—both physically and psychologically—and, with much more frequency than we care to admit, die because of neglect, abuse, or outright murder.

Bettelheim discovered a profound and deeply unsettling truth during his time in the Nazi concentration camps. He found that certain Jews formed an identification with their Nazi tormentors and mirrored their brutal behavior, directing it toward their fellow victims. Perhaps the same kind of protective mechanism has operated on women: As women have traditionally felt victimized by those in a more powerful position—the men—they have taken this rage about this injustice and created a new class of victims—the children.

The disturbing fact is that we cannot lay the mantel of child abuse at the hands of men exclusively. Mothers, as well as fathers, inflict child abuse.

Mussolini said, "War is to man what maternity is to woman." It is true, as he implies, that men are wont to express their aggression in noble (and not so noble) world causes. But his statement means more than he meant it to mean. Not only are both war and motherhood inevitable consequences of the respective natures of men and women, but also, mothering is often very like war. As often as not, children and their mothers battle each other for love, for possessions, and for nothing at all.

Some mothers allow their aggressive instincts to get the better of them and cross that all-too-fragile line that separates feeling from action. A battering mother generally has a distorted view of parent/child roles. She characteristically experiences herself as the child and sees the child as a hostile, persecuting adult. She speaks of the child as though he had an adult's capacity for deliberate, purposeful, and organized behavior. A mother who had victimized her young son said, "I can't stand it when he provokes me into a rage by manipulating the conversation so that it ends up looking like I'm at fault." The mother of a three-year-old daughter whom she had abused said, "Look at her give you the eye. That's how she picks up men—she's a regular sexpot."

Fathers, too, are subject to the same role reversal. Most cases of sexual abuse occur because the father sees in the child a much older person whom he imagines to be comfortable with her sexuality. Even more unfortunate is that some of those whom we entrust to punish the offenders are guilty themselves of the same thought disorder. A judge ruling on a case of a five-year-old victim of sexual assault described the child as "an extremely promiscuous young lady."

The recognition of childhood as a distinct and wholly different life phase has been the norm only for the last 100 years. Bettelheim has interpreted the historical lack of understanding of childhood as an indication of a cultural immaturity. Similarly, parents today who perceive their children as miniature adults, with the expectation of adult behavior, harken back to that earlier period in history. Parents who themselves were never babied properly are still, as parents, in need of babying. The quality of parenting in one generation depends upon the kind of parenting that the earlier generation gave. As William Wordsworth wrote: "The child is father of the man."

LEARNING MOTHER LOVE

Mother love, as we know it today, with all the tender loving care, nurturing, and understanding that good mothers bestow on their children, came about because a few million years ago there evolved an animal who, for the first time in history, had more information in its brain than in its genes. It's been uphill learning ever since. Mothering may be, only at its best, instinctively right, but the best news about it is that we can think, we can learn, and we can unlearn.

It is only in the conscious acknowledgment of our hate that we become free from the impulse to act hatefully. Knowing that you hate your child (whom you also love) is one of the most difficult feelings to accept, but it is a feeling that every mother has.

Our mothering capacity for our children is clearly affected by our own early mothering experience. But those mothers whose mothering was damaging need not pass on a legacy of destructive mothering. Love in childhood is clearly important. Without it, one is much more likely to be damaged. But, it is *not all*. If childhood, and the quality of mothering we received in it, were the only criteria for our later capacity for loving and productive relationships and lives, no mother would ever be able to improve upon her own mothering. And while there is a strong inclination to repeat the past, to visit the sins of our fathers and mothers upon our children, some of us do learn to do better. Our innate capacities are only our first lessons in who we are. Next, our childhood exposures help to shape us. But finally, and by no means least important, our capacity for growth—the sense of self that we can develop independent of our reflexive and learned responses as we learn to become a unique, creative "I"—can give us promise. Such is the real task of motherhood: dispelling the dark shadows at the heart of motherhood with the light of conscious awareness.

The relationship between mother and child is the first step in a long series of events that leads us to adulthood, and this relationship shapes the adult loves we seek and find. It doesn't take long, however, for the infant to discover that there is a world beyond mother. Family life, and the loves of our first family, father and siblings as well as mother, is the next step in our progression of lessons about love. So it is family life that we will learn about next.

CHAPTER 6

The Dark Side of Family Love: Violent Separations and the Children's Revenge

Seven thousand years ago someone drew a picture of three people—a man, a woman, and a child—the sacred family trinity that has been a recurring and pervasive theme in religion, folklore, and art all over the world. It was the invention of the family that paved the way for love to be a part of our everyday life. Although originally the family was created to increase the odds of survival, at some point in our psychic evolution love became an important ingredient of family life.

From our earliest years we are taught to respect and value family. We are taught that family is a safe haven in a dangerous sea. We are told, as children, to avoid strangers and to stay away from unfamiliar places and the darkness of the night.

It is, then, the great irony of family life that the most dangerous place for us all, by far, is the home. The most dangerous people in our lives are not strangers with whom we may have a tragic encounter, but our own family members, those with whom we are the most intimate. The likelihood of being assaulted, beaten, killed, or sexually molested in one's own home, at the hands of a loved one, far exceeds the chance of that happening anyplace else or by anyone else. We may, indeed, have an ancient picture of family members standing peacefully side by side, but we have an even older picture of one person killing another. As long as we have had family, we have had destructive hate as a part of family life.

Family love has clearly not fulfilled its gleaming promise. Family love, like its antecedent, mother love, has its own set of pitfalls. As the cast of characters increases, the permutations and configurations of all possible loves and hates grows greater in number and in complexity. It is no wonder that we experience family life to be so difficult.

THE MYTH OF THE INNOCENCE OF THE CHILD

For most of our history children were seen as neither good nor bad, neither innocent nor evil. Rather, they were utilitarian. They were valued for their contribution to the family economy. In the eighteenth century a group called the Romantics changed that view. The child was seized upon as the symbol of all that was good and innocent. The Romantics created, through their writings, a cult of childhood, whose legacy we are still contending with today.

In the late Victorian era the myth of childhood innocence was at its height. It was during this time that Freud shocked twentieth-century proper ladies and gentlemen by smashing the myth of the innocence of children.

Freud pointed out not only that children have sexual feelings, but also that if one looked deeply into the unconscious of a child, one would find a wish to destroy the parent. Given the pervasiveness of the unconscious wish of the parent to destroy the child (as we saw in the last chapter), it should not surprise us that at some point the child might want to retaliate.

These two pivotal themes, which formed the cornerstones of psychoanalytic theory—sexuality (Eros) and destructiveness (Thanatos)—converge in complex ways to create the various manifestations of the dark side of family love.

INTIMACY VERSUS SEPARATION: A LIFELONG DILEMMA

Our yearning for love begins with mother. At first, when the infant is still in symbiotic fusion with mother, there is no love—only need and need satisfaction. But soon enough it begins to dawn on the emerging consciousness of the infant that mother is separate from himself. We now know that at this point in the development of the child a second birth takes place. It is a birth that is every bit as monumental and as painful as the first, but its nature is psychological rather than physical. This is the birth of the psyche.

When the still rudimentary psyche of the infant begins to entertain the idea that somebody outside of himself exists, it is an essential step in the development of a personality. To the extent that this acceptance of separateness is accomplished, the mature personality is allowed to flower. To the extent that it is halted, the personality remains stunted in its narcissistic phase.

Once an "other" is recognized, impulses, sensations, feelings, and ideas become infinitely more complicated. They can be attached to this "other." Feelings about "aloneness" are aroused and are directed toward the apparent cause of the separateness. Frustration, and its accompanying rage, toward the separate mother are actually a guiding light for the developmental progress of the infant.

At the same time he feels frustration and rage at his mother for not fulfilling his every need at the instant of arousal—in short, for being different and separate from him—the child also feels an urge to explore outside the immediate orbit of the mother. The world beckons, and the infant's curiosity is piqued. Inanimate objects, as well as other people besides mother, are discovered. There develops for the child sources of satisfaction other than a breast flowing with sweet milk.

Throughout the rest of the individual's life, there will be a constant interplay between the need for warmth and security, as was experienced in the symbiosis with the mother, and a need for expansion and discovery, as represented in the world separate from mother. But always, there will be remembered this early state of union, and this memory exerts a powerful pull on each of us to return to it.

FATHER THE INTRUDER

Fathers are the forgotten victims of family life. It is a thankless job to have to break into the symbiotic union between the mother and infant. Fathers of newborns often feel abandoned, neglected, and unimportant. A father's role in the care of a newborn seems insignificant in comparison with the role of the mother. Both mother and child can experience him as an unwanted intruder, threatening to break up their symbiotic bliss.

Yet, the father has a special role to play in the undoing of the symbiosis between mother and child. It is the father's task to cut into the relationship of dependency between mother and child; the father must cut the psychological umbilical cord between them. This will free the child to have relationships with people other than the mother. The father, then, is, after the mother, the first real "other," and as such becomes a prototype for future relationships. If the father is absent or weak or tyrannical, the child will not make an easy transition to other relationships. The dependence on the mother in these cases will be too strong and will last too long. The child may grow into either a self-serving or a self-sacrificing narcissist. In either case, the maladjustment will prevent normal, loving ties as an adult.

THE STORY OF OEDIPUS

It is not an accident that Freud chose the two myths of Narcissus and Oedipus as the foundation of his entire theory of psychological development. They were both used as metaphorical paradigms with which to illustrate what Freud considered to be the main conflicts of psychological development. Between the two myths, all the information that is necessary to understand the central themes of the human psyche is represented. The story of Narcissus tells us about that essential phase in infancy when mother and infant are ineluctably bound, and how damage in this stage of development yields an emotionally stunted individual. The story of Oedipus picks up the developmental sequence where the tale of Narcissus leaves off. It is this Greek tale that Freud took as the illustration for the child's destructive capacity toward his parents. Infantile narcissism has been outgrown, and separation becomes the major developmental task. It is in this process of separation, and how well the challenge of this step is met, that love's destructive potential has its next opportunity to reveal its face.

The story of Oedipus begins with an allusion to acts of incredible physical and psychological trauma inflicted on a child by his parents, those whom we would expect to be his prime protectors. Instead of caring for their child, Laius and Jocasta order their infant son, Oedipus, to be put out to die. In a prophecy, Laius has been forewarned that his son is going to be a danger to him; Oedipus, so the prophecy goes, is going to kill his father and marry his mother. Laius and Jocasta, rather than rising to the challenge of parenthood and helping their son learn to put his potentially destructive aggression into constructive action, decide instead to simply get rid of the problem by getting rid of the child. The first act of aggression, then, is parent against child.

But Oedipus' life is saved by a sympathetic peasant who brings him home and raises him as his own son. Oedipus grows into a young man who, like many young men, has an urge to see the world beyond, and he sets out on a journey. During his travels the repercussions of his past, still unknown to him, begin to unravel. Traveling across the countryside, Oedipus comes across an obstinate old man who doesn't move out of his way fast enough, and Oedipus impatiently shoves him aside, knocking him down to his death. This old man, unbeknownst to Oedipus, is his father. Oedipus has wreaked his revenge; the retaliatory revenge of the child against father has been enacted. Oedipus continues his travels, apparently unaffected by his violent act. He correctly answers the question of the sphinx, enters the city of Thebes, and is rewarded the queen—who is in reality his mother—as his wife.

Freud used the Oedipus story to illustrate what he felt was the boy-child's universal drive of wanting to kill the father in order to have sex with the mother. Sexual longings exist, even among family members, between parents and their children, and between siblings. For the boy-child, like Oedipus, father is resented for interfering with free access to mother.

The part of the story that Freud did not emphasize, however, has to do with the reason that Oedipus remained unable to free himself from his fate. It seemed a mere coincidence that Oedipus would later run into his father on a strange road, and his mother in an unfamiliar town. The truth is, of course, much more complex. The hidden meaning of the Oedipus myth has to do with Oedipus' earliest experience with separation, and the underlying reason why Oedipus is led, seemingly innocently, to kill his father and marry his mother.

Our first clue that the story of Oedipus has to do with the urge to move beyond the narcissistic phase of mother/child unity is revealed in his name, meaning literally "bad foot." Soon after he is born, Oedipus is maimed by having a spike thrust through his feet. Since the child is enabled to explore the world through crawling and walking, locomotion has primary significance in the psychophysical development of the child. Movement away from mother is what will permit the experience of bodily separation and subsequent reunion with mother. We are told, then, on a symbolic level, that Oedipus has an inherent weakness in this area. Oedipus is destined to have trouble with the developmental process of separating from mother.

The irony of Oedipus' relationship with his parents is that at the same time they were forcing him away from them, they were actually impeding his ability to move away freely and independently. Their actions contributed to the very problem they wanted to avoid. Laius and Jocasta, despite their best efforts to rid themselves of this threatening son and the fate he promised to bring to them, have not seen the last of Oedipus. Because they have destroyed his ability to move freely away from them, his destiny remains ineluctably bound with their own.

CORE CONFLICTS

We are told in yet another way that separation is very much the issue at hand in Oedipus' life. Oedipus is called upon to solve the riddle of the sphinx:

What being, with only one voice, has sometimes two feet, sometimes three, sometimes four, and is weakest when it has the most?

For Oedipus, already sensitive to the issues of locomotion because of his own disability, it would not have been a great stretch of mind to arrive at his answer:

Man, because he crawls on all fours as an infant, stands firmly on his two feet as a youth, and leans on his staff in his old age.

The mystery to unraveling the riddle of the sphinx is, then, to focus on the process of locomotion in the development of the individual, from birth to old age. The riddle of the sphinx is not just a question posed to anyone; it is a question specifically for Oedipus—an invitation to him to think more deeply about the nature of his plight.

Each of us has, like Oedipus, our own personal riddle to solve, a core conflict that has the potential to impede our development or, when resolved, to free us to accomplish as much as we can dream. Our core issues are the ones that are both the most painful to us and the most perplexing. They originate in the earliest period of our lives, a time that none of us consciously remembers. These core issues are often deeply repressed in our unconscious. Although we don't know what they are, they will continue to affect how we live our lives.

Oedipus accepts the invitation of the sphinx to look inwardly for the answer to who he is—an invitation to discover for himself his core issue, his identity, which has been based on a falsehood. For Oedipus' success in solving the riddle—that is, in coming to know more fully who he is—he is awarded his life, the city, and his mother.

Oedipus, after solving the riddle of the sphinx, has all the accoutrements of success; he has a beautiful wife and is king of a city. But, like many of us who have material success, and even love, Oedipus still is not settled. His major life's difficulties are still before him. Oedipus, at this stage in his life, is very much a symbol of contemporary man: He has acquired tremendous external wealth, yet remains internally poor. Oedipus has not yet arrived at the deepest truth about himself. He understands from the sphinx's riddle his area of vulnerability—that he is still tied to his parents. Since he was rejected from birth, Oedipus was never allowed to go through the necessary safety and security of the narcissistic stage of symbiosis. For him, separation was fused with destructive aggression. What Oedipus has not yet understood about himself is that his adult dealings with his parents are defined by murderous aggression rather than a normally contained aggression, tempered by love.

It is inevitable that Oedipus' early history would come back to haunt him. Such is the prediction of the *repetition compulsion* that Freud discovered. Whatever unresolved core conflict remains from childhood comes back in later life with a vengeance. The Greeks called it Fate; Freud, in understanding that this compulsion to repeat the past is part of us rather than some outside force, called it the *unconscious*. After killing his father, Oedipus extracts his second revenge: bedding his own mother. As the story goes, Oedipus does not realize he has married his mother, so consciously his behavior is not vengeful. Even so, on a symbolic level all his rage has indeed come home to roost.

THE BETRAYAL OF THE CHILDREN

The core conflict that each of us struggles with is whether we were loved by our parents. This question is very much in the unconscious mind of Oedipus. It is a question that is so terribly painful and so frightening that each of us would rather, like Oedipus, live in a state of delusion than know the awful truth.

The fact is: All children are betrayed by their parents, sometimes in unavoidable, necessary ways, sometimes in trivial and easily forgivable ways, and sometimes, like Oedipus, in ways that are irreparably damaging. Some betrayals are conscious; some are not. Betrayal comes in a thousand different forms.

When I was eleven, and a big girl, I was taking the public bus to and from school every day. One day I alighted from the bus at the intersection where I needed to make my transfer to the next bus. I saw my mother negotiating the same intersection in her car. I yelled and ran, hoping to catch up with her and get a ride home for the final leg of my journey. As she continued to move with traffic, utterly oblivious to my efforts and my presence, my eyes filled with tears of abandonment and loss. It was all so silly. I would see her in fifteen minutes, both of us safe and sound at home. Yet, I felt betrayed. She somehow magically *should* have known I was there. I was mourning the rupture of our symbiosis; we were no longer fused as one, with her knowing and responding to my every wish. That was the betrayal. It was inevitable that at some point, through no fault of her own, my mother would fail to protect me from being alone in the world.

Then there are the kinds of betrayals that are deliberate and mean. For example, one of my patients is nutritionally minded. He believes, with great conviction, that his son's health depends in large part on the quality of his diet. His wife, however, is an inveterate junk-food eater. They have their differences, and they generally live with them fairly peacefully. But when it comes to food and their son, the son becomes a pawn in the war between them. Mommy takes Mikey out for a walk and says, "Daddy's not here. Let's have some fun. Let's get a hot dog and ice cream." What is Daddy to do? Can he forbid his wife to be alone with their son? This mother is betraying the father's dearly held beliefs, using the child as her pawn. Mommy's lesson to the child: *Daddies* (read males) *are to be rebelled against, not to be taken seriously. Females can betray males, and look how easy it is to get away with it.*

How many beliefs should a spouse be allowed to trample on before enough is enough? At what point does tolerating these betrayals become betrayal to oneself? And who is the ultimate victim of the betrayal? Surely it is the one to whom betrayal is being taught. Parents will always disagree, and this mother simply didn't share her husband's concern about junk food. Instead of agreeing to disagree, however, these parents mightily confused the child by setting up battle lines and using subterfuge to win the war. The mother's candy-coated treat was in fact a lesson in hostility.

Betrayal, too, comes in the form of passivity. What else can one call it when a father passively allows a mother to totally dominate her child's life? What else can we call it when a mother passively allows her husband to discharge his temper on the child? She hates every minute of it, she knows it's wrong and shivers whenever it happens. But she still goes to sleep in the same room with him at night and cooks his breakfast in the morning. To whom is her deepest allegiance, then? How else can the child experience these events—events formulated by the passive parent as much as by the abusing parent—but as betrayal? It is no wonder that these children will grow up hating *both* parents—justified in their rage toward the abusive parent but guilty about their rage toward the cringing parent. It is no wonder that these children grow up to be abusive mothers and fathers, and weak mothers and fathers, never trusting anyone. The "good" parent—the nonviolent or non-manipulative parent—turns trust into mush. Who has proven worthy of trust?

Texas teenager Shelley Sessions, molested by her stepfather, finally revealed her secret to the world. It was a secret that she had kept from the age of eight to sixteen, too terrified to tell her mother, her boyfriend, or her close girlfriends. When the secret came out, Shelley assumed that her mother would be on her side. How could her mother *not* be on her side? Her stepfather, Bobby, had been successfully prosecuted for the crime. He had been institutionalized for the crime. The world knew now, and her mother knew now.

Shelley thought her mother was on her side until, one night as she was preparing for bed, Shelley was "kidnapped." Shelley was carted off to a home for runaway girls and imprisoned behind locked gates. The kidnapping was her mother's decision, her mother's betrayal, heaped on top of all the betrayals of silence and ignorance through all those painful, lonely years of Bobby's abuse. Bobby was coming home, and, after all, everybody knew that Shelley and Bobby were like oil and water. One of them had to go. Shelley's mother's betrayal was every bit as scorching as the betrayal of outright abuse.

Dory Previn, songwriter, singer, and composer, is articulate about her mother's collusive passivity in her father's abuse. When she was a child, for four and a half months she, her mother, and her sister were locked in a room by her unstable, punitive father. Eighteen years later she was finally able through her writings to give words to her experience of growing up with an abusive father:

from then on
we were a family
we even had some fun
the boards
on the dining room door
came down
and daddy put away his gun and
I forgot it happened
like something
i'd been dreaming
till eighteen odd years later
when i suddenly woke up screaming

And it took about that long, too, for her to feel the effects of her rage toward her poor, pitiful, victimized but nevertheless destructively silent mother:

Actually we could have gotten out at any time. There was a door. The one that swung open into the kitchen. I was too small to stick up for my rights. But if Mama wanted to, she could have just taken us two kids and walked out of that rotten room. But she didn't. . . .

Previn finally came to the realization that her mother's passivity was, in the end, far more damaging to her than her father's psychotic ravings. It is from her mother that she expected protection and comfort. It was her mother who had promised to make the world a happier and more interesting place to be, to take her to see Barnum and Bailey's and the Statue of Liberty and to make her chicken croquettes. It was her mother's promises that didn't mean anything.

We've already seen that self-destructive people redirect their aggressive feelings against themselves. Passivity—the refusal to acknowledge rage, the refusal to fight—is another way of seeking obliteration. The true crime of the betrayal of passivity is that it crushes whatever psychic protection anger might have given. It teaches that hate is not permissible, and that "No" is not an acceptable answer.

And finally there are the worst betrayals of all—the betrayals of love that involve physical or sexual abuse. Yet, even in these cases the core question—am I loved?—is still tucked away in the recesses of the unconscious. Abused children are often much more forgiving of the abusive parent than anyone else, and will cling to any memory of even a fleeting kindness in order to assure themselves that they are loved. They will assure us that their mommys or daddys "didn't really mean it." Children need to be loved. Many will feel loved even when they are not.

THE CHILDREN'S REVENGE

Freud's belief was that all children, invariably, want revenge against their parents, for good reasons and bad. Feelings of wanting revenge begin in childhood, and all children are susceptible to them. In their dreams at night, and in their daydreams, play, and fantasy, children plot all manner of schemes to retaliate against their parents. Even with the best parenting, childhood is a frustrating time, and frustration cannot exist without rage and hate and the desire to pay back in kind.

Parents disappoint their children in myriad ways. They have other children, and thus prove to older children that they were not sufficient. They lack the foresight to predict the future, and so can't protect the child from unexpected, painful surprises. They lack the omnipotence to make the world exactly as the child would fashion it, thereby forcing the child to have experiences that he would sooner forgo.

Also, childhood is a time when restrictions are endless. We can't ride a bicycle (or own a Corvette) even though our older brother does; we can't touch every object we feel curious about; and on and on. Because no parent is ever omniscient, omnipotent, or all-gratifying, children are going to feel hate toward them. This is true whether the child has been whipped and beaten by a wrathful, punishing father or bathed in caring and sensitivity. Each child believes that the parent *could* have or *should* have done better. Each child asks, "Why didn't you love me more, or better?" No amount of love can forestall the question, since no amount of love can create a frustration-free childhood.

Although all children may plot revenge in their wishes and fantasies, only some actually take their revenge. Ordinarily, it is only vindictive parents themselves who, like Laius and Jocasta, later become the objects of their child's actual revenge.

Children may exact their revenge upon their parents, or when they are grown, upon their own children. The most common expression of revenge is when parents treat their own children as they themselves were treated. They are able, at long last, to extract a long-deferred revenge for the indignities and suffering they endured while they were at the mercy of their own parents' parenting. Parents rarely recognize the hate in their behavior. They give respectable rationalizations, such as, "That's the way I was brought up; maybe it hurt a little, but I'm none the worse for it"; or the popular refrain of "That's the way they did it in the good old days." The parent, under the guise of teaching obedience, control, strength, and fortitude of character, is really giving to the child the lesson that "might makes right." It is the superior size and strength of the adult that puts him in the position of power. It is inevitable that the child will look forward to the day when he will inherit the superior position. And, though he may pledge as a child—as did his father before him—to do better ("When I'm a parent, I'll remember the frustrations of childhood"), his own unsatisfied rage may, at times, get the better of him. He, too, in order to aggrandize himself, will punish and restrict those who are weaker than he.

As they grow up, children, especially teenagers, seek revenge on their parents directly. Parents become vulnerable targets for the expression of the vindictive rage of their own children. Rebellious behavior in teenagers is often an attempt to hurt the parent. Teenage sexuality and unwanted pregnancies are often as much about the relationship the teenager has to the parents as they are about sexual interest.

In 1988, a scenario unfolded that grabbed the attention of all of New York City. The tabloids were alight with stories of the trial of Bess Myerson, involving corruption in the city. But soon enough it

became clear that the real drama that was unfolding was one between a mother and daughter and, like the Greek tragedy *Electra*,
involved a daughter turning vindictively against her mother in
order to ensure her downfall.

At issue was whether a particular judge, Hortense Gabel, had
acted illegally. Her daughter, Sukhreet Gabel, was the prosecution's star witness, absorbing more than nine days on the witness
stand, testifying as to what she did and did not know about her
mother's presumed participation in a conspiracy to reduce the divorce settlement of Bess Myerson's lover. Sukhreet's mother, Hortense, was a widely respected judge to whom this matter had
fallen. The corrupt agreement was simple: If the judge reduced
the settlement, Bess Myerson (commissioner of cultural affairs for
New York City) would grant Hortense the favor of a $22,000-a-year
job for her unruly and hopelessly unemployable daughter,
Sukhreet. This is, in fact, a case of mother love stretched to the
limit: a woman epitomizing for her entire life a model of decency,
fairness, and commitment to social justice throwing it all away for
the sake of an ungrateful, fair-weather daughter.

In one courtroom scene, Sukhreet revealed that without telling
her mother, she had taped a phone conversation between her and
her mother; she had then turned the tape over to the prosecutor.
The tape was played in the courtroom. Hortense, legally blind,
had been assisted over to stand near the tape recorder. When the
tape ended, the lawyers dispersed, the jury was dismissed, and
Hortense Gabel found herself suddenly alone, holding onto the
rail for support. Shana Alexander described the scene in *When She
Was Bad:* "She began creeping forward like an old, blind worm toward the witness box. When she reached the far end of the rail—as
close to the box where her daughter still sat as she could get—she
straightened up and clasped her hands behind her back. She was
perhaps five feet tall, wearing a navy-blue dress and what looked
like a blond wig slightly askew. Was there ever a more powerful,
tender image of unrequited love than what one could read in that
mother's straight, mute back?"

And, we might ask, as well, was there ever a more subtle yet
vicious case of revenge of child upon parent in Sukhreet's happy
willingness to indict and destroy her mother?

One other situation comes to my mind. It is the story of my own dying mother. I grew up hearing from her that she felt hated by her own mother. She said that she grew up feeling that her mother wanted her dead. It was hard for me to imagine the legitimacy of those feelings, knowing my grandmother as I did, as a wizened, weathered, almost deaf, short Jewish lady whose main sin in life seemed to be her ill judgment in having her hair dyed too red and having indulged in too many face-lifts, leaving her lips a thin line of hard color. But when I became a psychoanalyst, I learned that, indeed, children do often have the feeling that their parents want to kill them. Whatever went on in those early years between my mother and her mother, it left my mother with a permanent feeling of rage toward her mother.

As an adult, my mother arranged to spend as little time as she could with her mother. For the year that my mother lay bedridden, suffering from the cancer that would finally kill her, she received visitor after visitor, friends and relatives wishing her well. All except one. Her own mother came, day after day, banished to the front of the house, spending long hours waiting to be received into the bedroom so that she could say a final farewell to her oldest child. This privilege my mother denied her. My mother died, inflicting this last act of rejection on her mother, a powerful payback for her years of suffering when she herself was the vulnerable target.

In their acts of revenge, children are able to express their full rage at their parents' inadequacies, disappointments, and failings. However, not all children seek the same level of vengeance. Only when hate feelings have not been allowed normal expression do they turn into this kind of perverse malignity. Parents who try to prevent their children from hating them will find themselves hated anyway, but in far more destructive ways.

THE CHILDREN'S GUILT

Since all children will harbor murderous feelings toward their parents, it is inevitable that all children will feel guilt. For all the reasons—real or imagined—each of us has to hate our parents, we have just as many reasons to love them. As we make our way through childhood and adolescence, we survive in large part because of the dependence we have on our parents and their caring response to us. For that care, even when it is minimal, there is still some semblance of gratitude. When we feel rage and hate toward those parents upon whom we have depended, we cannot do so without feeling guilty.

The process of emotional separation—growing up—is fraught with guilt. Severing infantile emotional ties with the parent can feel, to both parent and child, like a murderous act. Children will eventually have the startling and unsettling revelation that their parents are as dependent on them as they have been on their parents. Leaving the parents, as all children will want to do when they mature, will be the moral equivalent of turning their backs on their parents' dependence. As psychoanalyst Hans Loewald has said: "The assumption of responsibility for one's own life and its conduct is in psychic reality tantamount to the murder of parents."

Guilt has everything to do with the conflict of separation. It is, sometimes, only in guilt that we are able to come together or leave each other. We see our parents on weekends because if we don't we will feel guilty. But we leave them because the claustrophobia of the relationship makes us act badly toward them, and we feel guilty.

Hiding behind guilt—a necessary by-product of separation—is the ever-present rage. Rage was our first response to separation when we were babies and were set down to do as we pleased when all that pleased us was to be held. With every progressive step of separation there is rage and guilt. Someone is going to want to leave or be left faster than the other wants him to. Guilt is inevitable in separation because what else can it mean other than: "You are not enough for me. I want more." And behind this dissatisfaction is the loss of the omnipotent mother of childhood, the time when mother was enough. In our unconscious we remain enraged with our mothers for failing to deliver us from every problem.

Children who have not learned that their feelings of hate do not have destructive power will remain convinced that separation will kill. When a parent dies, guilt tells the child all the manifold ways that it was his fault. I have not yet met *anyone* who did not have some twinge of guilt about his parents' deaths.

Mostly the guilt remains in the realm of the reasonable—for example, whether something else could have been done, perhaps to have made a parent's last days more comfortable or to have communicated more love. These are the inevitable guilts that accompany being a good child.

But when the rage has been particularly strong, and the concomitant guilt equally strong, there is, as well, the conviction on the part of the child that he has actually killed the parent. All those years of fearing the effects of our anger finally come true. We are guilty as charged.

Parents, too, may stimulate the guilt in their communications to the child. In Philip Roth's *Portnoy's Complaint*, Alexander Portnoy is the prototypical example of a child plagued with a legacy of guilt. His mother warns him about his father: "Alex, keep the back talk up . . . continue with this disrespect . . . and you will give that man a heart attack." Unfortunately, this kind of parenting is not limited to fiction. Parents do communicate to their children that their children are hurting them, or killing them, leaving the child to believe that they are, or are soon to be, murderers.

It is common for us to engage in the kind of magical thinking that characterizes childhood when we feel guilty about our rage. We think that our rage, even when unexpressed, has magical power to destroy. We give our wishes the power of actions. In *Necessary Losses*, Judith Viorst tells the story of a woman who had a bitter, quarrelsome relationship with her mother:

> Bitter and angry, quarreling with her every day, she fantasied one evening, as she drove there for a visit, that her mother had suffered a fatal heart attack. Arriving at the street, she saw an ambulance roar past, stopping with a screech at her mother's front door, and paralyzed with fear she watched a team of medics rushing in with a stretcher and out again with the body of the woman who lived upstairs from her mother.

The woman told Viorst:

> I was utterly convinced when I saw that ambulance that I had given a heart attack to my mother. And I have to confess that part of me still believes in some nutty way that my magic missed and got that poor lady instead.

This magical thinking is a vestige of our infantile narcissism. Most of us retain some aspect of this process, and we carry with us a corresponding amount of guilt.

INTIMATE VIOLENCE

Separation is such a conflictual issue for both parents and children and arouses so much rage that it is often accompanied by physical abuse. Fathers who refuse to acknowledge that their children are separate human beings, with their own needs, will assume the right to treat a child in any fashion their impulses dictate. The boy-child may become his whipping boy, object of all his wrath; or, the girl-child may become the object of his sexual need (or the object of his need for control, expressed sexually). Mothers may hit, scratch, and beat their children from rage that their children have needs or wishes different from theirs. Husbands abuse wives, wives abuse husbands, and siblings abuse one another. Every member of a family is a separate individual with separate needs. These needs are bound to conflict with one another with a fair amount of regularity, whether it's about something as mundane as which television show to watch or as profound as whether to take a kidney from a healthy child to give to an unhealthy child. Families in which differences are not well tolerated are families in which there is potential for physical abuse.

Family life in contemporary America is not doing well in containing violent impulses. According to one report, half the women in this country are physically abused each year by the men in their lives. Children are learning violence as part of family life. Physical punishment is still the preferred method of child rearing. In a recent survey, more than 70 percent of the respondents felt that slapping a twelve-year-old child is necessary, normal, and good. Many parents believe that children "deserve to be hit" or "need to be hit." The absence of physical punishment seems to be the deviant method of child rearing.

With physical abuse so prevalent in childhood, it is not surprising that the practice should find its way into the dating scene. Although we like to have nostalgic memories of our courtships, involving candlelit dinners and stolen kisses, unfortunately the truth is that hitting, beating, and abuse are as much a part of the American dating scene as are loving flirtations and affections. Studies have found that between 22 and 67 percent of dating relationships involve some form of violence. Sociologist June Henton reports that more than one-quarter of the victims, and three out of ten of the offenders, interpret violence in a dating relationship as a sign of love.

The statistics don't change much when marriage occurs. One out of four wives, and one out of three husbands, thinks that a couple slapping each other is normal and good. A battered wife may not leave because of her strong belief that she provoked the abuse and therefore deserved what she got.

The interesting twist here is that even an apparently innocent victim of spousal abuse may be experiencing unconscious feelings of vengefulness toward a parent. Frequently a child's vengeful feelings are only indirectly expressed, and both parent and child may not even be aware that this is the nature of the difficulty. The adult child, in forming a destructive marital relationship, may be proclaiming to the parent, in effect, "This is the legacy of loving you left me with. I was damaged by you, and this is the best I can do."

The story of Charlotte Fedders is a good illustration of this dynamic. Charlotte married a man with whom she was in love, and whom she felt to be a well-suited partner for her.

He was a prominent Washington, D.C., attorney, and during the marriage he earned the prestigious title of chief of enforcement for the Securities and Exchange Commission. What Charlotte didn't know, however, when she married this seemingly well-mannered, educated, and highly successful man, was that he suffered from what she refers to as "black moods." In these dark moods, he would withdraw from her, refusing to speak to her for days and weeks. When she asked him what was upsetting him so, he would reply, "Look in the mirror. There's our problem." Eventually his withdrawal turned into outright physical abuse.

Charlotte eventually began to turn her husband's loathing of her against herself, and became convinced that he was correct: She deserved his abuse. Her self-loathing became so intense that at one point she began slapping her own face. "I'm so stupid," she would say to herself; then whack. "I'm so ugly." Whack. "I'm so fat." Her husband would watch her do this.

Charlotte was finally able to break the cycle of self-blame and leave her husband. She detailed her painful journey of self-realization in her best-selling book *Shattered Dreams.* Her husband did not stop blaming her for the breakdown of their marriage, and a circuit judge apparently agreed with him. Charlotte's husband claimed that she should share the blame for his violence because she denied him emotional support during his periods of depression. Indeed, Mr. Fedders was awarded 25 percent of the monies earned from the sale of Charlotte's book.

Fedders was a dismal husband, but Charlotte could not have been susceptible to his dim view of her without some prior preparation for the role. That preparation came out of her witnessing her father's relationship with her mother and her siblings, and her own experience of her father. Her mother made sure that the house was quiet for him, exactly the way he wanted, and ensured that a thousand other things were exactly the way he wanted. No one else in the family counted. This family was a one-note song, and that note was Father. Charlotte's continuing refrain as she was growing up, modeled after her mother, was, "He's my father, he's a man, he must be right."

Charlotte's sister Martha gives a compelling account of the role of revenge in the family:

> I just didn't know Daddy that well. I wasn't scared of him like, "Oh my God, he's going to do this to me"; it was more like the kind of scared you feel when you're on a first date and you don't know the person. And you'd see him get mad at other people, so you didn't want to have him get mad at you . . . Dinner conversations would revolve around his day and how he had *gotten* somebody. That was what you were supposed to do, *get* someone who had crossed you. He wanted us to do the same thing . . .

In continuing to stay married for almost twenty years to a man who physically and mentally abused her, Charlotte was the ultimate good daughter. She deferred to her husband, as she, her mother, and her sisters had done to her father. Since she felt herself to be unworthy of this smart, successful, handsome man, feeling rage about his treatment of her was out of the question: "I felt privileged to be married to a man of his stature." But, through all the sufferings at her husband's hands, Charlotte was able to extract a powerful payback to her father, who had drummed into her head that revenge was the sweetest of all feelings. What better way to punish a parent than to live a miserable life, suffer indignities that you refuse to free yourself from, and become a slave to the fear that your own parent has instilled within you? Whether or not the parent is aware, or even cares, about the grown child's failed life is immaterial. The process that is playing itself out is the child's perverse destruction of his or her own life based on an internal need to punish the parent.

One of my patients suffered from a similar dynamic. Early in his treatment he was able to articulate the gratification of revenge against the parent. He lacked one final credit to get his B.A. from college. His parents had wanted him to be an attorney. He became an auto mechanic instead and refused, for twenty years, to return to college to finish his degree. He said, "They don't deserve to have a successful son. I wouldn't want to give them that satisfaction." The man has allowed the rage he feels for his parents to stunt his entire life.

The connection between revenge and the narcissistic need to self-destruct may not be all that obvious, but it is there nevertheless. If the lesson we have learned about rage is that the only proper place to direct it is against the self, we may collude in the realization of self-destructiveness. Such a collusion, however, will not take place without unconscious rage at the parent who has fashioned this contract for us. Self-destructiveness may be the only form of revenge we can permit ourselves.

THE SIBLING BOND AND SIBLING BONDAGE

Cooperation begets cooperation; exploitation begets violence. Scenes of domestic violence and psychological abuse within the family give important lessons to the children. Most often, children will grow up to model their behavior after the same sex parent, a process called *identification.* A girl child of an abused mother can come to accept abuse from men as natural, deserved, and inevitable. A boy child of an abusing father will easily embrace the role, later in life, of being a punishing father to his wife. Abuse does not need to be experienced directly for the lesson to be learned. It may be witnessed or only sensed through the pervasive tension in the family relations.

Besides parents hating their children, and children hating their parents, the children in a family often come to hate one another. If the lesson of the family is that abuse is tolerated, and if the parent is perceived as too powerful or dangerous, the child may feel that expression of hatred toward the parent is unsafe. In that case, the child may direct aggression toward less powerful figures. Siblings often meet this requirement. Hatred toward the parent is often expressed in sibling rivalry and sibling violence.

Aside from finding an easy victim, there is another compelling reason to hate one's sibling. Each of us, in our heart of hearts, wants to be our parents' only true love. On the deepest level of our narcissistic needs, we want all the attention all the time. Siblings, and their own demands, will take some of that attention away from us. We may be instructed that it is right to be our "brother's keeper," but more often, like the original brothers of our civilization, Cain and Abel, we end up wanting to do away with our siblings more than we want to love them.

It should not surprise us, then, that violence between siblings is more common than violence between parent and child or violence between spouses. Sibling violence is the most overlooked form of domestic violence. When the first research was conducted on sibling violence, the sociologist Suzanne Steinmetz had difficulty getting parents to discuss the topic. The problem was not that parents were ashamed or thought such violence to be wrong. Rather, the problem was that sibling violence was such an everyday occurrence that parents hardly thought it worth mentioning. Most felt that nasty behavior between siblings was normal and helped to prepare their children for the dog-eat-dog world that they would be encountering soon enough. Although most of the incidents of sibling violence consist of slaps, kicks, and pushes, there are, as well, some dangerous manifestations. According to Steinmetz's research, weapons—knives or guns—are used by one sibling toward another in three out of 100 cases of sibling violence.

Expression of hatred toward the parent may permeate the sibling relationship in far more subtle ways than physical violence. Children may develop a bond that excludes the parents or is protective of themselves against the parents. Research shows that when sibling bonds are intense and exert a formative influence on the development of personality, usually there has been a deprivation of reliable parental care. These siblings use each other, much as other children use their parents, in a search for personal identity. When parental relationships are not reliably available, siblings serve each other as substitute parents, and the sibling bond is activated to an intense degree. Whether or not this intensification of the relationship is beneficial or harmful depends on a great many factors, including the reaction of the parents, the personalities of the children, and the dynamics of the family as a unit.

Marsha came to me with cancer, interested in exploring whether or not her cancer was related to her emotions. Marsha is the child of politically active, liberal parents. Her father was active in the civil rights movement in the sixties and protested the war in Vietnam in the seventies. Marsha has a younger brother who has followed in the footsteps of their parents, and who has been jailed on numerous occasions for his involvement in political protests.

Shortly after Marsha and I began our work together, her cancer went into remission. Seven years after her initial diagnosis and two babies later, she remains cancer-free. Her own words, in a diary she kept during her treatment with me, describe eloquently what she discovered over the course of her journey of introspection:

> My mother was a very intense, but emotionally withdrawn woman. She clearly had an easier time being loving to my brother than she did to me. I remember her saying to me repeatedly throughout my childhood: "Stop torturing me." She would say it in Hebrew, and a literal translation would be: "Stop getting down on my life." I can still remember the feelings when she would say

that to me. It was always when I could no longer be the "good girl" and my jealousy at my younger brother for her affection toward him got overwhelming. It took some years of training to bury my poisonous feelings in my body and put on the act of the perfect girl. But what a tender nerve that left me with.

My mother had always taken for granted that everything would go well with me, and had given me the message that "you can do it on your own. You do not need me as much as your brother who is weaker and more needy." Again, I went along with her communication, but I found a loophole—sickness. Being sick was a sure way to get her attention. Being sick made me important. I have wondered whether my ploy of becoming a hypochondriac has anything to do with being trapped in this self-fulfilling prophecy of cancer.

When my brother was jailed for his political activities, I felt so guilty that, for a long time, I had difficulty doing anything that he himself could not have done in prison. And when I did do something that I considered pleasurable, I would think of his not being able to do it. It was as if I had gone to prison with him. But at the same time, I felt that my mother had gotten what she had bargained for—having a hero for a son, the right kind of hero, one who sacrificed his life for the right cause. She was so proud of him.

I developed bleeding colitis right after he was arrested, and continued to suffer from it on and off for years after that.

This conflict, between my brother's life or mine, repeated itself again, years later when a campaign was begun to release him from jail. I was supposed to be helping out with this. I was holding a full-time job and was studying full-time for a master's degree. I remember my bodily sensations during this awful autumn. It was like my body was stiff from tension, and the despair of constantly choosing his life over mine was just unbearable. It was about four months into this campaign that my cancer was diagnosed. I remember saying to myself "What I need now is some horrible disease." In my mind it could not have been anything else but cancer.

Marsha presents a clear picture of a child with an emotionally unavailable mother. In reaction to this deprivation of maternal care, Marsha forged an intense bond with her brother. Marsha's rage and desire for revenge against her mother became clear to Marsha during the course of her treatment with me. The brother, and the sacrifice of herself to his cause, served merely as an effective instrument with which to carry forth her self-destruction.

SIBLING REVENGE AGAINST THE MEMORIES OF PARENTS

Children may extract their revenge against parents by perpetuating sibling disagreements after the death of one or both parents. How siblings manage the issues involved in putting the affairs of a dead parent in order is usually related to emotional dynamics that were created in childhood. Children who were not taught cooperation, either among themselves or with their parents, will lack the skills and desire needed to cooperatively deal with one another in the absence of the parent. The most important part of their inheritance is the legacy of noncooperation they receive from their parents.

A friend of mine is one of three children, all in middle age. They were fortunate in that their parents both lived into their nineties, and both died painless deaths. All three children had established their own lives, and while they saw each other at family gatherings and were able to be pleasant enough to one another, there lay beneath the surface unresolved and potentially explosive family issues.

The oldest son, Aaron, harbored a long-standing resentment toward both his brother, Ed, and his sister, Lois. The parents had given money to Lois after she had been suddenly widowed at an early age. They had, as well, given their summer cottage to Ed, the youngest child, after he expressed a wish to live in it year-round and convert it into a permanent residence. Though neither of these gifts amounted to a great deal of money, and Aaron had been given money as a wedding present, Aaron persisted in the belief that the distribution of gifts and their values had been unequal. This sense of unfairness and favoritism was a constant unspoken point of contention among the siblings. Both Ed and Lois felt Aaron's feelings were unreasonable. Aaron's anger about the favoritism interfered with his relationship with his parents, and he was the least close to them of all the children.

After the death of the mother, all three children felt it was appropriate to put their father's affairs and his estate in order. When it came to selecting an executor of the estate, first Lois, then Ed declined the responsibility. Aaron, the most appropriate choice because he is the oldest, was elected by default.

When their father died, the first step in the managing of the estate was the probating of the will, normally a routine affair. Aaron delayed attending to it, and just when it seemed he was finally getting around to it, the dog ate the will. Next, there was a piece of property to be sold; the buyer had made an offer and both Ed and Lois had agreed to accept it. Only Aaron held out for more money, and the buyer was lost. After a year and a half of postponements and delays, finally the money was ready to be distributed. Still Ed and Lois waited, and when money finally did arrive, it was only a fraction of what they knew they were entitled to.

Up to this point Lois and Ed had both kept their peace. Though Aaron's explanations of the delays had never convinced them, they had deliberately shied away from rocking the fragile peace that silence created. Now, with this final act of blatant and antagonistic disregard, they called Aaron's attorney and asked what the problem was. He admitted that the settlement had taken an inordinate amount of time, and said that when he had asked Aaron why everything was proceeding so slowly and badly, Aaron had replied, "My brother and sister know why."

A year later, Lois and Ed remained in legal action against their brother, the estate not yet settled. Aaron had achieved a powerful payback to his parents by exacting his revenge against his siblings. The act of revenge that he wanted couldn't be carried out during the life of his parents, but was skillfully accomplished after their death.

LOVING IN SPITE OF IT ALL

Though we may prefer to believe that love and abuse are incompatible, our experience tells us otherwise. The bonds between the abused and the abuser do not necessarily disappear because of incidents of violence.

It is precisely the characteristics that make family life warm, supportive, and intimate that are also responsible for turning the family into a demonic unit of abuse and violence. We spend more time with our family, doing a wider range of activities; we know our family members better than anyone else. Family members know better than anyone how to make one another laugh; they also know how to provoke pain, fury, and hurt in one another. The depth of knowledge that makes loving intimacy possible also can be used to attack vulnerabilities and to escalate conflicts. The great irony of family life is that the very intimacy that gives support and security is also a potential explosive, ready to be set off with the right spark.

However, in spite of the limitations and dangers of family life, we are still better off with it than without it. The modern disruption of family life and the frequency of divorce is having an adverse effect on our mental and physical well-being, particularly that of our children. According to Leonard Sagan, children from divorced families perform less well than children of two-parent families on a wide variety of academic, social, and health measures. Children of single-parent families will have experienced the pain and anxiety that goes with the loss of a parent, and this loss is likely to affect relationships later in life. Children of divorced parents are themselves much more likely to get divorced. Children of single-parent homes are more than twelve times as likely to be physically abused than are children of a two-parent home.

According to researcher M. Winn, the impact of the prevalence of divorce does not stop with those who are directly involved with a divorce. Seeing the ease with which families become nonfamilies affects the children from stable families, as well. One ten-year-old child, after seeing *Kramer vs. Kramer* (a movie about divorce), said, "My parents had a fight the other day, and my mother walked out of the house. I thought to myself 'This is it,' and I cried and cried. But she had just gone next door to the neighbors." In the same study, another child said, "We're one of those families that aren't divorced," adding after a pause, "At least, not yet." In these times of uncertainty about family life, children are being deprived of their childhood.

Family life, at its best, may be a "safe haven in a heartless world," as Christopher Lasch has said, but the family functions not only as a haven but also as a strong foundation from which one moves off to investigate the world. After mother love and after family love, the next major love that we experience is romantic love. It is romantic love, with all its similarities to mother love, for which we yearn most ardently. With a need this great, we are bound to experience not only the radiance of romantic love but also the chill of the dark side of love.

CHAPTER 7

The Dark Side of Romantic Love: The Reemergence of Yearning

A colleague of mine once spoke of a patient who suffered from an insatiable need for sex. He felt compelled to satisfy his sexual appetite two, sometimes three, times a day. He discovered all manner of meeting women, but one of his most successful approaches was to walk up to an attractive woman on the street and remark that she reminded him of someone he knew. He found that if he communicated that what he felt about this reminiscence was warmth and pleasure, the woman would respond to him with positive interest.

This man continued the pattern for several years, and though his compulsion was taking up an inordinate amount of time, there seemed to be no cure for him. Until one day he noticed a particularly striking woman walking down the street. He was behind her, and as he watched her walk he realized that this time the woman really did remind him of someone, though he couldn't quite place the memory. As he approached her, readying his seductive invitation, she turned to face him, and he was startled—and horrified—to see that it was his own mother whom he had been pursuing. Shortly after this event, the man settled into a committed relationship with a woman whom he eventually married, his search for his mother having finally ended.

ROMANCE AND THE RETURN TO A PERFECT PAST

As the story suggests, in spite of our belief that what we seek in romantic love is something new and different, in fact we are searching for something that is old and familiar: idealized mother love. Just as we expect mother love to be the nearest thing to perfection on earth, so, too, do we make these same demands on romantic love.

It is true that to fall in love is a magnificent, expansive, enhancing experience. It energizes us; it connects us with the world around us through the relationship with the other person. It is a natural, creative, and beautiful experience, even sublime. It has to do with rapturous feelings of engulfment in a world that is completely and blissfully safe and warm and nurturing. It is the vision of Eden, before separateness and the pain of aloneness could even be imagined.

It is more than mere coincidence that the feelings that we experience in romantic love feel remarkably like feelings from another, earlier time in our lives. That time, too, our needs were perfectly understood, we had no fear or anxiety about abandonment, and there was utter completion. That time was, of course, the time of the intrauterine environment, before birth. Romantic love seeks the same completion and fulfillment that a mother's body gives absolutely perfectly to her unborn fetus. It is this sense of completeness that we all long to perpetuate even after our time in the womb has ended. Romantic love wants the same union of selves that is represented in this early, prebirth symbiosis, when our needs are perfectly met.

THE DISAPPOINTMENT OF ROMANTIC LOVE

While romantic love starts out with a glittering promise of eternal joy and satisfaction, eventually the dark aspects that are inherent in this kind of love emerge. Because romantic love re-creates most precisely the issues and conflicts of mother love, whatever unresolved conflicts remain from the earlier love will emerge later in romantic love. Our romantic dreams of lasting completion through the meeting of a beloved are, almost always, an illusion.

Just as the story of Eden has to do with the expulsion from perfection, just as birth has to do with separation, and just as motherhood has to do with hate and anger, so, too, does "being in love" have to do with the loss of that dreamlike state of bliss and unity. We can't begin to understand the intensity of the force of romantic love until we understand that it is our deepest and oldest longings that find representation in it. Romantic love is a refinding, a reedition of old wishes and feelings.

As visions and fantasies of wondrous harmony are evoked with romantic love, so, too, are the earliest memories and fears of loss and disappointment, the dread of aloneness and the nightmare of abandonment. Embedded within the very perfection of this blissful love is the inevitability of its ultimate dissolution. Perfect harmony between two individuals cannot exist for more than fleeting moments outside the womb—a truth we resist with all our hearts all our lives. In romantic love we search and search for our other half and the completion that we once had. The face of romantic love is turned toward the past, a memory of that one perfect, lost love.

All great poets and authors of great literature have recognized that the state of being in love is a fragile one. It may feel enduring and profound—the emotions it arouses are, indeed, intense and dramatic—but because romantic love is based on the past, its foundation is not always strong enough to survive the stresses and strains of everyday life. Romantic love turns dark when one misunderstands the true nature of being in love and attributes to romantic love more strength than it has.

THE STORY OF EROS AND PSYCHE

The myth of Eros and Psyche has been passed down tirelessly from generation to generation since the second century A.D. The legend of these two ill-fated lovers brilliantly illustrates the nature of romantic love. In the telling of the tale, we come to understand each of the aspects of romantic love and the dangers that are inherent in this illusory and elusive love.

The story begins, as do many tales of romantic love, with a desire born from destructive hate. The goddess Aphrodite can't stand the adoration that a beautiful young mortal named Psyche is receiving. In a fit of jealous rage, Aphrodite sentences Psyche to spend the rest of her life on the top of a mountain, isolated from other mortals and fated to become the bride of the monster Death. But before Psyche falls claim to the monster, the kind West Wind takes pity on her.

Through the West Wind's gentle breezes, Psyche is wafted down the mountain to a valley, where she is free from the clutches of Death. Here, she meets Eros, whose home is this valley. The two promptly fall in love.

But Eros is not being entirely truthful with Psyche. He harbors a secret. Eros' mother is Aphrodite, the very same goddess who punished Psyche for her allure and beauty. Eros doesn't want Psyche to know his true identity as a god, and as Aphrodite's son. In order to keep his identity hidden, Eros visits Psyche only in the darkness of the night, when his godly beauty and his golden wings cannot be seen.

Psyche is visited one day by her sisters, who keep asking all kinds of probing questions, and they start Psyche wondering. Who is her sweet lover who creeps to her in the darkness of the night? What would the full light of day—the awareness of all aspects of his being—reveal him to be? Psyche yearns to make her love a conscious one, to learn all that there is to know about her mysterious lover. She determines to find out. One night, before Eros comes to her, Psyche hides a lamp under her bed. As she leans over her sleeping lover to get a good look at him, a drop of hot oil falls onto him and awakens him. Eros awakens with a start, quickly realizes that Psyche has discovered the truth about him, and vows to punish her by abandoning her. As Eros flees, Psyche follows, but she trips, and instantly the peaceful valley where their love has flourished disappears, and Psyche finds herself once more alone, on top of the craggy mountain, waiting helplessly for Death to claim her.

UNCONSCIOUS LOVE

The love between Eros and Psyche is a love that is nurtured in darkness. Psyche, like all of us who fall in love, is content, initially, to allow her love to be blind. Romantic love is blind because it thrives on fantasy and illusion; it looks inwardly at one's own hopes and desires rather than at the reality of who the other person is. Since the lovers don't really know each other, romantic love is a perfect, idealized love, imagined to fulfill whatever it is that we feel we need or want the most.

But such an imaginative love is fragile. As happened with Eros and Psyche, when the truth is fully exposed, there is a tendency to flee. We experience shock and disappointment, even rage, as did Eros when he discovered that his beloved was not content to live in an unconscious secret love. When we discover the complete, unvarnished truth about our beloved—their imperfections and their all-too-human traits—we feel betrayed by both our lover and our love. Often we do not withstand the shock of our disillusionment, and rather than persevere with this love and ground it in reality rather than illusion, we destroy it altogether.

ROMANTIC LOVE AND SEPARATION

It is often in romantic love that we have our first chance to practice our ability to love and be loved outside of our immediate family. It is here that we first encounter one of the caveats of romantic love. In order to make room for a new love, old loves need to be given up. Mother is replaced as the primary love object. Romantic love is yet another step in the progression toward final psychological separation from the parent.

The story of Eros and Psyche is instructive in its lesson about this aspect of romantic love, as well. For a new love to be successful, it must take priority over previous loves and allegiances. Eros is a prototypical example of someone who is unsuccessful in making this transition, and he destroys his new love relationship with Psyche because of this inability.

Eros and his mother had not broken their symbiotic union. As long as Eros determined to keep his romance with Psyche a secret, he had not broken his tie to his mother. He remained within her sphere of influence, undeveloped as a man and as a separate adult.

It is, in fact, Psyche's burning Eros and seeing him that allows him to break free from his mother's domination. Although he is injured by the relationship with Psyche, he is finally *seen* for who and what he is. This freedom to be himself leads him to be able to individuate from his mother.

We learn, then, from the myth that our ties to our earliest loves can prevent us from making new loves. It is easier to remain in the shadow of the protective mother, unharmed and unrevealed, but it is only when we are willing to risk injury, hurt, and rage that we can come to know the fullness of our potential for new loves.

The relationship of a couple I saw for marriage counseling, Cindy and Mark, has similarities to the stories of the mythical figures of Eros and Psyche. When Cindy first consulted me, I was struck by the calm in her voice, in sharp contrast to the drama of the story that she told me. She and her husband had had a fight— their worst one yet, which ended in an unexpected and drastic action. In a rush of desperation, Cindy pulled open the china closet and, one by precious one, began destroying the dishes that were their most-loved wedding gift. Cindy had been imploring Mark for almost an hour to admit his psychological brutality to her. She had finally reached the end of her tolerance and threatened to continue with the destruction of the china until the entire set was wiped out unless he was willing to apologize for his incessant criticisms of her.

Only a year and a half earlier Cindy and Mark had fallen rapturously in love. The world had never seemed brighter. They were not newcomers to this game of attraction—she was forty-four, he fifty-three. They both had had their share of romantic relationships. After a whirlwind eight-week romance, they got married—a second marriage for both.

In the beginning of their relationship, each had had a strong sense that this love represented the culmination of their lives and was what they had been waiting and preparing for during all those frustrating and empty years. Their future promised a new, uncharted expanse that each was eager to explore. They seemed so perfectly suited that they felt, at long last, their soul mates had been found.

How could this ideal relationship have deteriorated so far in such a short time? How did a love life that sparkled with such promise turn into a frightening dark perversion of itself? No wonder Cindy and Mark were confused; their arguments were growing ever more frequent and increasingly destructive. Making up was sweet, and love was always refound, but in their loving moments they would have been hard-pressed even to adequately describe what their fights were about or how they began. All the intensity that had originally fueled the constructive power of their early love now seemed to be turned, with equal force, toward the goal of mutual accusation and destruction.

The marriage of Cindy and Mark, like the relationship between Eros and Psyche, was born out of the unconscious shadows of romantic love. To understand how two intelligent people could have come to this impasse, we need to know something about their histories—their earliest loves.

Cindy grew up with a very proper, ladylike mother. Cindy was well trained in the art of fine living: She threw the best dinner parties around, five-course events with each dish excelling the last; she was an avid admirer of fine wines and carefully selected color and vintage to match her choice of dishes. By the time Cindy met Mark, she had honed all this to perfection.

An essential requirement of a husband for Cindy was a man who shared with her the pleasures of this life-style. Many an ardent suitor had been rebuffed because of his ignorance of these sensibilities.

When Cindy met Mark, she knew at last that he was "right." Mark exuded an air of success. He was a wealthy man; he dressed expensively, drove a high-status car, and enjoyed eating out at fine restaurants. He met all of Cindy's requirements: He was, at first glance, exactly the man she had been looking for.

But Cindy's love for Mark at this phase of their relationship was an unconscious one. They felt they knew each other; they felt a sense of recognition in each other, two half selves uniting into one. But what Cindy was seeing in Mark (and Mark, in different ways, was seeing in Cindy) was a projection of her own unmet needs: the self she longed to be; the self that would make her whole. Cindy wasn't seeing Mark; she was seeing her incomplete self, finally reaching completion through Mark.

Mark, too, was a victim of his own projections, seeing in Cindy what he needed and wanted to see. He saw an independent woman, quite successfully managing on her own—a welcome relief from his former overly dependent, intensely possessive wife. Cindy asked him questions about his feelings, his ideas and dreams, and just plain how he spent his day—a stark contrast to his emotionally distant mother.

Once Cindy and Mark got to know each other more fully, they could no longer maintain their projections. Mark is indeed all of what Cindy perceived, but he is also much more. He is also a man who is demanding, critical, overly possessive, and suffocating. Shortly after the wedding, Mark listed his litany of rules: Cindy's dogs were not allowed in the house; she could smoke only on the patio; the dinner dishes should be done immediately after the completion of the meal, and Cindy was always to go to bed at the same time as he. For Mark's part, his cursory knowing of Cindy did not include her tendency toward histrionics when her life and her feelings got too overwhelming. He was unaware of her extreme defensiveness and inability to tolerate any expression of rage toward her.

The challenge of Cindy and Mark's marriage is to find a way to accept all parts of themselves and each other, and not to put into destructive action the pains and hurts and disappointments that constitute the dark side of their love. To do this, however, means giving up all the shimmer and glory of romantic love, all the dreams of idealized, perfect mother love. It is only when the "in-loveness" of romantic projections ends that cooperative love—the love between two separate identities—can begin.

INVISIBLE PARTNERS

The psychic mechanism of projection is not an inherently destructive process. It is a perfectly natural step in the developmental sequence toward cooperative love. Projection puts us firmly in touch with our deepest selves, the wishes and hopes and dreams that represent the best of our longings. Each time a projection occurs it gives us an opportunity to know our inner, invisible partners. Jung calls these invisible partners *animus* and *anima*, the masculine and feminine principles that reside in the depths of our psyches, and which lead us to seek a complementary whole of both. Projection, too, serves often as the initial spark that ignites the fire of love that inches its way toward its final and enduring version forged of cooperation, respect, and trust.

Eleanor Bertine, a Jungian analyst, uses the historical figures of Dante and Mark Antony to show that it is how we *use* our projections that determines whether the outcome of romantic love is constructive or destructive. Both Dante and Mark Antony were rapturously in love. Their loves also met the classic description of projection: They were instantaneous (what we call "love at first sight"); they were without ambivalence; it was the beloved who held the key to the other's happiness; and the element of surrender played an important role in these loves. Yet, in spite of the common elements of these projected loves, they ended very differently from one another. Dante used his love to create great literature; Antony's was used to destroy a civilization.

Dante first saw Beatrice when he was only nine years old, but he was smitten forevermore. Some years later, Dante described the impact of this meeting:

> Her dress on that day was of a most noble color, a subdued and goodly crimson, girdled and adorned in such sort as suited her very tender age. At that moment I say truly that the spirit of life, which hath its dwelling in the secretest chamber of the heart, began to tremble so violently that the least pulses of my body shook therewith; and in trembling it said these words: Behold a deity stronger than I, who, coming, will rule me . . . From that time forward Love quite governed my soul.

We see in Dante's words that this was love to which he surrendered. The real person of Beatrice was almost incidental. It was, rather, her representation of the feminine principle, the soft, flexible, giving nature of love, that was important.

It wasn't until Dante was eighteen that he saw Beatrice again, and this second meeting was their last. But neither that fact, nor the fact that Beatrice married shortly thereafter and died a year later, stopped Dante from his lifelong exploration of the meaning of Beatrice to his psyche. Dante dedicated many of his sonnets to Beatrice, and she reappears in his masterpiece *The Divine Comedy* as his guide in heaven. In allowing Beatrice to guide him, Dante came to know fully and consciously the feminine aspects of his psyche that would otherwise have eluded him as a man. In making transcendent poetry out of his exploration, he gave structure to his experience, thus making it available to the world.

Mark Antony had quite a different experience with his love. After Julius Caesar's death in 44 B.C., Antony became emperor of lands that included the home of Cleopatra, Queen of Egypt. Antony traveled to Egypt to receive homage from the various kings and queens now under his domain. In his initial meeting with Cleopatra, although it was she who was supposed to be the conquered one, she quickly dominated Antony through her seductive prowess, thus beginning one of the most famous, and tragic, love affairs in history. Antony surrendered to Cleopatra his good judgment, his competence, and his individuality. He acted, according to Plutarch, "as a man who had no proper control over his faculties, who, under the effects of some drug or magic, was still looking back elsewhere."

Soon enough Antony found himself in battle. Before meeting Cleopatra, Antony had distinguished himself as an honored and excellent general, whose very best was brought out in times of war. Yet now he followed Cleopatra's far inferior judgments about war: "So wholly was he now the mere appendage to the person of Cleopatra that, although he was much superior to the enemy in land-forces, yet, out of complaisance to his mistress, he wished the victory to be gained by sea." In the final moments of the war, with still a chance of winning even with the monumental disadvantages he had incurred, Cleopatra's ships suddenly took flight. To the utter astonishment of all engaged in the battle, Antony abandoned his fight, his ships, and his men, and set sail in pursuit of his beloved. Within a few months, Antony and Cleopatra, defeated and shamed, were dead by their own hands.

Antony's "love" for Cleopatra left no room for him to maintain his separate identity. His surrender was a complete surrender, not to love but to self-annihilation. There was no self left to love or to be loved.

Both Dante and Mark Antony were in love with an idealized image of a woman who existed more in their psyches than in reality, but only Dante was able to understand that his love was a projection. Modern lovers, too, are forced into the challenge of separating the real from the ideal in their beloveds.

Projections often predominate the beginning of romantic entanglements, when one's hopes and expectations (i.e., fantasy) are strongest, and when accurate information about the beloved is minimal, despite the fact that we may *think* we know the other person. Often in projected love there is a sense of recognition ("I feel like we've always known each other"). These projections *are*, in fact, familiar because they are *ours*. We are seeing the internal contents of our minds, our wishes and hopes projected onto another person.

Sally is a patient who came to me after her husband, Randy, left her. Randy had had a torrid love affair with a married woman before meeting Sally. He had waited three years for the woman to leave her husband before he finally despaired of the possibility and ended the affair. Randy and Sally married shortly after they met. When Randy announced to Sally four years later that he was leaving her, he confessed that he had never stopped thinking about the other woman. She had finally divorced and had contacted Randy to resume their relationship.

Randy's relationship with the other woman lasted five months. He came back to Sally, pleading for her to take him back, explaining that he now understood that he had been operating under an illusion about this woman and his love for her for all of those years. Sally by this time had come to terms with their separation and was not interested in taking up with Randy again.

Randy had correctly come to understand that his love for this other woman was a projected love. The woman that Randy thought he wanted was not the same woman he lived with for five months. The woman whom Randy had thought about longingly for four years was an elusive fantasy, fueled by memories of an illicit affair that involved more sex than it did day-to-day cooperation. The woman Randy found was a flesh-and-blood, slightly controlling, hotheaded woman who was, in fact, not too different from Sally. In mistaking a projected love for reality, Randy destroyed his marriage and ended up with neither love.

ROMANTIC LOVE AND SURRENDER

In romantic love we want to return to the prebirth experience of being merged with another. This longing to merge, to surrender to another, and to dissolve the boundaries between self and other constitutes part of the ecstasy of romantic love.

Both men and women can find contentment living in the shadow of another. When both partners have strong identities, this can result in a mutually satisfying arrangement. One of my colleagues has worked out a successful marriage based on her husband's desire to fuse his own ambitions with hers. She is an internationally known psychoanalyst. Early in their marriage he had a successful career in business. But as the demands of her fame became more pronounced, her husband made the decision to make *her* his career. He administers a psychoanalytic school that she founded and directs; he publishes her books, and he follows her around the country as she gives lectures and teaches.

When the decision to surrender to another is made willingly and with a strong sense of self as a foundation, the result is the best of what romantic love has to offer: transcendence of self and expansion beyond the confines of a single self. A union has been created, a "we" out of an "I." The self has been enlarged, expanded, and made stronger.

The paradox of romantic love, however, is that inherent in the desire to merge and surrender the self is the risk of losing oneself altogether. Although the power of romantic love has turned beasts into beauties, it has also enslaved countless numbers of men and women into blind obedience.

It is precisely in this paradox that the seeds for one of romantic love's greatest agonies are sown. Romantic love wants fusion. In romantic love, separateness is dissolved; either the "otherness" of the other is obliterated so that there is no "other" to be loved; or, the "otherness" of self is annihilated so that there is no self from which to love. Walking the thin tightrope between merging and maintaining separate identities so that mature love is possible is a feat not easily accomplished.

ROMANTIC LOVE AND FEAR

The one unequivocal piece of information we have about the phenomenon of romantic love is that despite its sweet appeal, it is fueled by all kinds of unpleasant emotions. Fear heads the list.

There is a precedent for this love born of fear. The link between love and fear is evident in the games parents play with their children. Peekaboo (I'm here; feel assured. I'm not here; feel frightened); tossing baby in the air (will I catch you or won't I?); and tickling (will I be nice and stop when you say to, or will I be mean and continue until you cry and plead for mercy?) all have the effect of strengthening a love bond by inducing fear and agitation. The message is strong: "Love me, be afraid of me, and trust me, because I can save you."

Some remnant of the ambivalent messages we receive in our childhood remains with us, and even in normal, mature love relationships a certain amount of fear and uncertainty can serve as a stimulant for passion. Too much consistency may feel safe, but it is not likely to stimulate the passionate feelings that we equate with romantic love. When the beloved, out of ambivalence or disinterest, creates uncertainty, we are enticed. Countless men and women are tormented by this all-too-common phonomenon of loving the very person who is the most ambivalent about returning their love. But if we see that mature love demands a complete emotional experience, and that we long to have *all* of our feelings stimulated, then we can understand the appeal of our beloved's ambivalence and inconsistency.

Some of us carry the link between fear and love to an extreme and are able to make romantic attachments only when fear is a predominant part of the emotional tone of the relationship. When pushed to the edge, the "love" of romance can quickly turn into a pathological dynamic that may *feel* remarkably like love but is in fact a love pretender, the destructiveness that accompanies any relationship that has fear as its defining characteristic.

The information that we have on the link between love and fear has been used and misused for hundreds of years. In recent years, we have even been able to put together a fairly reliable formula, based on the stimulation of extreme fear, that can produce a laboratory re-creation of the phenomenon of "being in love." In an experiment done on three litters of puppies, one litter was consistently mistreated, one was consistently treated well, and the third was alternately mistreated and treated well. Both the mistreated and well-treated puppies grew into dogs who acted independently of their owners. The on-again, off-again puppies, however, failed to make the transition to adult independence and remained devotedly attached to their unpredictable masters. They manifested devotion, fierce loyalty, attachment, and behavior that indicated an inability to function adequately without a master. Isn't the cringing attachment that these dogs manifested eerily close to the kind of attachment we feel when our "being in love" is accompanied by visions of loss?

This same principle of alternately blowing hot and blowing cold to induce fear and uncertainty has been a technique used all through the ages, from the religious inspiration of the ancient shaman to the modern brainwashing techniques of war. In both these situations an emotional response that looks and feels very like love is stimulated.

During the Korean War, a group of captured American prisoners were physically abused, frightened, isolated, and deprived of their toilet facilities by their Korean captors. They were then exposed to another group of Koreans who cleaned and bathed them with gentle reassurance. In a very short period of time, the soldiers were open to believing as absolute gospel anything that the kind Koreans wished to tell them. Through the simple induction of fear and then the relief from that fear, the captors were able to erase all vestiges of rage and rebelliousness in their prisoners and replace them with gratitude and devotion.

The vision of helpless puppies who are at the mercy of the whims of their trainer, or of frightened soldiers grateful for any small act of kindness by their tormentors, may bring us uncomfortably close to our earliest, usually repressed, memories of having once been a helpless child, entirely dependent on mother to rescue us. It is precisely because we have already known the experience of needing to be rescued that we can be brought back so easily to that fearful, dependent, infantile state. Some of us never quite leave this meaning of love. Actress Robin Givens, ex-wife of boxing champion Mike Tyson, made the point of the link between love and fear succinctly: "I loved the danger. He was exciting. I think what people don't realize with a certain type of woman is that there are times when she wants the man she is with to be . . . a man." Mike Tyson, who made his living assaulting and weakening his opponents and was later imprisoned for rape, could certainly, by Givens' definition, be called a "man." And the thrill of the danger could be mistaken for love. But any love based on fear is not a love that will foster mature growth and respect between two people.

Some people are attracted to danger and fear, but any of us can, under the right circumstances, be brought to the state of loving devotion even against our will. Without the benefit of knowledge about either scientific or brainwashing technology, many of us practice and perfect these techniques on one another.

In her book *In the Name of Love,* Jill Tweedie points out how relatively easy it is to get someone to fall in love. Isolate the person; throw her (or him) into new surroundings so she feels threatened and fearful; upset her, humiliate her, and disorient her, and just as she is most tired and most disoriented, appear as her savior. Comfort her, soothe her, and promise her anything that will assuage her fear. Sleeplessness will augment the effect. By alternating threats and soothing protectiveness, within an astonishingly short period of time she will inevitably declare her undying love.

Two contemporary works of art illustrate this manipulation. In her novel *Possession*, Ann Rule brilliantly portrays the phenomenon. She tells a gripping tale of a psychopathic killer who sets out to make a woman his sexual slave. He follows the key rules

illustrated by both the prisoners-of-war and the mistreated dogs:
He kills his victim's husband (leaving her terrified and alone); he
kidnaps her (leaving her defenseless) and carries her off to the top
of a mountain, where her survival depends on his good wishes
(leaving her dependent). At first the sex is forced. But as her memory gets disorganized and her thought processes become chaotic,
she is able to retain only one fact: He loves her; he will protect her;
and he will never leave her. She knows that this is so because he has
told her. Her mind, exhausted and emptied of all else, becomes a
willing receptacle to his message.

> No one else would ever love her this much. He would never leave
> her. He had told her these truths over and over until his words
> made a little rhyming hum, and she could hear melody behind
> them.

When her "lover" is finally captured and killed, she clings desperately and devotedly to his lifeless body.

In her film *Swept Away,* Lina Wertmuller makes the point that
even the most strong-willed individual can be brought to her knees
through the use of the blow-hot, blow-cold treatment. Her pro-
toganist is a bitchy, wealthy woman who finds herself stranded on a
desert island with a man whom she considers to be her social and
intellectual inferior. Yet, it becomes evident that his skill at living
off the land will enable him to survive. It is only when she demonstrates a posture of humbleness and dependency that he helps her
or is kind to her.

It's a simple Pavlovian reinforcement schedule: He rewards her
for signs of dependency with food and affection; he punishes her
for signs of anger or independence by withholding food and assistance. She returns to civilization contentedly and peacefully "in
love" with a man whom only days earlier she considered to be a
savage.

While Rule's and Wertmuller's stories both have exotic locales
and both represent an extreme version of the induction of fear in
another person, modifications of the principle occur in almost
every relationship. For instance, the element of isolation: It is a
commonly known fact, verified by research, that romantic and sex-

ual ardor is increased when people are away from their homes. Business trips, for instance, are a fertile ground for affairs. The relative isolation of the housewife leads to an exaggerated emphasis on her relationship with her husband. The upset and humiliation element is evident in relationships in which one partner is overly critical; the other will lose self-esteem and feel grateful that the partner tolerates such an undeserving person. The inconsistent alternating of loving protectiveness at one moment and rage at another is perhaps the most common dysfunctional pattern in relationships in which there is alcoholic abuse by one of the partners. For most of us, some of these elements are present in our ordinary relationships and our love relationships are shadowy versions of the ones in Rule's and Wertmuller's stories.

ROMANTIC LOVE AND FRUSTRATION

Romantic love, as well as being fueled by feelings of fear, is also stimulated by the feeling of frustration. This, in fact, was Freud's basic understanding of how love originates. The greatest frustration, Freud felt, was inhibited sexuality, and it is when this barrier is erected that romantic love, with its ever-present sexual overtones, is most likely to reveal its face:

> Some obstacle is necessary to swell the tide of libido to its height; and at all periods of history whenever natural barriers in the way of satisfaction have not sufficed, mankind has erected conventional ones in order to enjoy love.

Wartime romances, adulterous and extramarital affairs, and unrequited love are all loves whose passion is fueled by frustration. As the saying goes, it is often true that absence does, indeed, make the heart grow fonder. Most of the great romance tales all through the ages are stories of frustrated love. Writers of erotica have honed the description of the arousing effect of sexual frustration to perfection, with most erotic stories portraying the protagonist as brought to the point of insatiable hunger for satisfaction out of frustration. Being deprived in love seems to be as powerful a stimulant to romance and sexuality as being gratified.

ROMANTIC YEARNING AND ADULTEROUS LOVE

Romantic love, in the face of reality, must transform itself into something else. At best, it can be turned into a realistic love, which involves admitting the strengths and weaknesses of the other person. At worst, it can become an experience of intense disappointment. In this case, we almost always blame our beloved rather than the fragility of romantic love. Narcissistic individuals, who remain more interested in their own feelings than in developing a cooperative relationship with another person, will remain perpetually tied to the idea of a perfect love, and will continue to search for it without success.

Romantic yearning can be replaced, but it cannot be satisfied. This is what makes some people susceptible to affairs. The "other" beloved always seems more appealing—more right, more perfect, more deserving—than the spouse. Unattainability is at the heart of adulterous love, which holds particular fascination for us. Western literature begins with a tale of adultery, the story of the Trojan War, a battle precipitated by Paris' abduction of Helen, another man's wife. According to researcher Tony Tanner, "it is the unstable triangularity of adultery, rather than the static symmetry of marriage, that is the generative form of Western literature as we know it."

Adulterous relationships are, by definition, triangular relationships. There are the two beloveds, always waiting for their precious few moments, and then there is the other, the impediment, the perceived obstacle to the fulfillment of the true love of the lovers.

Adulterous love is as much as anything an imaginary love. It exists in stolen moments, romantic escapades, and most of all, it exists in the world of imagination. Adulterous love feeds on fantasies, and its very nature of secrecy and removal from the mundane world is precisely what sparks its extraordinary quality. It is a love that is separate and better than everyday togetherness.

Adulterous relationships feed on their frustration. The fact that the beloved is not always available, and that the culmination of the love is fraught with danger, are both the thrill and the frustration, the bliss and the agony.

Adulterous love, on closer examination, bears a striking similarity to the love between two parents and a child—the original love triangle. As we begin to separate from our dependency on mother and leave infantile narcissism behind us in order to make our entry into the world as independent competitors, so do adulterous lovers make forays away from their spouses and into the forbidden love of another.

Similarly, adulterous love finds its appeal precisely in its prohibition. In choosing an unavailable individual to be the beloved, the incest taboo has been re-created all over again. Whoever is forbidden is precisely who will be desired. It is interesting to note, as well, that many affairs involve someone who is part of one's social circle of friends. It is all too common that affairs are conducted between siblings, cousins, friends of spouses, next-door neighbors, or others who fall under the rubric of the larger family of friends and community—people who are all the more forbidden because they are so close. Like mother (or father) originally was.

THE INCEST TABOO

In virtually every case of breaking the incest taboo, the love that is created is one of enslavement and dominance. The incest taboo may create unconscious frustration in family members, but there are powerful reasons why it exists.

When original sexual yearning of a child for the parent is stimulated, there is potential for tremendous destructiveness. A chilling example of this is found in the following account:

> Continuing softly, he said, "When you were a little girl, did you ever want to make love, to your father?"
> I was stunned. My mind went blank, and then raced swiftly over images of my dad. I'm afraid I giggled again. "Don't be silly," I said. "No."

"I know you have," he said. "You must be honest. Every girl at some time wants to make love to her father." I was silent.

This is not a scene from a psychoanalytic session, as it may seem, urging a recalcitrant patient to face up to the truthfulness of her incestuous feelings.

"You've got to be free of all your inhibitions and your fears. They're weighing you down. They are choking you. You've got to break free."

He moved his hands over my body, continuing to watch me in the mirror . . .

"Make love with me." His voice was even lower. "Make love with me and imagine that you are making love to your father. You must break free of the past. . ."

This is Susan Atkins' account of her seduction by Charles Manson. It is, as well, her induction into the group that called itself "the family." It is a recounting of a particular kind of "love"—a kind of love that included mass murder.

Manson's technique to get Susan, and his other women—Krenwinkle, Fromm, Van Houten, and Kasabian—to lay themselves at his feet, willing to "love, honor, and obey" him, followed standard mind manipulative techniques.

All your roots are cut. You are freed from your families and all their old hangups. You are cut loose into the now. You are free. And because we are free, we can become one. The Bible says we must die to self and that's exactly true. We must die to self so that we can be at one with all people. That is love.

Charlie Manson may be evil for wanting to dominate his women, but these women were willing to submit to his domination. Surrender is the sine qua non of romantic love, but surrender finds its darkest representation in submission. In their book *The Mind Manipulators*, Alan Scheflin and Edward Opton describe why these girls were such easy prey for Manson: "They all felt alone and afraid in the world around them. They did not have clear identities in search of a place. Rather, they searched for a place to obtain an identity." Surrender, without a nucleus of a self to return to, yields submission. In states of extreme submission, even murder is possible.

Vincent Bugliosi, prosecuting attorney, described the sustaining strength and inner peacefulness that their love (and their new-found identity) gave them:

> For them all the questions had been answered. There was no need to search any more, because they had found the truth. And their truth was "Charlie is love."

Susan's book recounting the story of her participation as a Manson girl is called *Child of Satan, Child of God.* The title of the book tells us all we need to know to understand her experience. Susan, and each of us who "loves" by subjugating our own identity into the whims of another, are, indeed, children—children who want their minds to be filled, their identities to be formed. In matters of love, we all have a tendency to be children. Like children, we want to dominate and we want to submit. We do it in lovemaking, and we do it in our running of the household. Some of us, like Susan Atkins, make it the full definition of our self and, as Bugliosi described her, remind us "less of human beings than of Barbie Dolls."

IN THE NAME OF LOVE

If the state of excited arousal, whether from fear, frustration, or inhibited sexuality, is an aspect of what makes the heart grow fonder in romantic love, how is it that we attribute the label of "love" to these aroused states?

Many of us define love by the way it makes us feel. Unconsciously, we may be taking our physiological pulse in order to determine whether we are in love. We put together an equation that reads: Pounding Heart + Sweating Palms + Trembling Knees and Hands = Love. Of course, the same formula = Fear and Frustration, as well as Love.

Several studies have documented the ease with which these emotional states can get mixed up. Most notably, S. Schachter and S. E. Singer established that when an individual is in a state of emotional arousal, the mind is particularly receptive to surrounding circumstances. In their experiment, subjects were injected with a drug that created the physical arousal symptoms of trembling, increased breathing rate, and disturbed pulse and heartbeat. They found that the emotions that the individuals reportedly connected to these feelings depended on the way the experimenters manipulated the environment. When placed with a companion who acted happy and playful, the subjects reported feelings of euphoria. But when placed with companions who complained and fretted, the subjects labeled the same state of arousal "anger." In each state the feelings needed an environmental interpretation.

Our ability to label arousal states depends to a certain extent on how our infantile states of excitation were managed and interpreted for us. As newborns we have a limited repertoire of emotional states. The only truly distinguishable emotions are excitement and relaxation.

If our needs in infancy are properly met, we learn that states of excitation are eventually balanced with states of relaxation. We learn to deal with arousal in ways that bring about comfort. But if our infantile needs are not met, the normal excite/relax pattern can become disordered, so that later in life we don't know how to calm ourselves. Or, we don't know how to deal with or label feelings of excitation, so we give them too much meaning. For example, a man who decides to marry a woman based solely on how he feels in her presence is giving too much importance to his own feeling state.

As we develop and mature out of infancy, we take cues from our parents and our environment that teach us how to label our feelings. If our mothers panic each time we fall down and call it love, in our aroused state we may come to associate panic and pain with love. If our fathers, in the name of love, rage at each mistake we make, as our hearts pound in fear, we might soon associate our feelings of incompetence and terror with love. And if our teenage sweethearts cheat, lie, and deceive us, and then to calm our hurt and anger hold us close with assurances of love, we may learn to associate deception with love.

Excitation, for any reason, can feel remarkably like love. A man I know explained why he had been conducting an affair for the last three years with a much younger woman: "She makes me feel the way my wife did when we were still sixteen. I was still everything to her." It is easy to be "everything" to a naive sixteen-year-old. A thirty-five-year-old man, however, still looking to be everything to a woman, is interested more in the thrill of idealized love than the reality of cooperative love.

When panic, deception, anger, and fear mix in an environment that offers candlelight, soft music, and a pleasant smile, the thrill begins as mere excitement. In states of fear and frustration we may do all manner of things in the name of love, without being anywhere near love's door.

CHAPTER 8

The Dark Side of Marriage: The Death of Dreams

In a way, marriage is a death. As we joyfully join our spirit with another to whom we are pledging eternal love and devotion—a love that has no end—why, then, in the midst of this promise of immortality must we suddenly remind ourselves of its inevitable end? Although we never consciously think about it, just a bit of thoughtful analysis reveals that the "till death us do part" refrain in the marriage ceremony protrudes like a jagged edge.

Marriage signifies the putting away of individual concerns. It is, in fact, the last hurrah for infantile narcissism. While individuality is still maintained in marriage, it is done only within the context of "otherness." First, there is only one "other"—the spouse; but then later, there may be more "others"—the children. The task of marriage, then, is the final act of putting away childhood dreams and assuming mature responsibilities to others.

MARRIAGE AND THE DEATH OF DREAMS

It is in our dreams of marriage that we allow our fantasies to roam most freely. We imagine perfect love and sweet contentment from the eternal companionship that marriage promises.

We don't like thinking of marriage as the time in one's life when we must give up our dreams. Such thoughts make marriage sound depressing. We much prefer to think of marriage as a time when dreams are fulfilled, longings realized. Yet, most married couples, talking honestly about marriage, will say that the preservation of their marriage does in fact depend upon their having to give up childhood dreams—dreams of complete happiness, dreams of the "perfect" spouse, dreams of success. We Americans like happy endings. Marriages, however, have realistic endings. Our challenge is to accept the happiness of compromise rather than to relentlessly pursue the unattainable ideal.

Marriage represents a death because it is only in the renunciation of infantile narcissism that cooperative love relationships can grow. Legitimate relationships can take place only when the distinction between self and other exists. Marriage, then, gives us the opportunity to be a self relating to another, and the opportunity for a mature love relationship.

Marriage is, however, also an opportunity for sleep. We may enter marriage with the idea that our struggle to be a self is over. We may put our inclination for individual growth away and become parasitically attached to our spouse. Conversely, we may decide that the act of becoming married has fulfilled our obligation to maturity, and refuse further emotional gratification to our spouse. The extent of both partners' awareness of their individuality determines whether the destructive forces of love's dark side will predominate, or whether the relationship will blossom into cooperative love.

Eros, god of love, had a special quality about him that made his fashion of love particularly dangerous. It was said of Eros that he "relaxes the limbs, and in the breasts of all gods and all men subdues their reason and prudent counsel." The description, of course, bears a striking similarity to another state that the psyche finds itself prone to—the state of unconsciousness, as in sleep and death. For the Greeks, the similarity was deliberate and meant to suggest the relationship between love and unconsciousness. To the extent that Eros, limb-relaxer, rules a marital relationship, the marriage will be an unconscious one, and ultimately a destructive one.

MARRIAGE AND THE REPETITION COMPULSION

Psychoanalyst Theodor Reik once said that there were only two decisions he had made about himself from his unconscious: his choice of a profession and his choice of a wife. He is not alone. Most of us make the choice of our spouses from our unconscious.

One of my patients, Claire, told me that she knew that she and the man she married were bound to each other for life from their first meeting. It was certain, she described, from the way his hands looked. She assured me that it was his hands that she had first fallen in love with, and that even now, when she watches him use his hands, she feels this same wave of love enveloping her. After some analysis Claire was able to come to some understanding of the unconscious meaning his hands held for her—hands she described with great feeling: elegant, sensitive, clean, and pure. It was the purity of her husband's hands that most attracted her.

Claire's father was a mechanic. He was perpetually, and it seemed uselessly, scrubbing his hands. As a child and adolescent, she had wondered often how her mother tolerated those dirty hands. She herself often felt repulsed by her father's hands, and longed for a father who was like the fathers of her girlfriends, a doctor or a lawyer—a man in a clean business suit rather than a greasy uniform, and a man whose hands would not dirty whatever he touched.

Claire needed to have the feeling that she was marrying a man different from her father, so that's what she did. But some of us have the opposite desire—to find a spouse who is like a loved figure from childhood. Another of my patients, Steve, had his first moment of uninhibited joy with Marie when she used a southern expression that he hadn't heard since he was a child. It was a favorite saying of his grandfather's, who had, like Marie, grown up in the South. Hearing the words again, after so many years, brought back nostalgic memories of being cuddled by his bear-hugging grandfather, and these feelings from the past enveloped his feelings for Marie.

Our choice of a spouse is often based, as it was with Claire and Steve, on issues and memories from our childhood. As much as we may want to think that as adults we have attained emotional maturity, most of us, when we get married, have not yet put our childhood concerns behind us. In the process of choosing our mates (and of being chosen) we are, most often, ineluctably bound by the patterns of loving that we learned early in life. Marriage is, as psychiatrist H. V. Dicks observed, the "nearest adult equivalent to the original child-parent relationship."

As Maggie Scarf elaborates in *Intimate Partners:* "It is in marriage that we resurrect not only the intensity of our first attachment feelings, but the miseries of old frustrations and repressed hatreds as well. And what is so frequently sought out in a mate—and then fought out with that mate—is some unresolved [and thus unconscious] dilemma about a parent."

In the two main tasks that create a marriage—first, the choice of the partner, and second, the dealing with the feelings engendered by an intimate relationship—we are greatly influenced by our early experiences of love and hate. Sometimes we choose partners who will re-create our early psychological histories, thereby duplicating the kind of emotional experience we are familiar with and have come to expect. When we are impelled to repeat our past in this way, we are just as likely to be tied to a damaging past as to a nourishing one. Freud found that the strength of our tie to our past, and our need to re-create our past in the present, is often stronger than our need to create a satisfying love, and he thus declared the repetition compulsion to be "beyond the pleasure principle."

Some of us will react against our past and make deliberate choices that are as far from our original infantile experiences of love and hate as we can manage. In either case, whether one is attempting to repeat the past or avoid it, the tie to the past is a powerful bond.

A successful marriage entails the abandonment of the past and a confrontation with the unconscious. This is seldom achieved smoothly and without crises. Marriage provides us with yet another opportunity for an awakening into consciousness, but as Jung said, "There is no birth of consciousness without pain." Marriage is a fertile ground for the repetition compulsion, but it also provides an unparalleled opportunity to free ourselves from the chains that hold us in our past.

Returning to the past, to a regressive mode of functioning, is most often the source of difficulty in a marital relationship. Emotional regression permits all of the early, unresolved issues of love and hate to come to the fore, thus making past hurts and pains and disappointments more real and more powerful than any gratification from present loves. Marriage starts to look like a no-win situation: The reason it is so beneficial is that it is so difficult. The very intimacy of the relationship, and the fact that marriage is a commitment for life, is precisely why the feelings that are stimulated are so difficult. Whatever the predominant negative feelings were in childhood—whether they were hurt, pain, betrayal, abandonment, rage—will be the same feelings that are resurrected in an unconscious marriage. In a momentary encounter, it is easy to hide the regressed aspects of one's personality. In the marital relationship, however, these unresolved aspects of one's psychological functioning invariably come to light, one by one.

THE NARCISSISTIC MARRIAGE

Many people get married, or hope to marry, believing that marriage will make them feel better. They imagine that all their needs will be magically met. In fact, just the opposite is true. Marriage is like the Trojan horse, bringing our unresolved problems even closer. As lonely or unpleasant as being single may be, it is, for most people, easier to maintain a pleasurable life alone than a happy marriage. With all its advantages, marriage also brings more responsibilities, more expectations, and more disappointments; it curtails freedom; and it arouses more uncomfortable feelings. Unresolved infantile needs, which may not have been troublesome while single, often become problematic in a marital relationship.

For example, Jan is a man I know whose early history continues to define and destroy each of his love relationships. When Jan was five years old, he was diagnosed with a rare bone disorder for which the treatment was his being placed in a full body cast in a hospital. For the first year of this treatment, his mother came to the hospital every few days. After this time, though, Jan's father was relocated and the family moved away. Jan remembers the painful day when his mother came to the hospital to inform him that she would be able to visit him only every two weeks, because of the distance.

Jan has had three adult love relationships, and the pattern manifested in each is exactly the same. When he is not in a relationship, he functions well and does not drink. For the first year of each relationship, he also is able to refrain from drinking. But a year into each relationship, Jan starts going on drinking sprees, sometimes for as long as a month at a time, and during his alcoholic binges becomes abusive to his lover. Although it has taken different periods of time for each woman to reach her tolerance for Jan's behavior, ultimately each woman left him. After each failed relationship, Jan wails that women always abandon him, that no woman loves him enough to stay with him.

In his love relationships, Jan is unconsciously repeating the same psychological drama that he experienced when his mother moved away. It is significant that this pattern reasserts itself only when he is with a woman. When he is alone he is able to remain detached enough from the conflict not to drink.

When we are compelled to repeat our past in this manner, it is far easier to blame the other person than to understand one's own participation in creating the drama. Everyone will recognize the familiar refrain: "No one makes me this angry except *you*"; or, "I never had this problem until I met *you*"; or, "Why does everyone else think I'm fine?" Each partner in the marriage brings unresolved issues to it that often interfere with the spontaneous enjoyment of the relationship and which provide a breeding ground for repetitions of emotional conflicts having their origin in the past.

Most often, people unconsciously expect to find in their marriage partners their ideal parent—someone to appreciate them, know them fully, take care of them, protect them. The expectation is that the marriage partner will miraculously "fix" their lives—on an unconscious level, sweep away whatever unfulfilled needs linger from their relationship with their parents. In this expectation, the emotional needs of the partner are almost completely overlooked. When both partners are focused exclusively on their own needs, the marriage is destined to be difficult and destructive.

The dark side of marriage, then, becomes manifest when one or both partners regress to functioning emotionally from one of the infantile stages of psychological development. Romantic love is usually characterized by a return to the symbiotic stage of development, but in marriage any of the phases of the birth of the psyche— symbiotic fusion, separation/individuation, or rapprochement— are represented.

Each of the marriages I am going to describe has returned to one of these narcissistic phases of development. These are marriages in which a significant aspect of the psychological processes moves regressively rather than progressively. These couples are reliving, through their partners, unresolved psychic difficulties, and are using their mates in an attempt to resolve and master issues that have grown out of their early primary relationships within their original families. And, as we saw earlier, when narcissists latch onto other narcissists, emotional maturation is that much more difficult.

REPEATING THE SYMBIOTIC PHASE OF DEVELOPMENT

On December 10, 1936, in the midst of Hitler's ascendancy and England's chaotic response to Germany, the king of England had matters on his mind more pressing than politics and the struggles of his country. On this day, he announced the abdication of his throne for the sake of the woman he loved. Although this king had been groomed from the day of his birth to assume the responsibility of leadership, and although he knew well the rigors and sacrifices of public service and the debt of duty he owed to his country, King Edward VIII revealed to the world his commitment to, above all else, love.

The love affair between Edward and Wallis Simpson, an American divorcée, has gone down in the annals of history as one of the most remarkable examples of the triumph of love. Scores of women despaired that their own love lives were colorless compared to the enviable romance and passion of these two lovers. It was, to all appearances, a storybook romance, igniting our imaginations and affirming the power of love's magic.

But the love story of Wallis Simpson and the Duke of Windsor (Edward's appointed position after his abdication) has a dark side that our imaginations could not see. Edward did not simply love Wallis; he felt that his very life depended upon being with her. Because he truly believed that he could not live without her, he decided, against advice, that if Parliament would not allow the king to marry a divorced woman, then he would not be king. Edward gave up his identity, his future, and his dreams, because Wallis Simpson stimulated in him some deep, unmet childhood need that had remained hidden until the development of their relationship.

It is now known that during a six-month forced separation from Wallis, Edward's psychological condition deteriorated dramatically. Without her he became quite dysfunctional. His friends described him as appearing like a pathetic child—lost, abandoned, and in constant need. He seemed to have no will of his own. Since his actions and feelings were determined entirely by the woman he loved, he was lost without her. Had this romance taken place some centuries earlier, we would have felt confident that Wallis had slipped Edward a magic love potion.

Edward may have drunk a love potion, but it was a concoction made not from the devotion to another but from the elixir of unconscious needs. Wallis was able to bring Edward under her spell because she instinctively understood something about his repressed childhood conflicts that made him a vulnerable victim to her modern-day potion.

The pattern of "loving" that Edward and Wallis fell into meets all of the criteria for a symbiotic relationship—the earliest infantile relationship. Edward's need for Wallis was a much more important aspect of his attraction to her than pleasure. Wallis, on the other hand, encouraged in Edward this extreme dependence. Their "love" was a folie à deux of symbiosis, both partners playing their roles of infant and mother supremely well.

It is likely that even before Wallis met Edward, she planned how she would make the king feel that she was indispensable to him (as a mother is to an infant), and thus he would fall in love with her. She understood something about the king that had eluded his confidantes, mentors, and advisers, as well as each of the women with whom he had been romantically involved. Wallis knew that Edward wanted to be controlled. He wanted to be challenged, rebuked, chastised, and led.

Though he made a dashing and handsome figure while traveling the world and aligning himself romantically with beautiful women, there was no joy for him in the assumption of mature, leadership responsibilities. And so, according to plan, Wallis' first communication with the king was one of reproach.

When Edward found himself sitting next to Wallis at a dinner party (a position she grabbed with a calculated and aggressive move), he politely remarked, "You must miss control heating, Mrs. Simpson." To which she replied, with startling effrontery, "To the contrary, sir, I like the cold houses of Great Britain." And, feeling the excitement of the moment, she dared to continue, "I am sorry, sir, but you have disappointed me. Every American woman who comes to England is asked that same question. I had hoped for something more original from the Prince of Wales."

Edward was hooked. He came back for more, again and again. Wallis treated him as though he were a spoiled child, once even publicly slapping his hand when he picked up a lettuce leaf with his fingers, and brusquely ordering him to use a knife and fork in the future.

Edward may have been groomed for the job of king, but his training neglected to address important emotional issues, so that in adulthood he was still functioning, psychologically, on the level of an infant. Edward's upbringing, in fact, has elements in common with the childhood training of many who experience the destructive aspects of love's dark side. He received no guidance or help that would have enabled him to meet the challenges of emotional maturation. Biographical accounts of Edward tell us that his father was a harsh disciplinarian who treated his sons as though they were midshipmen, perpetually on parade. His mother, Queen Mary, did nothing to soften her husband's harshness, and her devotion to royal duty outweighed any lingering maternal instincts that she might have conveyed. With such a distant and stringent upbringing, Edward remained emotionally on the level of a boy, living forever in the dream world of money, parties, and golf.

Wallis astutely sensed this maturational gap and conveyed the kind of emotional communications that fostered deep dependence in Edward; she skillfully elevated herself while denigrating the king.

Wallis, too, had her own brand of regressing back to infantile narcissism. Although it appears that Wallis was never "in love" with Edward, she, too, had her own unrealistic expectations about this romance. She remained deeply ambivalent about whether or not she wanted to marry Edward, but she was always fully committed to the goal of reaping the benefits that a close tie to the king would bring her. In her book *Oneness and Separateness: From Infant to Individual,* Louise Kaplan, a student of Mahler's, describes one of the love difficulties of people who inadequately pass through separation/individuation:

> They idealize those whom they can coerce into becoming the all-giving, perfectly holding partner who will sustain their image of self-perfection. Although they idealize their partners, they use them ruthlessly as though they were mere extensions of the self; they use them to manipulate and destroy potential enemies; they use them in order to experience the pride that comes from possessing a perfect partner.

As Wallis entered womanhood, she quickly learned that her beauty and femininity gave her the power to command men to give her what she wanted. By the time she met Edward, she had married twice, but each husband had failed to give her the sense of satisfaction for which she yearned. Surely, then, she must have thought, a king would have the power to slay the dragons of dissatisfaction that haunted her. Surely there was no more perfect partner than a king. Wallis married Edward, in love with the kind of perfect life that she imagined a marriage to him would give her—a social whirlwind of enviable parties and gatherings—thinking that the riches and thrills of the high life would calm the ever-present tension of desire and hunger within her. Wallis needed Edward as much as Edward needed Wallis, in order to fill a deep, abiding emptiness.

By all accounts, the marriage of Edward and Wallis was tragically empty, joyless, and full of pain and disappointment. Fairy-tale marriages that glitter and shine on the outside can never be made real, based as they are on unresolved and repressed childhood conflicts that in later life find pathological expression.

REPEATING THE SEPARATION/INDIVIDUATION PHASE OF DEVELOPMENT

Tara and Bill had been married only a year when Tara first consulted me. Her concern was her sense of unreality in her marriage. She felt that she had been carrying on an elaborate masquerade for the sake of Bill. Tara had married Bill in spite of grave reservations about his suitability as a marriage partner and in spite of not knowing whether or not she loved him. The nature of the masquerade was that Tara felt it essential that Bill think that she had married her "ideal" and that she was exquisitely happy, without an ounce of ambivalence about him. Yet, in spite of her efforts to convince Bill otherwise, he became suspicious of Tara's dissatisfaction with him and confronted her: "You feel you settled in marrying me, don't you?" Tara cried and denied it and cleverly manipulated Bill into feeling guilty for even thinking such a thought.

Tara's complaints about her marriage had to do with how different she and Bill were. Tara loved sex; it seemed that Bill's sexual appetite was much less than hers. Tara loved socializing and was extroverted and talkative; Bill was withdrawn and quiet. Tara wanted to be close to her mother, who lived in the same apartment complex; Bill wanted them to keep as much distance from her as possible. In spite of the differences, Tara said that she went to great lengths to try to make herself over in Bill's image. In fact, she made herself as like Bill as possible. She pretended to be satisfied with sex once a week; she toned down the sexually explicit way she had dressed before her marriage; she grew quieter at parties, and deferred to Bill as much as possible in conversations; she asked her mother to stop by the apartment less frequently and always to call first.

When Tara described why it was important for her to make Bill think that she is just like him, she began to talk about her past. She said that she remembers from childhood that her mother had had a constant and intense fear of abnormality. Her mother was a vigilante of mental illness in the family, convinced that there was a genetic flaw in her background and that her children were at risk of some ill-defined but nevertheless terrorizing mental illness. Tara grew up with a profound fear that there was, or would be, something wrong with her.

Tara explained that all of her life she had gone to great lengths pretending to be just like the people around her—fading into the wallpaper, as it were. Her fear was that if people were to perceive her as different, they would see her as strange, peculiar, as if there were something wrong with her. The safest route for Tara to take was to hide any aspects of herself that defined her differently or uniquely.

Yet, Tara did in fact have different opinions, preferences, and desires than others. In spite of her fear of discovering her own individuality, her personality developed in its own fashion, sometimes imitative of those around her but sometimes not.

Adolescent years were particularly difficult for Tara. Every relationship she formed risked a criticism from her mother. "Why are you friends with her?" "He's not good enough for you." Any movement toward another person was interpreted by her mother as rejection of her. The confrontations, explanations, and denials were exhausting. It was easier for Tara to live a pretend life, hiding her true self—her separate self—from her mother.

As it happens, Tara's sister was blatantly rebellious and overtly angry at their mother, and never hid the fact that she intended to be both a different sort of person from her mother and to live a different sort of life. She was constantly criticized for her individuality: "Why does Sasha always have to be kissing Alex?" "Why is Sasha always telling me to do things differently?" The complaints about Sasha were made to Tara, and the message was clear: "If you want to be loved, be like me." Tara determined, early on, to be the "good" daughter, the one who would please, imitate, and "love" her mother.

Tara did not have the benefit of a mother who would guide her successfully through the difficult process of separation. Her mother wanted Tara to be both near her and like her. Tara paid for this deprivation in her adult love relationships.

Tara could not have replayed this scenario from her past had Bill not been a willing, albeit unconscious, participant. Bill was the perfect partner for Tara to repeat this past conflict with. He was, in many ways, like her mother. He lived in a world of doom and gloom, always expecting financial ruin to befall him. While he professed his love for Tara, he rarely acted in ways that would have demonstrated real interest in her. With Bill, Tara's secret self remained undisturbed. The similarities between her husband and her mother were not lost on Tara:

> I feel when I'm with Bill like I did with my mother. I don't feel loved. I don't feel understood. I don't feel interested in by either of them. My mother never gave me what I needed, and neither does Bill. Family life when I was growing up was basically unexciting. We never had family outings, we didn't laugh together. I was jealous whenever I looked at the other families and saw how they enjoyed themselves. My relationship with Bill feels the same. Bill can be fun sometimes, but basically he doesn't really know how to let loose. Now instead of feeling jealous of kids with great parents, I look at all the other couples and feel jealous, knowing that they're all having more fun and are more in love than Bill and I.

Tara and Bill were able to improve their marriage only when they were both able to reconstruct their pasts, and saw how their unresolved issues were affecting their present relationship. Becoming a self, and loving oneself, means first and foremost being interested in who that self is. Cooperative love occurs only when the stage of separation/individuation has been mastered, and it arises out of loving oneself enough that revealing that self is possible.

REPEATING THE RAPPROCHEMENT PHASE OF DEVELOPMENT

In describing the way the desire for security and the desire for freedom alternate in the toddler, Bowlby says:

. . . slipping free from the mother, a two year old would typically move away from her in short bursts punctuated by halts. Then, after a more prolonged halt, he would return to her—usually in faster and longer bursts. Once returned, however, he would proceed again on another foray, only to return once more. It was as though he were tied to his mother by some invisible elastic that stretches so far and then brings him back to base.

The ambivalence that characterizes the rapprochement phase of the struggle for independence and separation, lasting from fourteen or fifteen months to about twenty-four months, is described well in the title of a section in Louise Kaplan's book: "Clinging and Pushing Away, Shadowing and Darting Away, Holding On and Letting Go."

Gordon and Nina had a marriage in which this wanderlust, representing a return to the rapprochement phase, was the essential dynamic of the relationship.

Nina lost interest in having sex with Gordon shortly after the birth of her child. She proceeded to have an affair, and was able to keep her affair secret from Gordon for the year that it lasted. She soon became disillusioned with the man and ended the affair, making a renewed commitment to her marriage.

Nina's commitment to monogamy, however, was short-lived. Before too long, she met yet another man who excited her even more than the first. She felt that she was, for the first time in her life, head over heels in love. She could not bear the thought of walking away from this powerful relationship. She decided to tell Gordon about the affair, file for divorce, and marry the other man.

Gordon and Nina spent months working out a legal separation agreement. They argued endlessly over who would get what, and over the custody and visitation arrangements for the child. Almost a year later, with the end of the marriage in sight and two weeks before the final divorce decree was due, Nina and her lover had an argument.

This wasn't the first time that Nina and her lover had disagreed, but this argument focused on their respective religions and appeared to be an unresolvable issue. The bickering frayed their tempers and stimulated in Nina intense feelings of betrayal and anger. Nina's religion had always been important to her, and she couldn't imagine marrying a man who did not share her religious faith. Her lover had a different religion but had agreed to convert. Now, almost at the point of no return for Nina's marriage to Gordon, her lover declared his inability to convert to Nina's religion. Then he went even further. He also expressed ambivalence about having children, although he had originally agreed to follow Nina's strong desire to have children.

Upset with his lack of constancy and his unpredictability, Nina felt that she had made a terrible mistake. She called Gordon and begged him to stop the divorce proceedings. She pleaded with him not to sign the papers and to allow her another chance to work out their marriage.

It was not, however, Nina's great love for Gordon that inspired her wish to return to him. It was, rather, her need for the safety, security, and predictability that Gordon provided. Nina was using Gordon as though he were the early mother, from whom she would venture out in the world to see what's there, have a little excitement, but then come back to for security. Her husband was home base, as in childhood games in which "base is safe."

The dating years are, of course, the appropriate time to repeat the rapprochement phase in relation to love partners. Nina had no difficulty during those years, since exploring and seeking adventure is the developmental task appropriate to that stage. But Nina was unable to move to the next developmental challenge of committed cooperative love that takes the other person's wishes, needs, and feelings into account.

In his observation of toddlers, Bowlby noted that when mother is around, the child is not that interested in her. He makes sure that she's still there and contentedly sallies forth. But if suddenly she's not there, he becomes obsessed with finding her—and will manifest agitation or depression until her reappearance. He'll forgo his adventuresome spirit until he has regained the security and sense of safety that her presence elicits.

Though Nina's behavior was quite painful to Gordon, he was a collusive partner. He agreed to try the marriage again. Gordon, unlike some men who would never tolerate such a situation, willingly provided Nina with a replication of the rapprochement phase of development. In marriages in which the rapprochement period is being repeated, it is the willingness of the surrogate mother to tolerate the role that is the determining factor in whether and when the marriage breaks up.

Bowlby's description of toddler behavior exactly applies to adult love that is based on the rapprochement phase of development. After a year of therapy, Gordon came to the point where he no longer wanted to be home base for Nina and was ready to proceed with a divorce. Until this point Nina had been the model of confidence. She felt in control of her life, enjoying her freedom and her halfhearted attempt to salvage her marriage all at the same time. She dated during this year, keeping Gordon unsure but hopeful of her ultimate ability to commit to him. When Gordon finally filed for divorce, Nina's world went topsy-turvy. She found herself in the midst of a major depression. She tried reconciling with Gordon, who had finally came to experience the role of the rapprochement mother as distasteful. Like the infant who looks frantically around for an absent mother, and who cannot sustain his bravado of independence without her, Nina became desperate. Gordon explained:

> When we were proceeding with the divorce, she got really desperate. She would tell me that she was going to kill herself. Her parents didn't know how to manage her. I felt like it was all in my hands, and I felt that old familiar feeling of being needed and how good it made me feel, and important and confident. She would drive around at 4 A.M., call me up and tell me that the insurance policy was in the top drawer, and shake a bottle of pills in the phone.

In spite of his urge to continue to fulfill the role of surrogate mother, Gordon managed to turn down Nina's offer of reconciliation. Nina found it difficult to maintain her affair, and that, too, fell apart. She ended up alone, never understanding that her unconscious repetition of her past had led to the dissolution of her marriage. Gordon began dating other women, eager to find a more appropriate marital partner for himself.

Although I have used infidelity to illustrate repeating the rapprochement stage, the phenomenon is not limited to affairs. A wife or a husband may not necessarily find a sexual partner. Instead, he or she may find another interest—a hobby, work, or traveling. What remains constant is the use of the spouse as home base, just as the child uses Mommy in the original rapprochement phase.

BRINGING CONSCIOUSNESS TO MARRIAGE

When Freud discovered the importance of loving children, it became equally apparent that children are better loved by parents who love each other. Freud himself broke with old Jewish tradition and married for love. We have been doing it ever since, and nowhere is the tradition stronger than in America.

Imbuing marriage with love brings us the possibility of using marriage as an instrument of transformation of consciousness. Jung likened the development of consciousness to the rising of landmasses out of the depths of the ocean. At first, consciousness appears as separate little islands, a few here and a few there, which only gradually unite to form a continent, a continuous landmass of consciousness. Out of consciousness, we are enabled to form relationships, to know one another.

Most of us enter into marriage in an unconscious state, bringing infantile and unrealistic expectations to bear on the relationship. When our love is based on our infantile narcissistic needs, rather than marriage being a free choice it becomes a compulsion, victim to the unpredictability of unconsciousness. The success of the marriage depends on having two developed, individuated selves entering into a conscious relationship with each other.

If we do not take up a relationship with our unconscious—enter it and know it—then that unconsciousness will be the basis of our relationship. It is through going inward, seeking a relationship with our inner world, that we come to know the outer world. As Jung said, "Individuation does not shut one out from the world, but gathers the world to oneself."

Commitment to another is certainly a main ingredient in whether or not a marriage will succeed. Even more important, though, is the commitment to first be a self and to know oneself. Together these strengths can help transform a relationship born of need into a relationship built on cooperation.

PART III

OUT OF
THE SHADOWS
AND INTO
THE LIGHT

If we can imagine a parent sufficiently skillful to replace each satisfaction of which the child is deprived by another satisfaction which the child could accept as approximately equivalent, without disloyalty to the requirements of reality, we should expect to see in the progeny of such a parent an ideal person, not one without aggression but one without a sense of being thwarted in the adventures and misadventures of life, and without hate for anything except those things which should be hated and fought against in defense of his own ideals and best interests.

KARL MENNINGER

CHAPTER 9

The Hate That Heals

What we as individuals need is not more love but more constructive hate. Love alone is not enough.

Life would, of course, be much simpler if we were able to exist on love alone. Then the rules would be clear; everybody would know what they were supposed to be feeling. There would be no child abuse, no divorces, no wars. But, we are more complex creatures than this and we, of course, feel much more than love. To try to pigeonhole our feelings into one simple category and to outlaw all our other feelings as unacceptable, wrong, or unnatural is as useless and ultimately destructive as an attempt to pray that we are "blessed" with only sunny, clear days.

Hate is neither a disease, nor a disorder. It is a basic biological adaptive mechanism. It is necessary in dealing with threats, irritations, and frustrations. Hate is constructive when it is used in self-defense, and is a vital reaction to have available. It becomes pathological only when it is fused with unfulfilled infantile needs, and destructive only when it is translated into action.

Psychoanalyst Melanie Klein has this to say about hate:

> . . . we need [people] for two purposes. One is the obvious one of getting satisfactions from them, both for our self-preservative

and pleasure needs. The other purpose for which we need them is to hate them . . .

She continues by explaining the stabilizing function that hate serves:

> . . . so that we may expel and discharge our own badness, with its danger, out of ourselves on to them.

Hate, contrary to how we generally think of it, helps to keep us sane.

HATE IS THE FIRST FEELING

Immanuel Kant observed that the cry of the child just born has the tone not of lamentation but of wrath. Psychoanalysts from Freud on have for the most part agreed. As Rebecca West put it:

> After a tideless peace of prenatal existence, the child is born into a world of uncomfortable physical experiences and terrifying incomprehended controls; it must beat with its hands and plot evil against its aggressors.

Hate is, in fact, the first feeling of differentiation. It is only out of the rage and bitterness of separation that the infant comes to understand his own individuality. Through each of the stages of separation that we make, from infancy through adolescence, we are propelled away from the past, which is no longer satisfying, toward an uncertain but exciting future. When one phase is no longer enough for us, our displeasure with it propels us into the next phase. This is an extremely constructive use of hate's energy.

For some of us, however, our inevitable feelings of hate do not find normal, constructive outlets. In these cases, the constructive hate that fuels normal separation is thwarted and we end up with separation problems. Usually this means we are stuck in a narcissistic phase of development, unable to move ahead until our separation problems have been addressed.

When constructive hate is prohibited, people develop the idea that their rage and hate are not just feelings; rather they are extraordinary weapons. To stifle the impulse to use these weapons, they remove their feelings from consciousness, thereby losing any opportunity to express them. With no avenue of discharge, the intensity of the unfelt, unexpressed feelings rises to volcanic proportions.

Those of us who prohibit ourselves from hating will find that we hate anyway, but that our hate has become a force for destruction. The hate is redirected away from a beloved and toward the self. This is the basic mechanism of the narcissistic defense that we use to destroy ourselves and our love relationships.

It is only when hate is made conscious that we are relieved of the myriad ways we have of destroying love. When hate is made conscious, we learn a lesson different from the lesson we learned in childhood. We learn that our feelings are not lethal weapons. We learn that we can safely discharge any amount of hate and rage, as long as the mode of discharge is words, or the forerunners of words, dreams and fantasies.

LOVE IS NOT ENOUGH

Unexpressed feelings accumulate like dammed-up pools of water. It is only when there is a release of dammed-up hate that love can be felt. When hate is bottled up in an individual, no amount of love offered to the person can cure this condition. In fact, love and concern offered to a person in need of discharging hate often has the effect of intensifying the blockage and making the person feel worse.

Sissy, for instance, is a much-loved woman. She has a winsome personality, has been a great friend to a good number of men and women, and remains close to her family. Love has always been an important part of her life, and she has largely succeeded in surrounding herself with it.

Two years ago, though, Sissy's life took on a different flavor. Until that time, she had been married to a man who wanted her to be his caregiver. Sissy was used to that role from her original family. She had spent her youth comforting her mother when her father went on his alcoholic binges. Marrying a man with whom she continued the caregiving role seemed natural. Sissy and Win might have gone on happily with such a clear division of roles, Sissy gratified in her sense of importance to Win, and Win happily divesting himself of the responsibilities of care of himself.

But circumstances intervened and disrupted this fragile equilibrium based on Sissy's sacrificial posture. Sissy was in a car accident and two disks in her back were ruptured. Immediately after surgery she had an allergic reaction to a drug and suffered a stroke. Though Sissy recovered fully from the aftereffects of the stroke, the experience left her with an unfamiliar sense of vulnerability and fragility. It was she, now, not her mother and not Win, who was in need of comfort and care.

Sissy's marriage did not survive the strain of this shift in roles. Win felt her emotional vulnerability to be a demand that he neither wanted nor felt capable of fulfilling, and he left. Now beset with both new feelings of dependence and the pain of the divorce, Sissy sank into a deep depression. But the love that Sissy had given out to her friends and family so freely earlier in her life found its way back to her. Everyone in Sissy's circle of loved ones rallied around her. On lonely nights, when missing Win was the only thing on her mind, there was always a friend or two keeping her company, valiantly trying to distract her attention away from her wayward husband. Her family gave extra family get-togethers, finding any occasion at all as an excuse to help Sissy get out of the house.

But, no matter how much love and concern her friends and family showed her, Sissy's depression did not lift. It seemed that all of her friends' and family's pleading and cajoling were useless. They beseeched her: "Just forget about him. There are other fish in the sea. Our love will surround you and make you well." All to no avail.

Sissy was being fed the wrong kind of medicine. Love was not the exclusive tonic Sissy needed in order to get over her depression. Sissy couldn't benefit from love—either her own or that from others—until she had come to know, first, her own hate and rage. She needed to be able to verbalize her rage about everything that had happened to her. She needed to be able to feel and express her hate for the doctors who had given her the medication that caused her stroke. She needed to verbalize her fury at her husband's abandoning her as soon as she was in need.

Sissy found herself in a position that is familiar to many of us. We have been taught to value love and to appreciate kindness. But there are times when our own feelings of hate, rage, or disappointment are so intense that what we feel contradicts what we think we should feel, and contradicts what our loved ones want us to feel. It is only with great difficulty that we can accept that our heart is filled with hate and desire for revenge when everyone around us is telling us how much they love us.

The situation Sissy found herself in illustrates a basic fact about the nature of feelings. It is, ironically, only when we allow ourselves to *have* our feelings that we can be released from them.

Sissy's depression was a signal that she was refusing to allow certain feelings into consciousness. Understanding and experiencing the immense amount of rage and hatred that underlies depression is the most difficult aspect of depression, but it is the only way that the depression can be healed. Depression is, like the crying of an infant, a wail—a wail without tears and a wail without words.

There is also a more subtle point to be understood here. Sissy's depression was not just a sinking into the pain of her life; it was not just repressed rage at all those who had betrayed her or injured her. It was, as much as any of those, a complaint against those very people who loved her the most and who were trying their mightiest to help her to heal. It was, in other words, a wail against those who would seem to deserve it least.

If Sissy had been able to acknowledge what she felt and put it into words, she would have told her friends and family about her rage at them. She would have explained that their blithe reassurances were of no help at all, that they couldn't take away her pain, and that they should stop telling her to just set it aside, as though her pain were a china cup that she could pick up or set down at will.

In staying stuck in her depression, Sissy was saying to those who loved her that their love was not enough. Her family's mistaken assumption that they could cure her through love is a mistake that most of us make, and with the best of intentions. When we see someone we love suffer from painful feelings, our urge is quite naturally to try to assist the person not to feel the feeling, not to feel the pain. Out of our own feelings of inadequacy and guilt over not knowing how to take the other person's pain away, we try to cajole or "love" the person out of the feelings. But when depression is chosen over hate, trying to help the person to "forgive and forget" or to "move on to something new" will serve only to intensify the depression. Loving a person who suffers from dammed-up aggression will only intensify that person's tendency to turn his aggression against himself. Love as the cure for unexpressed hate only worsens the condition. This person needs help in discharging the rage.

Ron Kovic's autobiographical book and movie *Born on the Fourth of July* illustrates the same phenomenon. It is a phenomenon that repeats itself over and over again after every war. A young man, both witness to and participant in savage acts of brutality, returns home to family, friends, and love. Yet, being surrounded by all this love doesn't ease his nightmares or his cold sweats. He rambles on and on about his war stories, and often prefers the company of his army buddies to the warmth and love of his family. His rage at innocuous events seems more suited to a war zone than to the calm suburbs he has returned to.

What is necessary for this young man is not love but help in verbalizing his rage at the sacrifices he has been called on to make. He needs help in talking about his rage at having his childhood innocence ripped from him, and support of his rage at his family for wanting him not to be angry at these things. Without verbal expression of these feelings, the young man cannot mourn his losses and cannot move into the next stages of psychological growth. Gratitude for his life having been saved, pleasure in the rebonding process with those who love him will come only after the acceptance of the hate.

DREAMS, WISHES, AND FANTASIES

For most of us, it is only in our dreamlife that we are close enough to our unconscious that we allow ourselves to know our own hateful nature—our own potential for violence and abuse.

The Greeks emphasized the importance of the limb-relaxing qualities of love (Eros), sleep (Hypnos), and death (Thanatos) because they believed in the soul. The soul, for them, is encased in the body, and it is only when we are supine, when the muscles of our body are relaxed enough, that the soul is set free. When the constraints of the body are relaxed, the soul is able to fly.

When it comes to knowing our feelings, then, it is in the state of dreaming, or its waking equivalent of fantasy, that our feelings are most free. In our dreamlife and in our fantasies we can feel anything at all—love, hate, rage, compassion, hurt, revenge—and there is no danger. In our dream and fantasy lives we can burn houses; we can target-practice with our dearest ones; we can blow up the entire world. We can do all of these things in our minds, but no destruction has been wrought. We are not bound by reason, sanity, concern, altruism, rationality, or justification. In our dreams and fantasies our feelings, like our souls, fly.

Fantasies begin for us even before we have the ability to form words. Fantasies are our first mental processes. They are psychic representations of our most primitive needs having to do with love and destruction. We love the most and best in our fantasies; we also hate the most and best in our fantasies. For some of us, we hate *only* in our dreams and fantasies.

The animal in the wild threatened with the "hate" of another animal has only two choices available to it: fight or flight. Since most of the threats we humans receive today are psychological threats, we have learned to adapt this basic survival tactic. We have learned to fight psychologically and to flee psychologically. Fantasy is psychological flight.

The animal who knows that it can't win a fight will always resort to flight as its defensive maneuver. Similarly, when we feel open rebellion is not a realistic option, fantasy becomes our only way of expressing our hate. Fantasies of escape serve the function of hating a beloved without having to engage in destructive behavior.

Often these fantasies are unbeknownst even to the beloved, thus rendering them even safer.

Tammy is an example of someone who coped with the hate in her marriage by escaping into a fantasy world of better love. Tammy felt locked into her marriage. She was financially dependent on her husband, and any thought of separating from him was quickly squelched as soon as she thought of the consequences to their four children. They adored their father, and rightly so. He was affectionate, attentive, and always available to play with them, listen to them, and give fatherly advice.

It was only when Tony had his periodic bouts of depression that Tammy felt she wanted out of the relationship. For days at a time he would become uncommunicative, and what little he did say were complaints, blaming her for the fact that he didn't make more money, that their social life had dwindled, and that he had no control over his life. She read the message from him very clearly, that his life had changed since he had married her, and that he felt he would be better off without her.

Even at its best, life with Tony was not how Tammy had, in her youthful zeal, imagined it would be. He wasn't as adoring as she would have liked; he rarely complimented her without being prompted. He seemed simply to take it for granted that she was there and would continue to be there. The stability of the relationship was its strongest point. For the most part, Tammy had made her adjustments.

But, during Tony's depressions, Tammy would retreat into memories of the past and the boyfriend she'd had before Tony. Early in her relationship with Tony she had continued to date Dennis. Tony was ready to get married after only a few months of dating, while Dennis wanted to wait until he finished graduate school. Tammy married Tony, never certain he was right for her. Dennis had since married but was always glad to hear from Tammy when she called.

Tammy and Dennis were not exactly having an affair. They were not having sex, though they did, with some frequency, express to each other love and a desire to be together permanently. They were having an affair of the heart, if not of the body.

Most of Tammy's calls to Dennis were during the midst of a particularly bad time with Tony. Either Tony would storm out of the house, or Tammy would sneak out and, in her agony, call Dennis. She longed to hear reassurances about what a wonderful person she was and how much Dennis loved her. Being hated by one man didn't feel so awful when she knew she was loved by another.

Dennis provided Tammy with a fantasied way out of a marriage that at times felt intolerable. Tammy needed this flight of imagination even though, through fifteen years of marriage, she never needed to act on it. She needed only to feel that being with Dennis was possible.

Through our fantasies we are able to find creative ways to sidestep our inclinations to act destructively. When we can find momentary escape in our minds we often don't need to find permanent escapes in our actions.

Children, too, find ways of escaping painful realities through flights of the imagination. One of my patients says that her parents were so damaging to her as a child that she constructed an elaborate theory about who her real parents were and how she would eventually be reunited with them. Another of my patients lived an hour every day in a carefully constructed world, where mothers and fathers didn't scream at each other, and sisters and brothers weren't competing for the small morsel of parental love available. He was well aware that this world existed only in his imagination, but this world made the other world tolerable, and this world was his refuge.

FANTASIES OF REVENGE AND THE STABILIZATION OF THE EGO

When we have been hurt, betrayed, or abandoned, and when we allow ourselves to feel our hate and rage, the idea of revenge is, as they say, sweet. However, we have learned from childhood that the desire to get even is neither noble nor mature. We know, for instance, that it is not appropriate for individuals to "take justice into their own hands" and exact revenge over a private feud. The criminal justice system, we solemnly assure ourselves, is based on our commitment to fairness and to the need for punishment appropriate to the crime. Revenge, we are told, has no place in the restoration of order.

Yet, in spite of our moral stance of recoiling from revenge, we are fascinated by it and embrace it. Revenge has been a favorite theme in art, from the Greek tragedies to Shakespeare. Revenge is a leading theme in modern movies and in detective and spy fiction. In the widely popular movie *Death Wish*, there is scarcely a shudder when the hero starts killing, picking off one punk after another, in revenge for the murder of his wife and the rape of his daughter. Instead, a cheering audience gives its approval of this behavior.

Popular entertainment depicts promiscuous vindictiveness, not a solution to which a thinking, moral person would want to aspire. Although we think we shouldn't want revenge, we do anyway. As a theme in entertainment, revenge is so popular—more popular than the church, which tells us not to seek revenge but to forgive—because characters are depicted doing what we all want to do. *Death Wish* gives us license to feel what we can't help feeling anyway.

Our wish for revenge is strongest in matters of love. For each first blush of love there are as many dashed hopes; for every delighted lover there are as many disappointed, angry, wrathful lovers dreaming of avenging the wrong inflicted upon them. This desire for revenge is never, ever going to go away.

Our promiscuous attitude toward revenge in matters of love is evident in the verdict of the trial of Richard Herrin. Richard had been having a college love affair with twenty-year-old Bonnie Garland. After a summer abroad, Bonnie decided that she wanted to date other men, and wrote Richard a postcard to that effect. Uninvited, Richard traveled from Texas to New York and pleaded with Bonnie to honor their love and not to break up with him. Although she reiterated what she had written, Bonnie, with perhaps some guilt and with certainly some sympathy, held out her arms to Richard and they made love one final time. The next night Richard crept up to her second-story bedroom and bludgeoned Bonnie to death with a clawhammer as she lay sleeping.

It was perhaps the normality of the story, until the murder, that made Richard's defense so convincing. Who, so the reasoning of the defense team went, could not remember some event in their past when rejection led them to want to extract revenge? It is not infrequent that two lovers find themselves back in bed together even as they are trying to separate. Who could not feel pity for a man so coldly cast aside after such a blissful night of renewed love and sex? Who could not forgive this man, who was so desirous to right this wrong of lost love that he was, as his attorney worded it, overwhelmed by such a "terrible flood of emotions" that he had the "inhumane thought" of wanting "to kill the person [he loved] more than anyone else in the world?" No one. Or, at least not one of the thirteen jurors who decided his fate. In spite of the prosecution's reminder that his "inhumane thought" was, in fact, an actual murder, Richard Herrin was found guilty not of murder but of the lighter charge of manslaughter mitigated by extreme emotional disturbance.

Contrast, on the other hand, Herrin's trial with another, equally famous case, also a murder by a spurned lover. Three years later, in the same affluent county of Westchester, New York, Jean Harris, headmistress of a prestigious finishing school for young women, was convicted of premeditated murder in the slaying of her lover. The conviction of Harris was for a more serious crime, and carried a harsher sentence than Herrin's, yet the actual crimes were the same. In terms of sheer brutality, Herrin's crime was, by far, more violent and caused more pain to its victim. Why, then, was Harris penalized so severely?

Harris had become convinced, like Herrin, that she was losing her lover. After a twenty-year relationship with Herman Tarnower, author of the famous Scarsdale diet, Harris was being replaced by another, younger woman. Unlike in Herrin's defense, however, Harris was presented to the jury as a woman incapable of such ignoble feelings as wanting revenge. Ever the lady at her trial, Harris gave the impression that she, and her relationship with Tarnower, was not susceptible to any unlofty emotions such as jealousy, anger, or bitterness. With this deliberate presentation of herself, she was prompted to add that the only thing she and Tarnower fought over was the "use of the subjunctive." Harris claimed that her only purpose in bringing a gun to Tarnower's bedroom that night was to kill herself, and seemed to fail to recognize that suicide in front of a loved one is one of the greatest of all forms of acting out a revenge fantasy. For the perception of her as being above any primitive urges, the jury was unforgiving and Harris will be in prison for a minimum of fifteen years, and if parole is denied, for the rest of her life.

Richard Herrin and Jean Harris are people who, in acting out revenge fantasies, crossed the boundary separating the normal from the pathological.

When our desire for revenge remains a fantasy, however, it actually serves several constructive psychological functions. For example, the desire for revenge, directed toward another, can serve as an internal gyroscope. Vengefulness maintains the balance of the destructive drive by directing it away from the self. In this, a desire for revenge is self-protective and stabilizing to the psyche. It marks the beginning of movement away from narcissistic self-involvement by allowing another person existence enough for blame. When someone has been wronged, a psychologically healthy response is to direct rage at the wrongdoer rather than turn it against the self. Wanting revenge is part of the healing process of hurt and anger.

King Lear is a prime example of how revenge serves this stabilizing function for the psyche. Lear is motivated entirely by revenge. His daughters have abandoned him in his old age, and he becomes obsessed with fantasies of revenge. He plots revenge on them both so that "all the world shall know." Although he hasn't quite articulated the exact manner of the retribution he intends, he assures us that these deeds will be "the terrors of the earth."

But Lear begins to think better about his revenge fantasies. Immediately before his descent into madness, he begins to feel a little sorry for his daughters, the "poor naked wretches." He even begins to blame himself for their suffering. In the last line before his madness overtakes him: "O, I have ta'en too little care of this."

As Lear's rage toward his daughters softens, he turns this same fury back on himself, blaming himself for their hard hearts. It is a classic twisting of rage back toward the self in order to protect the beloved others. Three centuries before the discovery of the concepts of narcissism and narcissistic defense, Shakespeare surely wants us to make the connection between Lear's setting aside his revenge fantasies and the dark madness that overcomes him.

In addition to keeping one sane, fantasies of revenge maintain a bond with the person toward whom the revenge is directed. As long as one is busily occupied with fantasies of revenge, the other person is not really *given up.* If the feelings of separation or grief are too painful to be tolerated, holding onto the hate is a way of holding onto the relationship with the person.

As was the case with both Kelly Ann Tinyes' family and Medgar Evers' widow, Myrlie, hate can provide a force for life when life doesn't seem worth living. I have spent many therapeutic sessions with spurned lovers plotting the most dastardly revenge, successfully forestalling suicidal behavior that was threatening to emerge whenever the feelings of grief and loss got too intense. Revenge fantasies can actually sustain life. It is only when it is clear that the deeper process of mourning the loss can be tolerated without destructive action that the foundation for the vengefulness can be eradicated.

Vengefulness also serves as a defense against feelings of hopelessness and powerlessness. The hope of vindictive triumph makes life more bearable and makes us feel less like helpless victims. By imagining the world the way we would like it to be in our revenge fantasies we escape the real world. In our fantasies we control our environment; we are powerful enough to give our story whatever ending we like. The bad guys can all end up dead. Nothing beats revenge fantasies for feeling good about yourself. You're powerful, righteous, and the number-one winner all the time.

Revenge fantasies are important healing tools, because they help us to use thoughts and feelings in the service of harnessing our impulses and controlling our actions. Revenge fantasies are a way of acting without acting.

HEALING DREAMS

Some of us have taken our childhood lessons not to hate so much to heart that we obstinately refuse to recognize any aggressive inclinations within ourselves. Even our fantasies may be muted. Our lack of conscious recognition does not mean, however, that our hate and wish for retribution are not there; rather it means that our feelings are so submerged into the unconscious that we become aware of them only when we relax our vigilance, so that our unconscious speaks in spite of our conscious wish to silence it.

Freud called dreams the "royal road to the unconscious," because dreams represent the most direct access that we have into our unconscious. Conflicts that remain unresolved in waking life, feelings that remain unfelt in waking consciousness, find their way to expression through dreams. Dreams tell us what we cannot say.

When hate is not felt in waking life, dreams are often violent and nightmarish. Hate denied in waking consciousness permeates our dreamlife. But even in the relaxed state of sleep we need to disguise our thirst for destructiveness. As children we dream of witches and goblins; as adults we dream of knife-wielding villains and cars careening out of control. We attribute hate and destructiveness to other figures in our dreamlife. Hate and destructiveness appear, then, to come from the outside, rather than being our own. These disguised dreams serve as a release valve, reducing the amount of pressure from our unacknowledged and unexpressed feelings.

When the distance between our conscious and unconscious feelings is not too great, or when the unconscious has only a thin layer of protection over it, hate dreams enable the hate to rise to the surface of consciousness. Such was the case with Terri Lee Timmons, a devout Mormon whose religion taught her only to love and never to hate. It was only through a dream that Terri could allow herself to come face-to-face with a feeling that seemed to go against everything her religion had taught her.

Terri's story started when she was fifteen. She had been menstruating for a year and had had severe pain on her right side each month as her menstrual cycle approached. It was logical for her to consult Dr. Story, a popular local physician and one of only two doctors in the tiny town of Lovell, Wyoming. Each month Dr. Story examined Terri's pelvic area by internal examination. She had gotten used to the routine, even though Dr. Story always failed to find anything wrong with her. On one occasion, though, the doctor deviated from his usual procedure. As Terri describes it:

All of a sudden, as I was laying on the table, my feet in the stirrups, I felt something start to push against my bottom in the area of my vagina that was very, very warm and fleshy and yet hard.

I didn't know what to think. I had never been taught by my parents or anyone what intercourse was. I had no idea what a penis looked like, or anything like this. All of a sudden I felt it push inside of me. I started to cry, because it really hurt. It was much larger than his finger, and it was not a hand with a plastic glove on it. It was bare skin.

At this point I couldn't imagine what he was doing, and yet I trusted him because he was my doctor. He kept pushing it in farther and I just cried really hard because it hurt very bad . . .

. . . all of a sudden I felt a warm fluid go all over my bottom on the outside and down on the table underneath me. I had no idea in the world what this was at that time.

After this happened, he started to fuss around. He grabbed hold of the paper that covers the table that they always pull down for a new patient out from under me and he wadded it up and threw it away, and started wiping me off. After this happened, he told me to sit up and to get dressed and he would be back in a few minutes, and so I did. Before he went out of the room and asked for me to sit up, he said to me, "You did real good," and then left.

I got off the table and proceeded to clean myself up. The tissue which I used to clean my bottom was bloody and I was bleeding. I was very upset and in a lot of pain. I got my clothes on and sat there and a few minutes later he came back in and told me he could not find anything wrong with me, that he couldn't explain my pain. I left.

Terri's description of her rape by her doctor was paralleled by many of the women in this town. For almost twenty years, Dr. Story had systematically raped the women of Lovell, Wyoming, while giving them "routine" pelvic examinations. Most of the women were Mormons and if they had had sex, had had it only with their husbands. They were a conservative, reserved lot, bound by their religion to be devoted wives, loving of God, respectful of authority, and, importantly, reticent to discuss sexual matters. Whatever misgivings or puzzlements or outright suspicions these women may have had about their experiences in their doctor's examination room were all quickly laid to rest. He was their doctor and they trusted him. Their need to love, not hate, prevented many of them from even acknowledging what had happened. They politely asked how much they owed him and wrote their checks; most scheduled new appointments. Those who allowed themselves to be aware of the rape wondered if they had done something to bring on the attack. Personal embarrassment and fear of ridicule prevented them from ever discussing their experience, even with members of their own families. Each remained alone in her shame, sure that she had committed adultery and would be excommunicated from the church.

Healing from the pain of their violation was a long time in coming for most of these good-hearted women. Hate was not a part of their emotional repertoire. They were more likely to pray for the strength to forgive than to allow themselves the feelings of rage and betrayal.

Such was Terri's circumstance when she found herself, years later, having to testify at Dr. Story's trial. Bringing up the past was itself stressful. As Terri described the experience in Jack Olsen's book *"Doc,"* she began to suffer physically as well as emotionally. Finally, Terri had a dream:

> Story was shopping at the fabric store in Powell and I was in the back where he couldn't see me. I shook and started to faint, but then I found a gun in my hand and I walked out and said, "Okay, you little son of a bitch, strip." I made him walk down Main Street naked. I yelled, "Now everybody's gonna see what they think they've been missing." A cop took me away, and I laughed and said, "This has been worth it."

Terri reported the therapeutic effect of the dream:

> That dream helped. I needed to have that power over him, to control and humiliate. I began to feel better. My lymph gland stopped swelling, the headaches went away . . .

Experiencing one's hate empowers. Denying one's hate amounts to cutting off an essential part of oneself.

Yet another even more astonishing illustration of the healing power of dreams is reported by psychoanalyst Gerald Schoenewolf in his treatment of a sexually abused patient. This woman reported the somewhat mysterious phenomenon of having nightmares about her sexual abuse and then waking up with bruises on her body. Apparently the dreams were stimulating actual physiological changes in her body. The nightmares were always the same: She was lying in a crib as an infant, with her arms tied; a man stood before her, smiling and masturbating, then touching her genitals. She tried screaming "no" but found herself gagged and unable to cry out for help. Her mother seemed to be nowhere in sight, though she was aware of a hopeless wish for her mother to rescue her.

While this woman's dream may not have been an exact replay of the sexual abuse she had experienced as a child, as with all dreams it crystallized her emotional experience. Schoenewolf decided to encourage the development of his patient's dream into a waking fantasy, thus giving her control over the outcome of the abuse, which had been denied her in the original childhood experience and which continued to elude her in her dreamlife. He asked her what she would like to do with this abusive man. "I'd like to kill him, but I'm too little." He made a recommendation: "Go back and kill him now. Imagine yourself as your own mother, walking into the room to defend yourself." The next day the patient returned to therapy smiling and feeling good. She said, "I feel so much joy. All last night I was going over the nightmare and killing the man. I never thought of it that way before. I never thought I could kill him. I killed him all night. I can't believe it. I feel so light, so full of energy. I started a new painting today. I called a friend; we're going out tonight. I hope this feeling never goes away. I've never felt like this before."

It is not an accident that these examples both involve sexual and status relationships. People who want revenge are people who feel victimized. Relationships in which there is unequal status, whether between adult and child, man and woman, boss and employee, physician and patient, are most prone to be abusive. After all, for abuse to take place there needs to be someone who is either

willing to accept the abuse or unable to escape it. These relationships leave the person of the inferior status feeling powerless, and
ultimately enraged. To the extent that the rage threatens to be discharged into action, the situation feels dangerous. Very often the
victim regresses back to narcissistic defense: better not to feel at
all; otherwise there may be a retaliatory beating, abandonment, or
attack. Hate dreams may seem like the only avenue of discharge
for these rageful feelings. When we are supine—unconscious and
unable to move, victims of the limb-relaxing quality of Eros, the
love that restrains us from destructive action—it is safer to let ourselves experience these feelings of vindictiveness.

OUR PSYCHOLOGICAL IMMUNE SYSTEM

The body has its own way of hating. The body's aggression, as it
turns out, is an excellent model for trying to understand how to use
our emotional hate for constructive purposes.

A healthy body will always recognize when it is in danger. It has
built into it a system of detection that, once activated, sounds an
alarm of danger so that defensive forces can be marshaled against
the offending stimulus. For the body, enemies come in the form of
germs, bacteria, viruses, or chemical pathogens, each with the
power to disrupt the body's delicate balance. Alternatively, the enemy may be internally arising agents, such as cancer cells, the ar-
terial plaque in heart disease, or the body's own waste products,
each also with destructive potential. This sytem, ever vigilant in
its protection of the body against both external and internal enemies, is called the immune system. When the immune system is
active it "hates" the enemy; it goes on the prowl, first ferreting out
the enemy, then destroying it. This is an aggression that has positive value. This is a hate that restores healthy functioning.

We have, as well, a psychological immune system that protects
us and tells us when we are in emotional danger. Like the physical
immune system, the psychological immune system detects both
internal and external enemies. The enemies for the psyche are destructive hate, the kind of hate that has its origins in narcissism.
Aggression directed toward us by others may be under the guise of

a seemingly friendly barb, such as "You use so much Windex I should buy stock in the company"; it may be as trivial as an unacknowledged hello, as irritating as "I don't like your hair cut that way," or as vicious as "You're an obnoxious human being and I wish all bad things would happen to you."

Our own aggression, too, runs the same gamut from irritation to wrath. The psychological immune system, when it is functioning properly, makes these fine distinctions, correctly determines the origin of the aggression (in self or other), and mobilizes its defenses so that we are not sitting ducks for the destructive potential of narcissistic hate. The constructive hate of the mobilization of the psychological immune system neutralizes the destructive hate of narcissism.

FROM NARCISSISM TO IMMUNITY

In the first few months of the infant's life, we are relatively certain that mind and body do not yet exist as distinct entities. Everything that happens to the infant happens on both levels. His experience of the world is, as Freud described, "oceanic," all things fusing into one great wholeness.

Both psychically and physically, the infant makes inadequate distinctions between himself and other. On the physical level, mother's suckled breast is experienced by the infant as an extension of self. On the psychological level, the infant experiences mother and self as fused.

In this state of narcissism of both body and mind, the infant is in the stage of his life when he is the most vulnerable. Psychologically, the infant is powerless: He not only does not recognize when he is in emotional danger, but he also has little capacity to defend himself.

The process of growing up is, then, about developing the capacity to defend oneself, on the level of both body and mind. The healthy functioning of both the physical and psychological immune systems depends upon adequately recognizing the difference between self and other. The immune system can't attack an enemy unless it is able, first, to recognize an enemy as an "other." The further we progress out of narcissism and the more clearly defined sense of self we have, the more properly vigilant our psychological immune system beomes. A properly functioning psychological immune system depends upon the emotional maturity of having a separate self.

Hate is the emotion of psychological defense. Just as the physical "hate" for enemies of the physical immune system is an integral part of having a healthy body, so, too, is emotional hate an absolutely necessary part of mental stability. Hate is, then, a progression away from narcissism and toward mature separation of self.

PSYCHOLOGICAL IMMUNE SYSTEM FAILURES

We can determine whether our psychological immune system is functioning properly by monitoring our thoughts and feelings. It is natural and healthy to feel a random assortment of feelings—love and hate, calm and excitement. Each of us has tendencies that are more emphatic in one direction, but in the psychologically healthy individual the other side is still present at least to a degree.

When there is a noticeable absence of a whole set of feelings, or a skewed preponderance of one set of feelings, we know that the psychological immune system is out of balance. For instance, if we never feel anger or hate, if our view of the world is that all is love and sweetness, then we suffer from an underactive psychological immune system. In this case we do not have access to our aggression. This is psychologically crippling, since it means we remain limited in our ability to channel aggression for constructive purposes.

Conversely, if we feel angry all the time, if we always blame other people for everything that goes wrong, then we have an overactive psychological immune system. In this case, aggression has become the predominant force and the counterbalancing influence of love is not available.

Finally, if we perpetually blame ourselves, if we find ourselves saying things like: "If I had only . . .," we have become the victims of our own hate turning back around on itself. In this case, the aggression is felt but is always directed against the self.

We also know that our psychological immune system has ceased to protect us when our thinking and feeling functions are out of balance. When we find ourselves perpetually trying to talk ourselves out of our feelings ("I shouldn't be feeling this"), we know that we are erring on the side of thinking. When we find that we act impulsively, purely from feeling, then we are refusing to let our thinking function serve as a counterbalancing force.

One of my patients, Margie, has suffered a low-level depression all of her life. She has talked continuously about her lack of self-esteem and her insecurity. She has never quite understood the origin of her insecurity and has steadfastly resisted the idea that it is related to her upbringing. It is true that Margie's parents loved her tremendously. She was their only daughter, and they showered her with love and attention. Obviously they adored her. Yet their love was not the kind of love that resulted in a strong foundation of self-esteem.

Shortly before the death of her father, when it became clear that her father was dying, Margie decided to take off a month from work in order to go home and be with her mother and brother to alleviate their burden of taking care of him. At this time, Margie had been living with Peter for three years. The nature of their relationship fell somewhere in the netherlands of no definition. Margie wanted to get married; Peter didn't. Margie maintained her own apartment for fear that Peter would ask her to leave. Much of the time Peter responded to Margie from his own self-serving point of view, rather than from any concern about Margie and her desires. Margie understood all this quite clearly, but her insecurity prevented her from thinking that she could do any better. She stayed with Peter, despite the ambiguity of the relationship and despite the pain this ambiguity caused her.

When Margie told Peter about her plan to be with her family for a month, his response did not surprise her. He told her that she might lose her job if she took a month off; he warned her that she was going to be away from her Weight Watchers group and would probably overeat and gain back all the weight she had lost; he threatened that he was going to be lonely for that month and couldn't promise that he wouldn't go out with other women. He said everything under the sun to convince Margie to stay. Margie had long ago gotten used to Peter's lack of support. It was her mother's reaction that took her by surprise. When Margie repeated to her mother all the silly, infuriating threats Peter had made to her, her mother's response was: "Now, Margie. Don't go upsetting Peter. You know how you can be." Then, to make matters even worse, her mother added, "Don't forget how good he has been to you."

Margie's mother's message was: *The other person is always right.* And the next message was: *Be grateful for whatever you get.* She had been "whispering" these messages to Margie all her life in every communication, but this time Margie's response surprised them both. She got angry.

This conversation basically jump-started Margie's psychological immune system. At last Margie was able to confront the fact that her insecurity and lack of self-esteem was related to her mother's persistent pattern of never validating Margie's point of view. If someone was blowing cigarette smoke in Margie's face, Margie's mother would defend the right of the other person to smoke. If Margie uttered a complaint about her boss not recognizing her talents quickly enough, her mother would tell her that she was expecting too much. Any expression of aggression by Margie toward another was met by her mother with a validation of the other person's point of view and an invalidation of Margie's point of view.

When the origin of the destructive hate is one's parents, it is particularly hard to detect the hate. Since as children we are inclined to see our parents as omniscient and omnipotent, it is only gradually that we can come to see that they do not always have our best interests in mind. We accept what they say about us as true, even when it is not, because children want to love their parents and accept what they say. We would rather hate ourselves than hate what is being said to us or who is saying it.

For all of these reasons, Margie had long ago repressed her feelings of rage about her mother's habit of not supporting her. Margie felt close to her mother in many other ways and trusted her. Rather than experience her anger at her mother, Margie incorporated her mother's message and made it a part of herself. She believed that she was, as her mother had told her on numerous occasions, overly dependent on men and ungrateful for the attention they paid to her. She became, then, a person who criticized herself just as her mother had; a person who did not believe in herself. By shutting off her psychological immune system and sacrificing her self-esteem, Margie was able to hold onto a needed idealized image of her mother.

It was only when Margie was able to look at the subtle dynamics of her relationship with her mother that the reason for her underlying depression became clear to her. When she was finally able to give herself permission to feel angry, she was able to claim for herself a confidence that she had never experienced. From that point she was able to feel anger related to other parts of her life. Soon Margie felt prepared to objectively evaluate the pros and cons of her relationship with Peter and to see whether or not it was worth working on and could lead to sufficient gratification to justify the effort. Allowing herself to feel hate was indeed a healing process for Margie, and she was at last using her hate constructively when she began to evaluate the circumstances of her life with a full range of feelings.

STRENGTHENING THE PSYCHOLOGICAL IMMUNE SYSTEM

There are myriad ways in which our psychological immune system can become damaged or out of balance. Happily, it can be mended. When we use both thought and feeling, reason and passion to guide our actions; when we recognize the essential differences between self and other and defeat our narcissistic tendencies; when we create a harmonious balance with all of the various functions of our psyche, *then* we can clearly read which feelings are coming to us from others and which feelings we have toward others. We may not have learned to do this well in childhood, but we can learn to do it in adulthood.

We can nourish our psychological immune system, and we can teach ourselves to listen to the signals that it sends out to us. Instead of denying our feelings of discomfort or depression or anxiety we can turn our attention to them, realizing they are signs that something is wrong. And then we can make new responses to old stimuli.

When our patterns of emotional response have become so set that they are automatic, we have lost the ability to respond uniquely to each situation. This is the arena of the dark side of love: unconsciousness. Without conscious direction, each of the shadows of love and the love pretenders will make their appearance. But we can learn to experience and respond to love differently. The beauty of the properly functioning immune system is that each situation is responded to appropriately.

Some years after my relationship with Richard had ended, I met another man, equally appealing. I imagined that he would be Richard's replacement, that I would soon have a nurturing, satisfying love with this man. Very shortly after we met we decided to go on vacation together. I looked forward to a heavenly week in the Caribbean getting to know this man. Two days before we were due to leave he explained that he was having some financial difficulty and asked if he could borrow some money for the trip. My alarm signal went off, just as it had the first night I met Richard, when the sole question he had asked me was about my tennis racket. I wanted badly to go on vacation with this new man, but all reason told me it was a bad idea to begin a relationship with his being in debt to me. We canceled the trip, but I remained interested in him, hoping against hope that perhaps this was just an anomaly, and wanting to give him another chance.

Our phone conversations were warm and intimate and hopeful of mutual love. We made plans to meet for dinner, and again I got excited at the prospect of seeing him and having a romantic evening at my favorite restaurant. He called at the last minute, announcing that something had come up. My psychological immune system was ringing loud bells by this point, and this time I decided to heed them. The up-and-down feeling of excitement, hope, and anticipation followed by disappointment and hurt was all too familiar. In spite of the appeal of this man, my strongest sense was that I would end up hurt in this relationship. I decided not to pursue it, and though I can never be sure that we would not have had a gloriously satisfying, loving relationship, my bet is still on the odds being against it.

For many years Marie and Barry had terrible fights with each other, always ending with the same tears and threats and screams. Something would anger one of them, and they would be off and running. Basically, they always ended up saying the same things to each other during these fights. Barry complained that Marie had invaded his life, that he had no independence anymore, and that he felt like a stranger with no rights inside his own home. *Her* choice of furniture filled their home, *her* clothes made the closets bulge, *her* dog needed walking and feeding. Marie countered that Barry's temper was unmanageable and that every time she wanted to talk to him about something, he ended up getting angry. She insisted that he was impossible to talk to. At this point in their fighting, things would get even more heated. By now Marie would be crying hysterically, and Barry would throw his hands up in the air despairingly and announce that he was going to move out. Marie would then sink into a suicidal depression.

Barry's threat of abandonment always touched a raw nerve in Marie. She had had two other serious relationships, and both had ended with the men walking out on her. Her father had left her mother, and Marie had grown up observing her mother's struggles and learning the difficulty of being a woman alone in the world. There was no more frightening idea to Marie than Barry's leaving her. If his intent was to hurt her or scare her, he knew just where to thrust the knife.

This is the way their arguing went on for years. When they weren't fighting, they were loving and supportive of each other. They had a wonderful, close relationship, which their friends envied. But the fighting was tearing their relationship apart. They couldn't seem to develop any rules about fair fighting, so each fight went the length.

One day it occurred to Marie that she had to acknowledge the fact that Barry always talked about leaving during these fights but that he never did. They would make up, and he would explain that he had said terrible things just out of rage. He would remind her about his ferocious temper, and that he did mean those things when he said them, and at the time it really did feel like that's what he wanted to do, and would do. But, he explained, that was apparently what he needed to say or feel when he was angry. Couldn't she remember that he was just discharging his rage? Did she have to take his threats so seriously?

Marie was experiencing firsthand how "old brain" and "new brain" functions do not always work together harmoniously. On the one hand she knew, logically and rationally, that Barry was right—that he was not going to leave her. Her new brain had a good, sound understanding of how they fought, and why, and the realistic consequences. But on the other hand, in the midst of the fights when he was threatening to leave her, she always forgot this information. Her old brain was so agitated that it knocked her new brain out of commission. Her reaction was always an overreaction, because her responses were based on her past experiences rather than on a true understanding of Barry.

With this new understanding, Marie was able to approach their arguments with a new awareness. Through the feelings of fear and dread that every argument stimulated, she was able to call up a part of herself that wanted balance and that had the rational understanding that her reaction was an overreaction. She was able to apply new-brain understanding to old-brain feelings. She was able to correct the overreaction of her psychological immune system.

Each of us can, like Marie, teach our psychological immune system when it is in error. A properly functioning psychological immune system helps prevent us from being victimized—not only by others but also by our own destructive aggression. Recognizing old patterns of reacting, and replacing them with more appropriate responses, is only possible if we are willing to learn from our mistakes.

HATE AND HEALTH

Just as we develop physical immunities as we are exposed to various illnesses over time, so can we, with experience, strengthen our capacity to make appropriate psychological responses to destructive aggression. For most of us, the hardest part of this process is simply becoming unafraid of constructive hate.

Coming face-to-face with hatred can indeed be frightening, particularly if we have been taught all our lives that hate is evil. However, once we acknowledge hate, we find that it need not be destructive—that in fact it can be our psychological ally and defender. The more attuned we are to aggression in its various forms, the more adept we become at managing hate and rage constructively. By emptying the caldron of bitterness that boils in our unconscious, we free ourselves to better enjoy the present.

CHAPTER 10

Cooperative Love and the Birth of Consciousness

Cooperation was, surely, the first form of love. For us to continue to live on this planet, it will need to be the last, as well.

Passionate and romantic love burn brilliantly but they risk being consumed by their own intensity. Romantic love cannot last because it places the self at the center of love. Cooperative love may have its beginnings in passion or romance, but for it to survive, the relationship, not the self, must take its rightful place at the center of love.

Long before language, there was cooperation. There had to be, because it was an evolutionary necessity. Whether the cooperation was in the form of worker bees going all out to make a lovely hive-home for their queen, in whom the entire future of their propagation lay, or of the mutual grooming in which monkeys engage, or whether it manifested itself in our human male ancestors going off to kill animals for food to nourish their women and children, cooperation was what made the difference between those who survived and those who didn't.

Cooperation was invented because our human or prehuman ancestors realized that their chance of survival was better if they had others around to help. "You scratch my back and I'll scratch yours" was the best attitude of all for the survival of the fittest. Cooperative love made the fit even fitter.

Cooperation is both a forerunner and the essence of genuine love. Today we have the luxury of advancing past survival issues and reaping the emotional rewards of cooperative love. Cooperative love is not motivated by fear, or even by mutual obligations and expectations, but rather by the promise of fulfilling our loving potential.

Cooperative love asks that neither the head nor the heart be neglected, even when their demands are conflicting. Passion and romance hold our attention because they are intoxicating and fresh. We feel giddy with expectation, wondering what joys we will savor next. Cooperative love is less flashy but more dependable—the sturdy car you would choose for a long trip rather than the sports-car in which you would go for a spin. Cooperative love derives no strength from our infantile needs that we are so used to and that we hold onto so dearly; rather it is a love that is a promise of what is new and different and possible within ourselves. It doesn't promise happiness, but it gives us the tools with which we may work to fashion relationships that are communicative, respectful, emotionally satisfying, and mutually enriching.

THE DEFEAT OF NARCISSISM

Cooperative love is based on the ability to realistically appraise the sensitivities and capabilities of another, and to maintain expectations in line with this objective evaluation. Cooperative love means that one will have developed the capacity to protect oneself, when appropriate, and to give generously of oneself, when appropriate, and to unselfishly be concerned about the welfare of the other, when appropriate.

The capacity for cooperative love begins early in life. Those of us who have been mothered and fathered lovingly will be able to be loving to ourselves first, and then to others. Loving parenting teaches us to orient ourselves to the reality, unpredictability, and dangers of life, and enables us to develop our own internal resources to cope with these contingencies.

Infantile narcissism is anathema to cooperative love. If we are totally absorbed in our own needs we will never be emotionally mature enough to sustain a mutually satisfying love, with all the self-restraint, compromise, and recognition of another's needs that it requires. If we are busy projecting our unconscious concerns onto another, we will never achieve true intimacy.

The precondition of cooperative love is self-knowledge. Only in coming to know ourselves are we able to truly appreciate what another person has to offer. Paradoxically, the only route to a fulfilling love relationship with another person begins with a journey inward—not away from the outside world but toward it through self-knowledge.

Mona is a patient of mine who needed only a little help in understanding her narcissism well enough that she could defeat it in her communications with her husband. She spent an entire therapy session telling me about her husband's reaction to a platinum wig she had bought. She had recently gotten a haircut; ten years of luscious dark hair was chopped off. When Mona looked in the mirror she almost didn't recognize herself. Giddy with her new image, she thought it would be fun to play around with other hairstyles and colors. She promptly went out and bought three outrageous wigs, one of them platinum blonde. Mona is Chinese and platinum hair is the last thing anyone would expect on her. But she loved the outrageousness of the look and went home excited to show Lars the "new" Mona.

Lars, however, was not as thrilled as Mona by her new look, and the two proceeded to have an argument over the wig. Lars told her she looked ridiculous. Mona got enraged and told him he was an idiot for not seeing the humor in it. He retorted that there is no humor in making oneself look silly. That statement even further enraged Mona, and she refused to speak to him for the rest of the day.

In our discussion about this event I explored with Mona why she wanted so desperately for Lars to agree with her, to have exactly the same point of view as she had, and why it made her angry when he didn't. Mona admitted that when Lars saw things differently than she did, she felt it called into question their entire relationship. It seemed not just that they were different but that Lars was wrong, and that she shouldn't be married to a man who saw the world from such a distorted angle. She was right, he was wrong, and what were they doing together anyway?

Mona was able to discern that Lars' inability to accept their differences came from the same attitude in himself. Lars felt, and communicated to Mona, that if she disagreed with him, it was *she* who must rearrange her bifocals and glean a new vision of the world.

The next week Mona fairly danced into her session, boasting proudly that she and Lars had had a disagreement. They had been watching a television show. She explained, "It was one of those inane TV movies, where the plot is evident in the first three minutes of the show, and Hollywood celebrities are paraded out just to pull in a TV audience. It's the kind of show that gives television its worst name." And, it's the kind of show that Mona loves and Lars hates. So when they settled in for the evening and Mona announced her intention of watching this show, she fully expected another argument. She knew that Lars felt the old familiar rage rising to the surface, with all its old critical nuances. ("Her taste is so pedestrian." "She'd rather watch television than do something interesting or valuable with her time.") Mona, too, felt the descent of her own criticism of Lars. ("He never just lets me be. He feels like a suffocating pillow to me.") As battle lines were being drawn, she remembered our conversation. She realized that she did not need to get defensive about wanting to watch television, and made a conscious effort not to become provoked. She reported the ensuing conversation:

> Lars: So you're really going to watch that piece of garbage?
> Mona: Yes. I enjoy these movies.
> Lars: How can you enjoy shit like that? You really have to deaden your brain to be able to sit in front of the tube watching that stuff.
> Mona: That's exactly why I like to watch it. I like to deaden my brain at the end of the day.
> Lars: Well, I have no intention of watching it.
> Mona: That's fine. There's no reason why you should like everything I like.

Lars: That goes without saying, but I still can't understand how you can like such trash.

Mona: That's what's so nice about being separate people. We can have entirely different tastes. I can like trash and you can like the highbrow stuff.

Not only was Mona able to leave her own narcissism behind her and accept the differences between herself and Lars, she was also able to make a communication to him that helped him to do the same. In a cooperative marriage, we know each other's weaknesses and tendencies toward narcissism, and rather than using these vulnerabilities as excuses for attack, we commit ourselves to the task of aiding our partners to be more mature in their dealings with us, as we try to be with them. Rather than complaining, we assist. We become, in effect, therapeutic partners to each other.

THE RENUNCIATION OF NEED

It is far better to base a relationship on mutual enjoyment of each other than on need. Although two people can come to depend on each other after a lifetime of sharing life's joys and trials, and even to need each other in certain ways, this is not the same thing as selecting a partner to fulfill unmet, infantile needs. Narcissistic need stems from one's early, unresolved conflicts. Any relationship that is defined primarily by unconscious need will have strong narcissistic components and, ironically, will leave either one or both partners feeling alone and isolated. These partners are not in love but in need.

Cooperative love is conscious love between two individuals who have matured beyond their narcissistic strivings based on unresolved infantile issues. True cooperative love is not based on thoughts of what someone will do for us or make us feel. President John Kennedy's message in the 1960s, "Ask not what your country can do for you; ask what you can do for your country," appealed to us precisely because it resonated with the mature part of us that wants to give as well as receive. With conscious cooperative love we are emotionally free enough to give; in need we are prisoners of our cravings.

No matter how much we may protest that those we need are those we love, the two feelings are not easily compatible. What we need and what we want may not necessarily come in the same package—and may, in fact, be mutually exclusive. Need may bind us to another, but the bond may be more of a prison than a cooperative love relationship. Cooperative love can come about only when need is not paramount.

The man who never learns to take care of household duties will need a woman to cook and clean. What he needs, then, will always have greater weight than his desires. I have seen widowed men who never developed domestic self-sufficiency remarry the first suitable woman who came along. In this equation, women are exchangeable; one is as good as the other if she presses shirts and puts dinner out on time. This is a limited "love" at best. Similarly, women who go "stupid" when it comes to balancing a checkbook or plugging in a telephone will need a man around the house because he's needed, not because he's wanted.

We cling to our needs by refusing to develop aspects of ourselves that foster independence and by holding tight to those aspects of ourselves that maintain our dependence on another. We may do it in the innocuous ways of never learning to cook or clean or to plug in a telephone. Or, we may do it in a much more significant way. We hold tight to our dependencies in the division we make of inner resources—rationality to men, and emotions to women. Staying tight in our little cocoons of gender identification leaves us dependent on the other sex for the expression of parts of ourselves that we have renounced as unimportant. We all know that women generally have better access to their feelings than men. (This is in large part why, historically, they have been considered the inferior sex. Feelings, after all, are trivial compared to the running of the state and wars and stuff.) But, to accept this division between what is appropriately masculine and feminine means the perpetuation of suppressing necessary parts of ourselves.

Before we are in any position even to begin to think about who or what we should pursue (and how, and what to do with them once we have them), we must be able to separate our true needs from our desires. Too often the choice of a spouse is made out of a need that has nothing to do with conscious preference. Freud, of course, showed us that much of the time when we think we are making choices we are, in fact, being buffeted about by unconscious forces. Too often our choice of a mate is based on an infantile compulsion to please (or displease) a parent; an infantile compulsion to be like (or unlike) our friends; an infantile compulsion to see ourselves in a pretty white dress and a wedding band. Because these compulsions are based on the feelings of helplessness and dependence—the needs—of a one-year-old, they have little to do with the maturity possible for a twenty- or thirty-year-old. Too little do our choices have to do with a genuine understanding and appreciation of the person we are marrying.

True love—not the variety of need that so often passes for love—can arise only when desire has replaced need as the driving force. Once we have left our infantile narcissism behind us, we can explore the selves of others, and our own selves in relation to others. We can feel our own boundaries and how they knock up against the boundaries of another, and how that feels to us and to the other. We can know from them when we are getting too close or when they are scrunching up against us before we are ready.

THE RENUNCIATION OF UNCONDITIONAL LOVE

With cooperative love we can learn the most difficult lesson of all. Parental love is like the love between adults. But the parallel is not exact. Unlike the unequal relationship between parent and child, true love between adults is love between equals. Furthermore, adult love is not unconditional. Of all the myths about love, the myth of unconditional love is the most pernicious and will create the darkest, most destructive moments in love relationships. Those who seek unconditional love are miserable because they haven't yet found it. They blame themselves or their beloved that the feeling of unconditional acceptance is absent. Destructive hate and rage accumulate around this unrealistic expectation.

Many people come to psychotherapy thinking that therapy will give them an answer to the mystery of how to attain unconditional love. Rather than question the attributes they ascribe to love, they question their relationships. They assume that therapy will help them figure out what has to happen for them to find unconditional love. Maybe they have to search harder. Maybe they have to trade in one inadequate spouse for a better model. It comes to them only with great difficulty and pain that unconditional love is a thing of the past, never again to be recaptured except momentarily. Unconditional love is a need that is pertinent to the infant that they once were rather than to the adult they should aspire to be.

FROM FEELINGS TO RELATIONSHIP

When we remain stuck in the narcissistic stage of development, we pay too close attention to our feelings and we neglect other aspects of our psychic functioning. We remain exclusively concerned with whether or not we are loved, or whether or not we love. We fail to ask ourselves *how* we might best love or be loved; we forget to use judgment about our feelings; and, of course, we make the assumption that hate is anathema to love.

Late in his life, Jung made some further reflections on the principle of Eros. From his earlier puzzlement about Eros as a "monster of a mountain" whose paradoxes had rendered him speechless, Jung came to grasp what he felt was the essential meaning of love:

> Love is a feeling, yet the principle of Eros is not necessarily loving, it can be hating too. Eros is the principle of relationship [underline mine].

And, as a warning about our inclination to confusing feelings and love:

> You must never mix feeling with love . . . [Feeling] has nothing necessarily to do with love.

And, finally, to reaffirm his conviction on the meaning of Eros:

Love is relatedness.

It is, then, through being connected to one another, and through all of the creative possibilities that connection lends itself to—loving and hating, feeling and thinking, experiencing and observing—that we form relationships. Love is a child of relationship, but it is only one child out of many. Eros, as we first saw him, as a young boy rebelliously searching for a love that he irresponsibly abandoned at the first sign of trouble, has now matured into a concept of relationship that demands full consciousness and full individuality. Eros, as the principle of relatedness, is the spark that is created between two separate selves, the electric circuit now able to reach to its completion.

FROM RELATIONSHIP TO COMMITMENT

The final connective leap from the individuality of our own self to another self is called commitment. Commitment in a relationship serves as a container, a structure that surrounds the thoughts and feelings that are generated in the relationship.

Jungian analyst Russell Lockhart reminds us of the etiology of the word "commitment." The Latin word *committo* means "to bring together," "into union," "in combination," "to connect." But the word has another, less familiar, meaning, and the additional meaning gives us insight into the inevitable dark side of love that will arise out of any committed relationship. *Committo* also means "to bring together in a fight" or "to carry on a fight." To be committed, then, means that Thanatos (aggression), as well as Eros, is going to be present. If we are going to be separate selves, uniting in relationship and commitment, we are going to have disagreements.

If we follow the etiology of the word "commitment" even further we find, as did Jung, that words, in telling us about our language, tell us as well about our psyches. The root word *mitto* means "to send away," "to cause to let go," "to release," "send off," "cast off." For us to be committed to one another we need to be willing to release our hold on our beloveds. We need to be our own self and allow our beloveds to be their own selves.

EQUALIZING THE INEQUALITY

Love has its earliest origins in the unequal relationship between parent and child. In some ways this is unfortunate since inequality often continues to be the emphatic definition of our relationships throughout the rest of our lives.

An infant is both smaller and less powerful than an adult. To skew this relationship even further, many parents, still angry about their own treatment in their childhood, relate to their children as though they have no rights. It is true that children are not yet as capable as adults, but they are not lesser beings because of their age. Children need and want to be treated with dignity and fairness. Their vote may not count, but their feelings do. Validating their feelings goes a long way toward equalizing an essentially unbalanced relationship, so that children grow up expecting fair treatment from others and wanting to give it in return.

In preadolescence our feelings of inadequacy are still acute. At this age we become aware that we are not the prettiest, or the smartest, or the richest, or the most popular. We want desperately to fit in, to be the same; we hope fervently that we won't be held up to ridicule, found inferior by the power group.

Adolescence is the time when the battle between the sexes begins and the inequality of male/female love is first experienced. If you know teenagers, you know there is always someone singing the refrain "Loves me, loves me not" and pulling petals off a daisy with lots of hope but with little certainty. Rarely is love received in exactly the same proportion as it is given. Such is the pain of love. It is never exactly as we would fashion it in the best of our dreams. More often than any of us would care to know, it more closely approximates the worst of our nightmares.

Since the beginning of civilization inequality has defined the battle between the sexes. For the most part, in subtle ways, it still does. It is, of course, women who, in every way possible, have been appointed to the inferior position. Ultimately any inequality leads to resentment that, if not experienced consciously, becomes a barrier against love.

Take, for example, financial inequality. Most women prefer to earn less than their husbands. Until divorce looms on the horizon, few of us think about the net of dependence this inequality casts. Many women have told me that they stay married because of their financial dependence on their husband. This is not as self-serving as it sounds. Children become the main victims when there is a sudden drop in family income.

Financial inequality is almost impossible to eliminate. Even when both partners make the same amount of money, attitudes about who pays for what can create an environment of inequality.

One of my patients works full-time. She is a professional and earns a good salary, as much as her attorney husband. They have arrived at unspoken rules about the distribution of money. Her money goes for household expenses, the children's clothes, and her own needs. His income covers their country house, their vacations, the children's private schools—all the luxuries her husband and children take for granted. But she knows that if there is an extra expense that would be entirely hers—say, a weekend at a spa—she must make the money to pay for it, or ask permission. He's a generous husband. He doesn't deny her much. But still, the rules have evolved that she must ask, even though money is not tight. There is no freedom for her in this kind of financial dependence. She lives part of her life based on permission. She lives part of her life on justification. For the wife of a less generous man, justification would before long give way to subterfuge and concealment. ("The dress was only $100," she would report, instead of the outlandish $200 that it was and that she paid for it.)

Another woman I know is supported entirely by her husband. She complains that they have sex too often. The definition of "too often" is whenever he wants. However, she refuses to mention this problem to her husband. She explains: "I don't have the right to have sex only when I want because he supports me." You can imagine the resentful feelings this woman has accumulated over time and the way they permeate other areas of this marriage.

Another form of inequality consists of devaluing all that is feminine. Societies have always been patriarchal, with men's status elevated and women's denigrated. The "masculine" emotions of aggression and assertion were the cornerstone of most cultures until recently; the softer, "feminine" traits weren't culturally valued until the last few hundred years. Now that they are emphasized, the problem with these qualities—being nurturing, empathetic, supportive, yielding—is that they are culturally encouraged only in women and serve to keep women in an inferior position.

A few years back I and a group of women friends decided to go hiking in the country for the day. We were obligated to baby-sit the thirteen-year-old son of one woman, so he came along with us. At one point on the trail we found ourselves not knowing which way to turn to get back to the car. We all took our guesses. The thirteen-year-old boy said his opinion with the utmost authority. Like lambs to the slaughterhouse, we followed his edict. His direction was wrong. We asked what had made him give his opinion with such assurance. He said that everyone else was offering their ideas, so he decided he would, too. Already, at thirteen, he had mastered the art of sounding like he knew what he was talking about. And, at the ages of thirty and forty, we women were willing to defer to the higher authority of a just-finished-with-childhood thirteen-year-old boy.

Jung said: "Where love reigns, there is no will to power; and where the will to power is paramount, love is lacking." If inequality is that deeply ingrained in us, what are our chances for equal love between two adults of the opposite sex?

If we are to have cooperative love relationships, first and foremost we need equality. Cooperative love is not two halves coming together. Plato, in his definition of love as two complementary souls meeting, had it wrong. It is, rather, two separate selves, two distinct human beings, each with a unique temperament and personal likes and dislikes, coming together. Cooperative love comprises two indivisible wholes, not the romantic notion of two complementary parts seeking completion. Cooperative love means two independent, self-defined, equal individuals choosing to be together and to work out their differences.

The growing equality of women is surely a hope for the future, for our individual lives as well as for our culture. By this I do not mean merely that women will one day earn as much money as men. Rather, I mean that the values women embody are increasingly becoming the values that our culture and the hierarchical leaders of our culture—the men—are beginning to value. Women are generally more connected to others than men are. Women like to talk about feelings and relationships. Women know both sides of inequality: the superiority of the mother and the inferiority of being a woman. Women, in other words, have qualities that are ideally suited to helping us find our way to equality in relationships.

THERAPEUTIC PARTNERS

The work that we need to do in our intimate relationships is similar to the work that is done in therapy. In therapy, one person—the therapist—assumes the more mature role. The patient, on the other hand, is allowed the entire scope of his (or her) emotional regressions, provided that the expression of the regressions stays within the framework of language. He can, for instance, feel vulnerable, scared, angry, or critical. But he does not curl up in the fetal position in his vulnerability; he doesn't cower in the corner in his fear; he doesn't throw objects in his rage; and he doesn't call the therapist obscene names in his criticalness. Rather, he translates all of these feelings into the medium of words.

Psychoanalyst Donald Winnicott emphasizes the importance of creating a "holding environment" in the therapeutic relationship—an environment in which the patient feels it is safe to experience all of his feelings and to put these emotional experiences into words. So, too, must we create a holding environment for the children and adults that we love in our everyday lives.

If the message we give to our loved ones is that we don't approve of certain feelings in either ourselves or in them, they will show their "love" to us by hiding these feelings. Once shame sets in, the feelings are likely to be submerged into the unconscious, and eventually will find a pathological means of expression.

Becoming therapeutic partners to each other means knowing the other person fully and consciously, and being able to see him or her without having to look through the distorting lens of one's own unresolved childhood issues.

An example of therapeutic partnering is seen in the relationship between Joan and Bernie. He grew up in a very serene household. He prefers quiet and calmness and feels disturbed every time Joan goes into one of her histrionic fits. For the first few years of their marriage, Joan's temper explosions caused the two of them great difficulty. Bernie frequently dreamed of divorcing Joan and finding a woman who had the calm disposition that reflected what he was used to.

After spending some time in therapy talking about his marriage, Bernie had an insight that enabled him to change how he dealt with Joan's tantrums. He realized that before Joan's temper exploded in full force there was always a warning. She would get irritable first. She would start complaining about how Bernie didn't straighten up after himself or that he was on the phone too much.

When Bernie was able to see that there was a pattern to Joan's tantrums, he got more interested in understanding the cause of her flare-ups rather than just hating her and wanting to be rid of her. He observed each time she exploded and thought carefully about what events had preceded the rage.

Bernie was able to understand Joan's rages long before she herself did. He detected the pattern that whenever Joan felt that an important decision needed to be made, she would begin to feel overwhelmed and incapable of making the right decision. This was the point at which her irritability would start. He would then react to her irritability by getting irritable himself; he would then tell her to calm down with a critical tone in his voice; this communication would further enrage her, and it would end with her histrionic fits.

Bernie came to understand that he could intervene therapeutically with Joan long before she reached her final breaking point. The proper point to intervene therapeutically was when Joan went into an overwhelm mode, before her emotional state took its downward spiral. Bernie took a therapeutic approach with Joan as soon as he detected that she was entering into a state of anxiety, fear, and the feeling of incompetence. He helped her to talk about her fears and feelings, to reason out her thoughts, and to arrive at her decisions.

Bernie was able to serve Joan as a therapeutic agent only because he was able to give up his own destructive hate. Rather than assuming the posture of a critical father in his communications to her, he got interested in her. Through this interest in understanding her and helping her he was able to assist her in resolving some of the emotional blocks that were preventing her from functioning in the marriage on a more mature level. This helped Joan, it helped Bernie, and it helped their marriage.

The caveat in being therapeutic partners to each other is, of course, the possibility of one person doing it for the other all the time. This is the natural relationship between an adult and a child; the parent's role is to help the child mature. However, a one-sided helping relationship becomes pathological, and codependent, when it is between two adults, one always playing the role of the therapist or the understanding parent and the other always being the patient or the child in need of assistance. Being therapeutic partners means knowing the strengths and vulnerabilities of both oneself and the other, and working constructively within those parameters.

COOPERATION

One of my patients quit a twenty-year smoking habit a year after he got married. His new wife was a nonsmoker and objected strongly to the smoke in the house. She didn't ask him to stop smoking for the sake of his health. She simply stated that she didn't want to smell the smoke in the house. For the first year after they married, this cooperative husband took his cigarettes outside. Since he was a heavy smoker, this meant that their conversations were frequently interrupted by his smoking breaks.

This man says that he finally quit smoking altogether because he realized that it was not fair to his wife. She should not have to be subjected to smoke if she didn't want to be. And she should not have to be subjected to the frustration of eternally interrupted conversations. In putting himself in her place, he was able to understand her feelings, her frustrations, and her desires. His quitting smoking was an act of cooperation.

Cooperation cannot occur in the presence of a strong destructive drive unless there is a commitment not to act out the urges. To cooperate with others, we need at times to subordinate our own impulses and drives for the sake of a mutual goal. The goal in love is the relationship. This means we do not say or do whatever we want, whenever we want, however we want. It also means, though, that this restraint is not a sacrifice to our own self.

True progress toward cooperative love can be made only when both individuals value a relationship enough to nurture and protect it, and are committed enough that they can face each other's destructive expressions of aggression unflinchingly. I know of one couple who never fought before marriage, yet after they married found themselves expressing more rage than they ever imagined they possessed. It was the first time for each of them that they felt comfortable enough with another person to let that person see and experience their rage. All that anger was not a sign of incompatibility. Allowing themselves to *know* each other, even the parts that wanted to stay hidden, was not a sign of weakness in their relationship but of strength.

COOPERATIVE TALKING

Freud said: "The man who first flung a word of abuse at his enemy instead of a spear was the founder of civilization." Freud understood that since hate, rage, and aggression are inevitable in any intimate relationship, there are going to be times when bitter feelings need to be expressed. The manner in which this is done is probably the single most important factor in the success or failure of a relationship.

Aggression is not the end of intimacy; it is part and parcel of intimacy. Aggressive impulses, when properly contained to mutually agreed upon areas (sex, of course, is one, but not the only; tennis can be another) can improve the quality of a relationship. When the "battle between the sexes" is tempered by love, the inevitable aggression will add variety and interest to a relationship.

Talking out one's feelings is one of the best ways to ensure that there is not such a buildup of unexpressed rage that destructive acts will follow. Talking defuses rage and hurt because it is an activity that demands the integrated use of the brain. When we react reflexively from feelings, we have regressed back to operating from the older, animal part of our brain. When we communicate verbally, we are operating from the newer neocortex. Talking about feelings allows us to use both sides of our brain simultaneously. Talking about *all* of our thoughts and feelings—even the forbidden ones—is the process through which we strengthen our psychological immune system. Letting ourselves experience and verbalize all of our thoughts and feelings rewires the brain into making new and creative connections. Talk that arises from an integration of both sides of the brain releases destructive impulses through verbal expression, thus invalidating the need for destructive action.

For talk to be cooperative and to heal, it must serve as a bridge between people. Communication is the balm that converts narcissistic love, self-involvement, into cooperative love, two separate people knowing each other. Even the most threatening feelings can be talked about if we are assured that the purpose of the talk is to communicate, not to harm.

Although it doesn't have to, hate often prevents communication. The threat of using words as weapons, rather than as tools for communication, will stand in the way of verbal communication. Discussing bitter feelings is undeniably tricky, and conversations can quickly go astray. Rather than say things that will possibly provoke retaliatory reaction, or abandonment, often we decide to say nothing at all.

There is the danger, too, that in the process of talking, one side of the brain will win out over the other. If the feeling side gains prominence, the talk may develop aspects of wanting to punish, judge, harm, or threaten. Or, alternatively, if the rational side takes prominence, talking may become simply an exercise in trying to intellectually persuade or coerce another's thoughts and feelings to be entirely logical and reasonable. For talking to be constructive, both of these pitfalls need to be recognized and avoided.

Another common pitfall in talking between people who are intimate is their expectation that they should be able to say anything. It is commonly believed, for instance, that there should be no privacy in marriage. We believe that in an ideal marriage, each partner should know everything about the other. The right to privacy is a privilege that is not abrogated by the marriage contract. Furthermore, it can be counterproductive to tell our partner absolutely everything that is on our mind or everything we have experienced.

Lea and Jack have a solid relationship with only one hitch, which was disturbing Lea. Jack liked to tell her every single detail of his day. If he had had a good day, he was generally in a good mood and Lea enjoyed hearing about his travails and successes. But if he had had a bad day, he liked to talk about that, too. Jack has a tendency to blame himself for whatever has gone wrong, and in the telling of these stories of failure he invariably presented himself as inadequate and incompetent. He wanted a sympathetic ear. Lea is, indeed, a sympathetic woman, and she prides herself on this quality. But the truth is: Much of the time when she was encouraging Jack, and supporting Jack, and reassuring Jack, she felt more like his mother than his wife. She resented the role, yet felt that she would be cruel if she told Jack to take his need for stroking elsewhere.

Both Lea and Jack were operating under the assumption that the "correct" behavior in a marriage was to say all and to hear all. But after several years of serving as Jack's confidante, mother-confessor, and forgiving-father, Lea began to see Jack, most of the time, as a child in need more than a partner equal in stature. They both had to learn that Jack's use of indiscriminate talking was inappropriate to the marital relationship.

Cooperative communication takes the other person's reactions into account. A partner's attitudes and likely responses should be carefully taken into consideration when decisions are made about what to say and how and when to say it. Information that will be hurtful or provocative should be given out only in certain circumstances and with care so as to lessen the negative impact.

Charles and Alice came to one of their marital therapy sessions after a particularly upsetting argument. The day before, Charles had found out that he had landed a much coveted role in a Broadway musical. He was thrilled; it was his first acting part for which he would get paid, and he rushed home to share the glorious news with Alice. He was crestfallen, then, when, after telling Alice, he looked at her face and saw that she wasn't smiling and could barely muster up a "That's nice, dear."

Charles felt unsupported and alone. He was furious at Alice's lukewarm response, too angry, in fact, to ask her why she wasn't happy about the news. In the therapy session, though, Alice was quite articulate about why her response was so ungenerous. Charles' news was certainly happy news for Charles, but it meant only more work and trouble for Alice. Charles would now be out of the house every night; Alice, who had a full-time job, would be left with the sole responsibility of feeding the children and getting them to bed. The precious little time that Charles and Alice had for each other was, with this new job, dwindling down to nothingness. It was these thoughts that Alice had after Charles reported his "good" news.

Alice explained to Charles that she could certainly understand his happiness, and that she wanted to share his happiness with him. It was his bursting in with the news without any awareness of its impact on her life that made it difficult for her to be joyous with him. Charles explained to Alice that she certainly could have voiced her concern *and* her happiness, rather than acting disinterested. It became clear that if Charles and Alice had been able to talk to each other, keeping in mind what they themselves felt and what the likely emotional response of the other person would be, Charles' "good" news would not have led to such a bitter misunderstanding.

Talking about one's thoughts and feelings is a skill. Talking, done well, is a wonderful opportunity to be fully who we are, and to meet the fullness of another person. As French philosopher Gaston

Bachelard says of unspoken words: "What is the source of our first suffering? It lies in the fact that we hesitated to speak . . . it was born in the moment when we accumulated silent things within us." A relationship that has learned the art of talking cooperatively and constructively (about even negative feelings) is a relationship that has the strength to withstand two mature, separate individuals being fully themselves, together.

COOPERATIVE FIGHTING

A fight in a relationship can be constructive, on occasion. It gives both people an opportunity to blow off some steam. It brings feeling into the relationship and opens up the opportunity for frank discussion. Relationships with no expression of hate are emotionally stilted, without the life energy that a good infusion of occasional hate can accomplish.

In marriage, the energy that is behind the hate in the partnership can be converted into sexual energy and can contribute to a rich and varied sexual life. Poorly adjusted couples, on the other hand, will use this same energy to psychologically assault each other.

Fighting is also inevitable among and with children. Children, because they are less fluent in the use of language, need to blow off steam more than adults. Because they are action-oriented, they need help in learning to gradually put their thoughts and feelings into words, rather than action. The younger they are, the more rudimentary their verbal skills; parental expectations need to be adjusted accordingly. Asking them to do what is beyond their developmental skill will only increase their frustration.

Children should never be punished for saying what they feel, even when it is embarrassing or is a negative feeling about their own parents. Yet, children also need to be helped to be aware of the impact their words have on others.

It's important that an adult who is expressing anger toward a child never lose control. Loss of control is terrifying to a child, who may not yet have the confidence that loss of control today does not mean abandonment tomorrow.

There are a few rules that must be followed to enhance the success of talking about hateful feelings.

1. *The person who is angry should try to figure out why he is angry.* This is not always as easy as it sounds, and it may require summoning up some objectivity—something particularly difficult to do when angry. For instance, hatred for someone may be misdirected. A person who has never come to experience and resolve his childhood hatred for his parents may feel it toward his marital partner. This is hardly fair for the partner, who happens to be on the receiving end of a lot of hostility.

2. *When one person is angry the other person needs to listen.* Arguing back or being defensive will only place both people in the position of operating from old-brain behavior. This means that nobody is going to be heard. None of us is required to agree with anyone else, but having the opportunity to express ourselves, to be heard, and to be understood is a privilege that each of us has a right to demand.

3. *After the anger has been given verbal expression, both partners should sit down and try to figure out how to solve the problem that precipitated the anger.* The anger, then, becomes a tool for people who love each other to work together on the normal problems of intimacy and living together.

4. *Children, especially, need to have their feelings acknowledged.* Children don't have the perspective that comes with emotional maturity, and they will often want things and want to do things that are not in their best interests. Parents don't have to give in to what a child wants, but they do have to listen to the child's feelings when he doesn't get what he wants. It is hard enough for a child to be as powerless as he is and to know that he doesn't make the rules. But to communicate to a child that not only does he not make the

rules, but his feelings about the rules don't count, is a message that will permanently damage a child's sense of a secure and confident identity.

5. *Parents should bear in mind that sibling hate is often misdirected aggression.* It is easier to hate a fellow child than to hate the larger, more powerful parent. Parents need to intervene with children's fights when there is danger that there will be injury (either psychological or physical) and redirect the rage toward the adult, who is more maturely equipped to tolerate it without retaliation.

Cooperative fighting is like riding a seesaw. One is up while the other is down; the game doesn't work otherwise. In fighting, people need to complement each other, not imitate each other. So, when one is up in the air, riled up about something and sounding off, the other needs to have his feet planted solidly on earth, stabilizing the relationship. With this kind of balance in fighting, things will not be carried to extremes and a constructive outcome is more likely. As Jungian analyst Anthony Stevens said: "Conflict is cooperation's shadow."

Hate itself is never the problem in working out a relationship. Rather, the problem is in the management of the aggressive impulse and the hate feelings that accompany this impulse. Too much repression of feeling can result in an accumulation of tension that will be discharged, finally, in an explosive release. Such uncontrolled discharge is frightening to the receiver and overly stimulating to the sender. Neither denying the feeling, nor indulging in it excessively will result in a constructive relationship. Self-control, where the feelings are meted out in a dosage that is comfortable to both sender and receiver, will preserve the foundation of love that is necessary for a good relationship. Understanding the origin of hatred and being able to verbalize the feelings in ways that are not destructive to either the self or the other will diminish the intensity of the hate feeling and mitigate its destructive potential. In this emotional environment, love, despite and even because of its inevitable dark side, can flourish.

COOPERATIVE SEX

One of the most difficult areas in an intimate relationship between a man and a woman is working out a sexual relationship to the mutual satisfaction of both partners. A satisfying sexual relationship, like all other aspects of intimacy, is not something that is necessarily accomplished without work. This fact is, of course, one of the great disappointments of marriage. Just as we want our partners to know our every need and our every wish without our having to tell them (and this is sometimes the criterion we use to evaluate the "rightness" of the person), so, too, it is in the bedroom. We resent having to tell our sexual partners what we want and what we like, and we refrain from asking them the same. Yet, talk in the bedroom about sex is every bit as essential for a good sexual partnership as communication about nonsexual issues is outside the bedroom.

We are at our most regressed when we are having sex. It is this regression that gives sex its divine pleasure. The pleasure of sexual activity represents us at the height of our narcissism, in our absolute delight in receiving pleasure. However, it also represents us at the height of our ability for cooperative love, in our generosity in giving pleasure. It is precisely because sex has the potential to represent us at our most infantile level *and* our most mature level that it is such a problem area for many relationships.

Silence is never so deafening as it is around the topic of sex. Many people have been taught that sex is not a proper subject for discussion. To believe this, however, is to believe that one's desires are not a proper topic for discussion. When we are comfortable with our desires, and feel entitled to having desires, sex becomes a comfortable area for discussion. This is, of course, the message that any loving person will want to communicate to a partner: that pleasure is worth discussing and worth pursuing.

At times, other concerns override a mutual willingness to communicate desire. When this happens the sexual relationship becomes unsatisfying. June and Ray, for instance, are a couple that I saw for marriage counseling because June had stopped wanting to have sex with Ray. They had a wonderful relationship in every other way and were completely satisfied with their choice of each other. In watching them, it was clear that they had a deep love for each other. Yet, in this one area of their marriage they were distraught. Ray wanted to have a sexual marriage, and felt sexually attracted to June. June, similarly, wanted sex in her marriage, but this wish remained only an idea. In fact, she never felt sexually interested in Ray and dreaded the nights when he would indicate that he wanted sex. Neither could understand how a marriage so good in so many other ways could be so bad in this one.

The problem, as we were able to unravel it, was that June and Ray loved each other so much that neither wanted to hurt the other. They both decided to keep themselves in the dark rather than know the truth of the problem in their sexual encounters. The fact was, Ray was quite inexperienced sexually when he married June. He was a fairly insecure man and looked to June for answers, much as a child would to its mother. Knowing Ray's fragility, June took on the role of bolstering his confidence. She always assured him that he was good-looking and smart and talented (all of which he is), and a good lover. Ray developed new confidence in himself and began to think about their sex problem in a new light. One day, he finally asked the fateful question: "Am I a good lover?"

June's response was immediate and instinctive: "Yes, yes, of course." And so she repeated over and over again, as she had all through their marriage. But Ray didn't accept the answer as easily this time. He had matured out of his little-boy "whatever you say is right" posture and was willing to challenge his wife. "You say this always. But the fact is, you don't ever want to have sex with me. I think we have to consider the possibility that I just don't know how to please you sexually." June was willing, with this invitation, to consider how Ray might become a better lover. When the idea became acceptable to Ray, June was able to think about it meaningfully. For the first time, they were able to have a frank discussion about their sexual preferences, without fear of injuring each other. In coming to understand their desires in bed as well as they had out of bed, June and Ray were able to develop a satisfying sex life.

Sexuality is an area in intimate relationships that is particularly prone to secrecy and misunderstanding. Concealing negative feelings about this aspect of the relationship will only lead to the discharge of these feelings in some other, indirect way. Sooner or later the true feelings will be sensed. However, when these feelings are brought out into the open, they can be looked at and solutions to difficulties discussed. Keeping sexuality silent and tucked away in the dark is only asking for trouble.

COOPERATIVE LOVE AND THE PSYCHOLOGICAL IMMUNE SYSTEM

Two people engaged in a mutually loving relationship may, over time, become complacent. Certain responses and ways of responding to each other can become habitual. If we aren't careful, we may let our psychological immune system shut down. At this point, we aren't exercising cooperative love; we are sleepwalking through love.

Even in a successful and mutually considerate relationship, our psychological immune systems need to stay active. Every day we need to make appropriate responses and adjustments, large and small, to aggression—our own and others'. *All* cooperative love has dark moments, and *any* relationship can slip into a toxic mode.

Jim and Sandra have been married ten years and have as good a marriage as any I've seen. They've successfully weathered many different phases of their relationship, and they are both deeply committed to their marriage. So why did they end up in my office for marriage counseling?

As it turns out, Sandra was ready to put more energy into her career now that all three children were in school all day. In a variety of fairly subtle ways, Jim simply wasn't helping Sandra achieve this goal. Consciously he expressed interest in Sandra's picking up additional clients for her interior design business, but at the same time he had sabotaged Sandra's plans several times. Once he had taken the car to be fixed on exactly the day she needed to go buy samples. Another time he had to stay at the office late instead of baby-sitting as planned. Sandra had to stay with the children and was forced to cancel an important meeting with a prospective client. When Sandra told Jim her great news that she'd landed a new account, Jim's reaction was decidedly ambivalent: He expressed great joy in her triumph, and with barely a moment's pause he proceeded to complain that there was "nothing to eat for dinner."

Sandra's psychological immune system became activated. Since Jim was truly unaware of his pattern of undermining Sandra's goals, they were having trouble engaging in constructive, cooperative talk.

Jim and Sandra didn't need to spend a lifetime in therapy to get past this stumbling block in their relationship. Jim came to see that basically he liked his life exactly the way it was, and though he wanted his wife to be happy, he also wanted her to keep managing things just as she had been doing. Sandra made it clear that those days were over. Together they are now redefining their roles and mutual expectations, bringing some new insights and experiences into their marriage. Jim will have to make some adjustments, and so will Sandra, but because Sandra recognized the problems and the two of them worked on mutually satisfying solutions their marriage will be strengthened, rather than weakened, by this new development.

COOPERATIVE LOVE AND OUR FUTURE

We depend on cooperative love for a stable future, both in our personal relationships and as a global community. When we nurture our young, they grow up healthier, more resilient, and more productive. But our willingness to cooperate cannot end at the narrow margin of what we define as our family, or our race, religion, or nation. We must push our definition of those with whom we cooperate to its outer limits. Our good wishes and altruism may have begun historically with the family unit, but our generosity is capable of being extended beyond the boundary of family so that eventually all of humanity is encompassed.

Anthropologist Irenaus Eibl-Eibesfeldt, commenting on our future as a species, observed: "Many deeply rooted impulses may become obsolete, having lost their species-preserving function. Aggression toward the 'outsider' may be one such." In so saying, he mirrors one of Freud's meanings of the cure of neurosis—the discontinuance of living the past in the present, the lifting of the veil of responses that have outlived their appropriateness and necessity.

Cooperative love, more than any other quality we humans embody, is what has brought us this far on this planet. And it is cooperative love that, in this day of potential global destruction, will determine whether we can go any further.

CHAPTER 11

The Reflective Light
of Psychotherapy

Many centuries after Narcissus, we are told of another mythical figure who had an experience gazing at her reflection. Her name is Alice, and in looking at her image in a looking glass, she is able to enter a virtual wonderland of sights and sounds, touches and tastes.

We are struck immediately by the difference between the outcomes of these two mythical figures. Narcissus' interest in his image led to a reclusive turning away from the world and eventual death. Alice's seemingly similar preoccupation with her reflection leads to a rich, expansive confrontation with life's complexities and contradictions, life lived at its fullest. Why the difference?

The reflective image of oneself is, in some native cultures, of great symbolic value. In many pretechnological cultures, photographs are thought to steal the soul. To them, the image *is* the soul. Perhaps they're not that far off.

The reflections of themselves that Narcissus and Alice happen upon are invitations to look into their souls, into the innermost depths of who they are. (That's the unique ability of a mirror. It confronts us with only ourselves; we see *only* and exactly *who* and *what* we are.) Narcissus stays focused on only the surface image of himself. Alice, however, is not satisfied with such a superficial experience. She looks into the mirror, and then through it, and in doing so is able to step into it, enter another world, the world of the other side, a world consisting of endless imaginative possibilities for the human psyche.

It is through the process of psychotherapy that we can join Alice in an adventure into the inner self. Contemporary psychotherapy provides us with a well-charted method of exploration. It gives us a mirror with which to look into our innermost selves. Through psychotherapy, we can take the same imaginative leap that Alice takes.

For some of you, the reading of this book will have sufficed and you will be content to take the insights you have gleaned and apply them to your lives. Others, however, will want to continue this process of self-exploration and will want the intensive experience of psychotherapy. It is for you that I have included this last chapter, an addendum of sorts. I include it because the path of psychotherapy is, I believe, the shortest route out of the narrow tunnels and dead ends that constitute love's dark side.

WORDS OF THE SOUL

Words, most of all, are the medium of psychotherapy. The use of words for the purpose of healing comes from the Greeks. They recognized speech to be man's greatest treasure, a gift from the gods that bestowed meaning to our earthly existence. Words name a thing. So important is the function of naming that in many premodern cultures the verb "to name" and "to be" are the same. Naming a thing with a word helps to give it existence. Naming, existence, and meaning are all found in the use of words. So important was this function to the Greeks that for centuries they sought to discover the secrets of words, the way in which words could be used to move the soul. Revered even more than the physician, who could heal the body and calm the psyche, was the person who could bring "cheering speech" to the ailing soul. Anyone who has been soothed by words can understand the meaning of Oceanus' pronouncement to Prometheus, "Words are the physicians of a mind diseased."

Words are, as well, the way of the creation of the world. God *said*, "Let there be light," and light was created, and all the rest of the world as well, through God's speech. The opening line of the Gospel of John is: "In the beginning was the Word, and the Word was with God, and the Word was God." Words are divine, words give birth to life.

Both Freud and Jung were interested in the ways in which the soul speaks to us and we speak to the soul. The first major work of psychoanalysis, of both Freud and Jung, was on words. Freud's first interest was in aphasia, a breakdown in the use of words due to a lesion in the brain. Later, he became interested in the method of free association. Freud simply asked his patients to say whatever came into their minds, to speak freely and without reservation. Similarly, Jung devised a technique that we know today as the Word Association Test, in which a stimulus is presented and the listener is instructed to say, as quickly as possible, the first word that comes to mind. When we silence the normal operations of our everyday conversational speech, when we temporarily cast aside reason and logic and our almost instinctual inclination to judge our thoughts and feelings, another language presents itself to us. Freud and Jung felt that this was the language of the unconscious. The unconscious is our inner speech. The unconscious connects us to our *soul*.

It is, then, this inner speech that is the province of psychotherapy, the speech we aspire to reach. Psychotherapy is a process of revealing to ourselves and to another our inner speech, the speech that represents who we are in the darkest, deepest depths of our being. It is, as Jungian psychoanalyst Russell Lockhart said, a "ritual of telling." One tells someone else these secrets of one's soul because telling another facilitates telling oneself.

It is perhaps not a coincidence that Freud began his exploration of the soul with the study of aphasia and that I, similarly, came to some insights about the healing nature of words through the words of an aphasiac. Not too long ago I read in *The New York Times* about a man who suffered from a stroke and as a result became aphasic. In the condition of aphasia, speaking is extremely difficult, and the meaning of the aphasiac's words are hard to grasp by even the most committed listener. The man about whom the article was written is Joseph Chaikin, until his stroke a well-respected director of plays. In his noble effort to learn to speak again, albeit haltingly and with great effort, Chaikin came to some startling insights about the nature of words.

Words, he said, and his inability to find them, are like the heavens. "So much feeling *between* words. It's endless . . . enough for endless planets and stars." Chaikin knows as much about those words that are unspoken as those that he is finally able to utter. It is as much as anything else the endless spaces between words, those unspoken silences, that give words their weighty meaning. These are the words we must learn to speak, the weighty ones and the ones that fall between the planets and stars.

The analytic edict that is given to patients is: "Put your thoughts and feelings into words." Words, when imbued with both thought and feeling, bridge distances between silence. Talking with both thought and feeling connects left and right brain hemispheres, love and hate, passion and reason, conscious and unconscious, spoken and unspoken. Words become precious. Words become expressions of our souls. As Joseph Chaikin finally concludes in his interview: "Words are important . . . 'love' . . . 'truth' . . . shouldn't be mixed up with 'eating candy' commercials."

As Freud and Jung were plunging into the depths of our souls, other scientists began the study of the historical roots of words and, similarly, plunged into the depths of the meaning of words. The interface of the two disciplines showed that words have meaning even beyond the resonance they have for each of our personal histories. Words are like Alice's mirror; they bring us deeper and deeper, even to the point of bringing us back to the origins of our construction of language. Words create cultural as well as personal resonance. Jung talks about the history of every word and sentence going back thousands and even millions of years, touching upon the historical fiber of our ancestry. Jung felt tracing back the lineage, a family tree of a word, would lead us to the parentage of our psyche.

Using Jung's ideas, we get interested in the etymological origins of words, and the resonant chords of history they strike. The word "psychology" has its etymological roots in the words *psyche* and *logos*. Psyche means "soul." Psychology is the *logos* of the soul. We have come to think of *logos* as meaning reason and logic, but its earlier meaning was "word" or "speech." Psychology is the speech of the soul, or "soul words."

The word *psyche* also means "butterfly." Words of the soul fly; they liberate us. Psychology, or its clinical application of psychotherapy, the therapeutics of the soul, leads us to the freedom and beauty that the butterfly represents. Our inner things (our thoughts and feelings), put to flight in words, are no longer imprisoned in us, nor imprison us in them. Such is the hope for psychoanalysis.

Too, butterflies originate as ugly, wormy larvae. One would never predict that a thing of such beauty could be transformed from a thing of such ugliness. We should not be so quick to reject all those ugly, wormy things in our psyches. From them may develop wondrous creatures of great beauty. Words affect transformation.

ECHO, THE FIRST PSYCHOTHERAPIST

With Freud's approach to therapy, the patient was not touched and was prevented from seeing the analyst, as well. The therapy became strictly a sound therapy; the only medium of exchange between patient and therapist was the sound of the words. Sounds alone were supposed to heal.

Before Freud, Echo had tried the same technique with Narcissus. She suffers disembodiment, and her only means of communicating with Narcissus is through words. But because of her limitation of speech, the only words she can use are Narcissus' own words. Echo is a sound mirror for Narcissus. In reflecting Narcissus back to himself in sound, she becomes a sound mirror of his psyche. She sends back to him exactly what he is sending forth to her. We can see through to our souls with the echoes of our sounds as well as with the echoes of our images.

Let's look at their dialogue. He calls out, "Is there anybody here?" Echo answers, "Here?" He hears her and invites her to be with him: "Come." She reciprocates the invitation: "Come." But she doesn't appear, and in frustration he beseeches her, "Come here and let us meet." "Let us meet," she answers. Finally, in despair turned to murderous rage, he flees from her with a threat: "Away with these embraces. I would die before I would have you touch me." She responds with the tantalizing prospect even still of a relationship: "I would have you touch me."

Echo echoes Narcissus' own questions and pronouncements. If Narcissus had been able to listen, he would have been able to find his own soul through the relationship. Instead, he turns away from his self, stumbles across his reflection in the pool of water, and satisfies himself with a mere chimera of self, a self without a soul.

Mirroring is an important process in childrearing. Children live in a world where feeling is paramount. Much of the time they are feeling. But if you ask children what they feel, generally they will say that they don't know or that they feel "good" or "bad." Their ability to define the feeling and put it into language is not yet well developed. It is the role of the adult to aid the child in developing this capacity. The adult does this by mirroring. The task of the adult is to reflect the child's feelings, to give word articulation to those inner processes that to the child feel unspoken, to make loud the "whispering of the walls." Mirroring reflects back to the child who he was, who he is, and who he is becoming.

When the emotional experiences of children are not confirmed by a significant adult, children lose their faith in their own experience. They develop a false persona that does not represent the center of their being. They lose their souls. Jung said, "If parents because of their own insecurity cannot accept sufficiently the basic nature of the child, then its personality becomes damaged. If it is beyond the normal bruising of life, the child becomes estranged from his center of being and feels forced to abandon his natural pattern of unfoldment."

Children who are not allowed to become themselves become someone else. They may become their mother or father, or the child their mother or father wants them to be, or the child their mother or father fears they will be. Whatever the case, they will have wandered away from their own being and will leave the home of their own soul uninhabited. They will develop a vague feeling of being "homesick even when [they] are at home." These are the children who become adults in need of psychotherapy. The psychotherapist must complete the job that the parents did inadequately, and help the person find his way back to the home of his own soul. It is in the dark caves of infancy, those places where shadows were first cast over our souls, that this journey back home begins.

HYPNOS AS A GUIDE

Without the benefit of modern scientific knowledge, Freud devised a therapy that enabled the patient to gain access to his unconscious. *The Interpretation of Dreams* was Freud's first major effort at uncovering the mysteries of the unconscious, and it was from this work that he concluded that "dreams are the royal road to the unconscious." Now, if only he could get his patients to have dreams with him while they were awake. In this endeavor, Freud experimented with hypnosis, but rejected it because its results were inconsistent and unreliable. And thus was he led to the technique that, still today, defines the practice of psychoanalysis. The patient lies on the couch and talks. He can talk about anything at all.

The patient evokes, then, the limb-relaxing quality of Hypnos. It is like sleep; he is in a relaxed position, arms at his side and legs uncrossed. But in spite of this bodily relaxation, his mind is awake and alert.

Modern science has demonstrated, in fact, that the state of consciousness that the analytic patient most closely resembles is the dream state. Dreams are characterized by what sleep researchers call REM (rapid eye movement), an internally active state. This dream state is different from both the rest of the sleep cycle and the waking state. William Dement, a leading sleep researcher, says about the dream state:

. . . during REM sleep a special mechanism is inhibiting or
blocking the effect of the central discharge upon the motor neu-
rons, so that the body does not move . . . We might conclude that
the brain is telling not only the eyes but also the body what to do
during a dream. One probable good fortune is that the muscles
cannot obey.

Hypnos, with his talent for limb-relaxation, allows us in sleep
and in therapy to contemplate the wildest thoughts and feel the
most extreme emotions—all without danger of action. In such a
safe haven of no-action, one can explore the deepest, darkest recesses of the soul.

GHOSTLY LOVE IN THERAPY

Freud began the technique of psychoanalysis by having the patient
lie on a couch. The patient's position on the couch was relaxed,
evoking the limb-relaxing quality of Eros and the state of consciousness in which the defenses are minimal. The consciousness
of the patient is not quite unconsciousness, as in Hypnos or
Thanatos, but in eliminating most sensory stimulation neither is it
ordinary waking consciousness. In fact, it bears the most resemblance to the state of being in love. With the limbs relaxed and
the vigilance of waking consciousness subdued, the soul could be
set free within the confines of the controlled analytic relationship.

Since baring the soul to another creates an intimate bond, patient and therapist develop a certain kind of "love." The trick was
to get the patient to fall in love with the therapist enough to cooperate with the treatment—that is, to set the soul free. (Freud almost lost his first patient, whom he shared with his friend Breuer,
when the patient developed a hysterical pregnancy, claiming
Breuer was the father. Too much love proved to be dangerous.)

It was, though, Freud's initial study of love that was the cornerstone of psychoanalysis as a therapy. He found that patients developed deep feeling for him, love even. (Since the patients were
in a state of Hypnos, he could have predicted as much.) At first
Freud felt that this love impeded the psychological progress of the

patient, turning both patient and analyst away from the true concern of the therapy—the patient's neuroses and reasons for seeking treatment. But Freud gradually came to understand this love in a different light.

He saw that the love the patient formed for the analyst was a repetition of personal history—a ghostly love, originating in the past, rather than a true love related to a genuine understanding and acceptance of the analyst. He also determined that it was this "transference" of feeling (the repetition of the past within the patient/analyst relationship) that was precisely what would enable the analyst to observe the infantile functioning of the patient firsthand, and thus to "see" what went wrong. The analysis of the "love" between the patient and analyst became the treatment. Interpretation, the rational explanation of the meaning of this transference love and its relation to the patient's illness, became the main therapeutic tool. The new-brain logic of the analyst was supposed to be persuasive to the new-brain rationality of the patient, and through rational understanding, cure would be effected.

The result of all this is that Freud, original excavator of the soul in the psyche, had devised a therapy that left the soul out of the cure. It is one of the great ironies of Freud's work.

Modern psychoanalysts have discovered that emotional difficulties that arise from patterns residing in the old brain are cured only by speaking the language that the old brain understands, the language of feelings. The classical method of analysis, providing interpretations to the patient or giving new-brain information to attempt to resolve an old-brain problem, is as useless as reading a bedtime story to a dog. Rationality and logic are persuasive tools of communication only when both parties of the communication are operating from the point of rationality and logic. Patients struggling with their feelings, however, need and want feelings from the analyst in order to get better.

THE DARK SIDE OF THERAPY

Hypnos and Eros, buddies as they were, with their common limb-relaxing quality, had a friend who surpassed them in this talent. I mean, of course, Thanatos. Thanatos: Death, or aggression and hate, as it has come to mean in contemporary thought; the final limb-relaxer. At the end of his life, Freud came to understand the real power of Thanatos in everyday life, and his last work, *Civilization and Its Discontents,* is a frank concern over whether human life will ever tame this force for constructive purposes.

But Freud was not at all interested in the presence of Thanatos in the patient/therapist relationship. This was unfortunate, since even a superficial thought about it would lead one to the idea that Thanatos *must* be present in the psychoanalytic treatment. How could Eros and Hypnos both be present without Thanatos? Freud's overlooking this fact is the major omission in his formulation of psychoanalysis, and the chief reason for the ninety-year-old disappointment with the curative results of psychoanalysis as a treatment of psychic disturbances.

It is not difficult, as Freud discovered, for patients to fall in love with their analysts and for analysts to fall in love with their patients. Revealing the secrets of one's inner self makes one lovable. No matter how despicable their acts, how morally offensive their lives, when patients tell the stories of their souls, they become knowable, recognizable, and ultimately lovable. Moreover, the gratitude of a patient for the nonjudgmental acceptance of his whole being can easily flower into love.

I spent the early part of my career, like many therapists, loving my patients and being loved by them. It is the predominant model of therapy, and since it was also coincident with what I and my patients were feeling for one another, I never questioned it. All that changed with my treatment of a young schizophrenic adolescent named Joan. We worked together—I thought quite successfully— for a couple of years. She seemed to like me, and I her, and she talked to me quite openly about her life and her plans. Though I couldn't exactly say I was "curing" her (I'm not sure that at the time I had even a concept of what "cure" meant), we nevertheless enjoyed ourselves. One day, however, our affection for each other descended into an unexpected and frightening fury.

Joan had been officially diagnosed as "schizophrenic with organic brain syndrome," a fancy label referring to the fact that she had been brain-damaged at birth, and had trouble dealing with her emotions. The brain damage meant that she would never function with normal intelligence, but with proper training she could probably expect to get a low-level job, and if the emotional pressures were not too great she could be expected to retain such a job. Unlike most of us, Joan was not instinctively drawn to people. Her feelings were too conflictual and confusing for her to sustain any but the most carefully controlled relationships. In the treatment I made a point of never imposing myself on her, never pressuring her for more closeness than she felt comfortable with. She had never had a friend, male or female. I was her only friend.

Throughout those first couple of years I felt very protective of Joan. When she told me tales of how schoolchildren had jeered at her, I would be sympathetic and accuse them of being mean and insensitive. She and I were a safe haven, together, in a heartless world.

On frequent occasions Joan pressed me to reveal her diagnosis. The thought horrified me. I justified my decision not to tell her by reasoning that learning the truth would be too much for her to bear. Both organic brain damage and schizophrenia are conditions that are certainly resistant to cure, if not outright incurable. Probably the real reason I never told Joan her diagnosis was that I was afraid if the truth were revealed, there would be no reason for us to be together. I did not believe that I could cure her schizophrenia, and I couldn't even begin to approach her organic condition. I was being paid simply to be her friend. Did I need a Ph.D. to be her friend? Did she need a Ph.D. to be her friend? The truth is, as I have since learned, one does need a special kind of training in the art of relating to be a friend to the psyche. It is a skill that few of us, as adults, possess.

During one of Joan's sessions I was called out of the room because of an emergency. I was gone for about five minutes and returned to find her brazenly sitting at my desk with her file spread open. There it was, right in front of her eyes: her diagnosis. She had read it.

I was terrified, for both myself and her. I was, of course, worried about the effect on her. But, as well, I worried that the director of the clinic would find out about this unfortunate occurrence and blame me for Joan's decline in mental health, which I expected to witness imminently. But even more than fear, I felt outraged. I was furious that Joan had intruded into my private files. I had never given her permission to do that, and I was enraged that she had presumed to do so without my permission.

Quite spontaneously, without thinking, I started yelling at her. I accused her of being deceitful and untrustworthy. I told her that after all the time we had been together, I expected more from her. She had no right to invade my space that way. I was so furious at her, I told her, that I had a mind to discharge her from treatment.

Equally spontaneously, and unexpectedly, Joan started yelling back at me. She screamed that she had been asking for that information for two years, that every time she asked for it, I sidestepped the issue; she had a right to know what was wrong with her, and if I wasn't going to tell her, she had no choice but to find out on her own, so that's just what she did. And by the way, she added, I didn't have to discharge her, she had a mind to fire me.

There we sat, looking at each other, amazed, energized, and feeling more for and with each other than we had during all the previous years when we had exchanged pleasantries and politeness. I realized that in her burst of anger, Joan looked and sounded more normal than I had ever seen her.

It began to occur to me at that moment that Joan's verbalizing her hate had had a curative effect on her, and that she was free enough to do it only because I did it first. That insight led me to the beginning of a two-decade-long exploration into the curative effect of giving oneself the freedom to experience and verbalize one's hate feelings.

GHOSTLY HATE IN THERAPY

The early analysts—Freud, Jung, and others—were often brilliant in their articulation of the forces of love that had made their patients neurotic and unhappy. As well, they understood intuitively what Spitz and Bowlby had been able to document scientifically: love heals. Yet, each made a fatal exclusion that eliminated large numbers of patients from therapy who were in desperate need of help. Once the discovery was made that love heals, hate no longer had a place in therapy. Patients who hated their analysts were not popular patients and were generally discharged from treatment and declared incurable.

Everything we know about love tells us that if the loving experience is inadequate in childhood, then it will be more difficult in adult life. There will be more darknesses, more destruction if the emotional feeding in one's early life was inappropriate to the emotional appetite of the child. Why, then, should it be any different for the therapeutic relationship?

People who felt loved as children are more likely to be comfortable with intimacy and to have a positive and cooperative attitude. These are just the kind of patients whom therapists most like to treat, and they are, as well, the kind of people who are least in need of therapy. The difficult patients—the ones who take offense at helpful suggestions, who won't be helped by anything the therapist says, and who lash out in anger or withdraw into depression out of frustration and rage turned inward—the ones who, in short, were the least loved, are the ones who will least love the therapist and the therapy. They are not the patients who say gratefully, "Thank you for your help in the last year—I feel I've made great progress." They say, "I've been coming for a year and nothing has changed." Or they may seduce the therapist into feeling wonderfully perfect and powerful by proclaiming their positive feelings for the therapist, all the while reporting that their lives continue to remain a shambles. Either initially or eventually the hate in the relationship is uncovered. The patient who does not get better stimulates hate in the therapist, and the patients who had an early diet of hate will begin to find hate in the therapeutic relationship.

There enters into the analysis, then, as much hate and anger, disappointment and hurt as there was in the original relationships of infancy and early childhood. It is a situation that doesn't feel good to either the therapist or the patient, and both will be tempted to either deny the feelings or flee from them. This is most often the point at which treatment is terminated. The patient, infused with negative feelings toward the analyst, will declare that the treatment is not working and will say that he will get better on his own, or will seek another therapist with whom he can find the first blush of love again, with the false hope that all negativity will be left behind as soon as the "bad" therapist has been replaced. Or, alternatively, the analyst may be tempted to act out his negative feelings toward the patient and say something that will be destructive to their relationship.

Freud felt that when these negative feelings were present in treatment, the therapeutic relationship ceased being helpful to the patient. He felt that only when the ghostly love of transference was reenacted could the treatment work. Early psychoanalysts felt that ghostly hate had no constructive use.

After my experience with Joan, I began to comb the analytic literature and found that I was not the only one who had happened upon the discovery that the expression of hate heals. Psychoanalysts Donald Winnicott, Harold Searles, and Hyman Spotnitz had each found that unexpressed hate was the main factor in their patients' holding onto destructive patterns. Hate, unfelt, unacknowledged, and unexpressed, put in front of love an impenetrable barrier that could not be breached. Only when the hate was dealt with first were the patients freed emotionally to love. Hate and love, we analysts learned, are inseparable, but hate is the first feeling.

My patients often assume that I will understand perfectly and support them in every way. It is very difficult for patients to experience the inevitable negative feelings about the therapist and the therapy, and to stay in the therapy with a necessary dialogue about these feelings.

Unfortunately, most therapists, too, don't like the idea very much and take it as an attack on themselves when the patient is dissatisfied with them. Often they find subtle ways of attacking the patient. (For example, "I think I detect some anger toward me in your voice," as though the patient shouldn't be feeling the anger.) If the therapist has his own unresolved issues of anger and hurt, then he or she will make the same mistake as the original mother and make the patient feel "wrong" for having these feelings.

It is always easy to hear anger about someone else. It's easy to hear the patient complain about his mother or spouse and to feel superior to those people because you, the therapist, know better how to treat the patient than the people in the patient's real life. This is a common feeling among therapists. The process of accepting someone's rage gets immensely more difficult, however, when the anger is brought alive into the present relationship. This is the moment the competent therapist waits for: when the real feelings, the difficult feelings, are in the therapeutic relationship. Now, in this emotionally charged present, the therapist can model for the patient a different way of accepting and talking about these feelings than the patient received originally. The therapist's permissive attitude toward *all* feelings in the patient presents the possibility to the patient of his having such acceptance of his own feelings. It is thus that we find our way back to our souls—to all of what we think and feel.

Sometimes simply accepting hate from an individual can be remarkably curative. Winnicott reports the case of a disturbed child whose initial communication to him consisted of biting his knuckles, which he allowed her to do. She then graduated to throwing objects on the floor, also permitted. The essence of Winnicott's message to her was: "I can take anything you can dish out to me. No matter how intense your hate and rage, I am strong enough to take it and not let it destroy me. And, I can still love you though you are hating me." Winnicott observed over and over again in his practice that such a message, given to children or adults, takes the destructive aspect out of hate and rage.

The caveat of this form of treatment is that its purpose is to defuse the danger of the explosive rage, rather than further ignite it. This neutralization is accomplished through showing the patient that expression of all impulses is permissible *only* through words, not actions.

What Winnicott and Spotnitz have both understood in developing these therapeutic techniques is that when we are told in childhood that our violent impulses are bad, or wrong, or evil, we can respond by denying that they exist, or we can respond by developing a compulsive need to act out these destructive impulses in order to punish those who have told us we are bad. It is as if to say: "If you think I'm bad now, you haven't seen anything yet. I'll show you just how bad I can be." By accepting the destructive impulse—but not destructive acts—the therapist enables patients to feel more comfortable with their hate. Eventually their impulses lose their destructive (or self-destructive) quality.

STRENGTHENING THE PSYCHOLOGICAL IMMUNE SYSTEM THROUGH THERAPY

Usually even a cursory acquaintance with someone will reveal the repetitive nature of his or her concerns. About love, people tend to ask the same questions and to voice the same complaints over and over again. This repetition reflects the neurological embedment of how we think and feel. We ask the same questions, and think the same thoughts, and feel the same feelings because they represent for us unresolved conflicts. We haven't yet found satisfactory answers and can't seem to apply our minds in ways that would lead to new and creative solutions.

Psychoanalysis is an effective means of rewiring the nervous system to gain freedom in our thinking and feeling patterns. In psychoanalysis, the patient is instructed to "say everything." In giving this recommendation, the analyst is suggesting to the patient that he return to the state of psychic development before thought and feeling patterns had become physiologically entrenched. "Say everything" means: *Have all your thoughts and feelings, even the forbidden ones, even the ones that your repetitive patterns of thinking and feeling have helped you to avoid.*

Although the analyst gives the patient the instruction to move through the walls of his defenses, it is in fact an impossible task for the patient. Most of our behavior in love relationships is governed by neurological pathways that were established in our first love experiences. We often don't ordinarily have conscious control over these pathways. We cannot always change our feelings, thoughts, or behavior simply by wishing them to be different. Similarly, we do not control our emotional blocks, and so no matter how cooperative or zealous we are as a patient, no matter how fervently we *wish* to be different, there will still remain areas of our psyches that are uncharted and unexplored, and will impede our emotional growth.

It is the task of the analyst to recognize and guide the patient through these unknown psychic lands that are creating emotional blockages. In helping the patient to first know and then to resolve these blocks, the analyst is, in effect, helping the person to tolerate new thoughts and feelings. In resolving the repetition compulsion—the patient's need to stay emotionally rooted in the past—the analyst is working on the level of neurology as well as psychology. Old nervous system patterns are deactivated, while new patterns are activated. Psychic change is created. Both love and hate are tolerated.

Creating the ability to "say everything"—that is, freely think and feel all thoughts and feelings, no matter how heinous and no matter how abhorrent they have been thought to be—doesn't unchain terrible monsters. In fact, it creates a well-insulated, balanced personality. Verbalizing emotions in the therapeutic setting serves an immunizing function, protecting the person from reverting back to old and useless patterns.

Learning to accept all of what we think and feel allows both old and new sides of our brain to be exercised, one serving as a calibration for the other. Our psychological immune system is able to function properly, neither ignoring nor exaggerating emotional pathogens. We know what we feel, what others feel toward us, and we are able to make judgments and decisions and base our actions on the sum total of our mental, cognitive, and emotional aspects.

Through therapy we learn to recognize when we are operating from old neurological pathways, and we consciously decide whether or not these patterns from the past are appropriate to the present. Through therapy we can devise new ways of reacting and relating, thereby freeing our loves from the shackles of the past.

BEING HUMAN

The etymological root of the word "infant" is *infans*, meaning literally without words. As infants, we are without speech, and our growing up is a process of learning to talk, to give articulation to our experiences and our inner world, to say what we see and think and feel, and to communicate.

Of course, expression is the beginning, not the end. We teach our children to modulate and moderate their language, as we should. Children, like Narcissus, say whatever they think and feel, without regard for the effect on other people. Being sensitive to the feelings of others is a skill that must be learned. But, more often than not, in teaching our children not to speak everything out loud, we teach them, as well, to quiet their inner voices, thereby depriving them of their feelings. And without feelings, words become meaningless. By the time most of us reach adulthood, our internal world, which our language is ideally suited to represent, has become as empty as Narcissus' pond.

We must find a way back to meaning. It is through relationships most of all that we can do this. To go through a relationship is to enter it, as Alice does—to separate from it, to see it, to merge with it, and to feel it. To let us move with it and be moved by it.

If we could stop trying to be gods or beasts to each other, if we could stop trying to find gods or beasts in each other, we could be human and find the humanness within those we love and hate. It would suffice. Dayanu.

References

Alighieri, D. *The Portable Dante.* New York: Penguin, 1977.

Ardrey, R. *African Genesis.* New York: Atheneum, 1961.

Aristophanes. *Lysistrata.* Translated by D. Sutherland. New York: Harper and Row, 1961.

Bacheland, G. *The Poetics of Reverie.* Boston: Beacon Press, 1969.

Bakan, D. *Slaughter of the Innocents.* Boston: Beacon Press, 1972.

Bank, S. P., and Kahn, M. D. *The Sibling Bond.* New York: Basic Books, 1982.

Bar-Levan, R. *Thinking in the Shadow of Feelings.* New York: Simon & Schuster, 1988.

Berscheid, E., and Walster, E. "A Little Bit About Love." In *Foundations of Interpersonal Attraction.* Edited by T. L. Huston. New York: Academic Press, 1974.

Bertine, E. *Human Relationships.* New York: David McKay, 1958.

Bett, H. *Nursery Rhymes and Tales: Their Origins and History.* 2nd ed. London: Methuen, 1924.

Bettelheim, B. *The Uses of Enchantment.* New York: Vintage, 1977.

Blanch, L. *The Wilder Stories of Love.* New York: Simon & Schuster, 1954.

Bowlby, J. *Attachment and Loss.* Vol. 1. New York: Basic Books, 1969.

————. *The Making and Breaking of Affectional Bonds.* London: Tavistock Pub., 1979.

Briggs, K. M. *The Fairies in English Tradition and Literature.* Chicago: University of Chicago Press, 1967.

Bugliosi, V., with C. Gentry. *Helter Skelter.* New York: W. W. Norton, 1975.

Chekhov, A. "Sleepyhead." In *The Tales of Chekhov.* Translated by C. Garnett. New York: Ecco Press, 1984.

Collier, J. P. *Punch and Judy.* New York: Rimington and Hooper, 1929.

de Rougement, D. *Love in the Western World.* New York: Pantheon, 1956.

Dicks, H. V. *Marital Tensions: Clinical Studies Towards a Psychological Theory of Interaction.* New York: Basic Books, 1967.

Dixon, N. F. *On the Psychology of Military Incompetence.* London: Futura Publications, 1979.

Durant, W. *Caesar and Christ.* New York: Simon & Schuster, 1944.

Eggerton, J. *From Cradle to Grave.* New York: Jove Books, 1990.

Eibl-Eibesfeldt, I. *Love and Hate.* New York: Holt, Rinehart and Winston, 1971.

Escolona, S. "Emotional Development in the First Year of Life." In *Problems of Infancy and Childhood.* Edited by M. Senn. Ann Arbor, Michigan: Josiah Macy, Jr. Foundation, 1953.

Farr, L. "Tall, Dark, and Homicidal." In *Elle,* March 1992, p. 152.

Feldman, L. B. "Dysfunctional Marital Conflict: An Integrative Interpersonal Intrapsychic Model." *Journal of Marriage and Family Therapy* 8, no. 4.

Fine, R. *The Meaning of Love in Human Experience.* New York: John Wiley, 1985.

Freud, A. "The Concept of Developmental Lines." *Psychoanalytic Study of the Child* 18. New York: International Universities Press, 1963.

Freud, A., and Burlingham, D. T. *Report on Hempstead Nurseries* (issued by the British Foster Parents' Plan for War Children, New York Headquarters), 1942.

Freud, S. *The Standard Edition of the Complete Psychological Works of Sigmund Freud* (24 vols.; 1892–1939). London: Hogarth Press, 1953–1974.

Friday, N. *My Mother, My Self.* New York: Dell, 1977.

Gaylin, W. *The Killing of Bonnie Garland.* New York: Simon & Schuster, 1982.

Gelles, R. J., and Straus, M. A. *Intimate Violence.* New York: Touchstone, 1988.

Greenleaf, B. K. *Children Through the Ages.* New York: McGraw-Hill, 1978.

Harding, M. E. *The Way of All Women.* New York: Harper Colophon Books, 1970.

Harlow, H. F., and Harlow, M. K. "Social Deprivation in Monkeys." In *Scientific American* 207: 136–146, 1962.

Hate. (Television documentary conducted by B. Moyers.) PBS, 1991.

Hatfield, E., and Walster, G. W. *A New Look at Love*. Lanham, Maryland: University Press of America, 1978.

Henton, J., et al. "Romance and Violence." *Journal of Family Issues* (Sept. 1983): 467–82.

Higham, C. *The Duchess of Windsor: The Secret Life*. New York: Charter, 1989.

Homer. *The Illiad*. Translated by E. V. Rieu. Harmondsworth, England: Penguin Books, 1950.

Horney, K. "The Value of Vindictiveness." *American Journal of Psychoanalysis* 8: 3, 1948.

Jacoby, S. *Wild Justice: The Evolution of Revenge*. New York: Harper and Row, 1983.

Jung, C. G. *The Collected Works of C. G. Jung*. New York: Pantheon Books, 1954.

Kaplan, L. J. *Oneness and Separateness: From Infant to Individual*. New York: Touchstone, 1978.

Kernberg, O. F. "Barriers to Falling and Remaining in Love." *Journal of the American Psychoanalytic Association* 22, 1974.

————. *Borderline Conditions and Pathological Narcissism*. Northvale, New Jersey: Jason Aronson, 1975.

————. "Mature Love: Prerequisites and Characteristics." *Journal of the Amer. A.P.A.* 22, 1974.

Kirman, W. "Revenge and Accommodation in the Family." *Modern Psychoanalysis* 14, no. 1, 1989.

Klein, M. "Hate, Greed and Aggression." In *Love, Hate and Reparation (Psychoanalytic Epitomes, no. 2)*. Edited by M. Klein and J. Riviere. London: Hogarth Press, 1937.

————. *Psychoanalysis of Children*. New York: Norton, 1932.

————. *The Psycho-Analysis of Children*. Translated by A. Strachey. New York: Delacourt Press, 1975.

Klein, M., and Riviere, J., eds. *Love, Hate and Reparation (Psychoanalytic Epitomes, no. 2)*. London: Hogarth Press, 1937.

Kohut, H. "Thoughts on Narcissism and Narcissistic Rage." *The Psychoanalytic Study of the Child* 27, 1972.

Lasch, C. *Haven in a Heartless World: The Family Besieged*. New York: Basic Books, 1977.

Lasky, J., and Silverman, H., eds. *Love: Psychoanalytic Perspectives*. New York: New York University Press, 1988.

Lockhart, R. A. *Words as Eggs: Psyche in Language and Clinic*. Dallas: Spring Publishers, 1987.

Lorenz, K. *On Aggression*. London: Methuen, 1966.

MacLean, P. D. *A Triune Concept of the Brain and Behavior.* Edited by T. J. Boag and D. Campbell. Toronto: University of Toronto Press, 1973.

————. "Brain Mechanism of Primal Sexual Functions and Related Behavior." In *Biological Foundations of Psychiatry* 1. Edited by M. Sandler and G. L. Gesse. New York: Raven Press, 1975.

Mahler, M. "On Human Symbiosis and the Vicissitudes of Individuation: Infantile Psychosis." New York: International Universities Press, 1968.

————, et al. *The Psychological Birth of the Human Infant.* New York: Basic Books, 1975.

Margolis, M. *Mothers and Such.* Berkeley: University of California Press, 1984.

Martin, J., review of *The Intimate Correspondence of the Duke and Duchess of Windsor. The New York Times Book Review*, June 29, 1986.

McDougall, J. *Plea for a Measure of Abnormality.* New York: International Universities Press, 1980.

McNeill, W. H. *The Pursuit of Power: Technology Armed Force and Society Since A.D. 1000.* Oxford: University of Chicago Press, 1982.

Mead, M. *Cooperation and Competition Among Primitive Peoples.* Boston: Beacon Press, 1961.

————. *Male and Female.* New York: William Morrow, 1949.

————. *Sex and Temperament in Three Primitive Societies.* New York: New American Library, 1935.

Meadow, P., with H. Spotnitz. *Treatment of the Narcissistic Neuroses.* New York: Manhattan Center for Modern Psychoanalytic Studies, 1976.

Menninger, K. *Love Against Hate.* New York: Harcourt Brace Jovanovich, 1942.

————. *Man Against Himself.* New York: Harcourt, Brace and World, 1942.

Miller, A. *Drama of the Gifted Child.* New York: Farrar, Straus and Giroux, 1981.

————. *For Your Own Good: Hidden Cruelty in Childhood and the Roots of Violence.* New York: Farrar, Straus and Giroux, 1983.

Murstein, B. I. "The Relationship of Mental Health to Marital Choice and Courtship Progress." *Journal of Marriage and the Family* 29: 689–96, 1967.

Neumann, E. *Amor and Psyche: The Psychic Development of the Feminine.* Princeton, New Jersey: Bollinger, 1956.

Norwood, R. *Women Who Love Too Much.* New York: Pocket Books, 1985.

Olsen, J. *Doc: The Rape of the Town of Lowell.* New York: Dell, 1989.

Otto, H. A., ed. *Love Today.* New York: Association Press, 1972.

Ovid. *Metamorphosis* (Loeb Classical Library, 2nd ed.). Cambridge, Massachusetts: Harvard University Press, 1951, vol. 1, book 3, pp. 149–161.

Peele, S. *Love and Addiction*. New York: New American Library, 1975.

Person, E. S. *Dreams of Love and Fateful Encounters*. New York: W. W. Norton, 1988.

Piers, M. W. *Infanticide: Past and Present*. New York: W. W. Norton, 1978.

Pincus, L., and Dare, C. *Secrets in the Family*. New York: Pantheon, 1978.

Plato. *The Symposium*. Edited by B. Jourtt. New York: Tudor Publisher, 1956, pp. 315–318.

Plutarch. *Plutarch's Lives* (Harvard Classics Edition). Translated by Dryden. New York: P. F. Collier and Son, 1909.

Previn, D. *Midnight Baby*. London: Elm Tree Books, 1977.

Reik, T. *A Psychologist Looks at Love*. New York: Rinehart, 1945.

————. *Masochism in Modern Man*. New York: Farrar, Straus, 1941.

Renneker, R. "Cancer and Psychotherapy." In *Psychotherapeutic Treatment of Cancer Patients*. Edited by J. Goldberg. New York: Free Press, 1981.

Robson, K. S. "The Role of Eye-to-Eye Contact in Maternal–Infant Attachment." In *Journal of Child Psychology and Psychiatry* 8, pp. 13–25.

Roth, P. *Portnoy's Complaint*. New York: Random House, 1969.

Rule, A. *Possession*. New York: New American Library, 1983.

Sagan, C. *The Dragons of Eden*. New York: Hodder and Stoughton, 1978.

Sagan, L. *The Health of Nations*. New York: Basic Books, 1987.

Scarf, M. *Intimate Partners*. New York: Random House, 1987.

Schachter, S. "The Interaction of Cognitive and Physiological Determinants of Emotional States." In *Advances in Experimental Social Psychology*. Edited by L. Berkowitz. New York: Academic Press, 1964.

Schefflin, A., and Opton, E., Jr. *The Mind Manipulators*. New York: Paddington Press, 1978.

Schoenewolf, G. *The Art of Hating*. Northvale, New Jersey: Jason Aronson, 1991.

"Seeking Words to Shape an Uncommon Life." Interview with J. Chaikin. *The New York Times*, May 19, 1991.

Sessions, S., with P. Meyer. *Dark Obsession*. New York: Berkeley Books, 1990.

Shakespeare, W. "The Merchant of Venice" and "Antony and Cleopatra." In *The Complete Works of Shakespeare*. Edited by G. B. Harrison. New York: Harcourt, Brace, Jovanovich, 1948.

Shengold, L., *Soul Murder: The Effects of Childhood Abuse and Deprivation*. New Haven, Connecticut: Yale University Press, 1989.

Short, S. "The Whispering of the Walls" (unpublished manuscript).

Smith, R., news editorial; WPIX-TV (New York), April 7, 1990.

Spitz, R. *The First Year of Life*. New York: International Universities Press, 1965.

Spotnitz, H. *Modern Psychoanalysis of the Schizophrenic Patient.* New York: Human Sciences Press, 1985.

_____. *Psychotherapy of Preoedipal Conditions.* Northvale, New Jersey: Jason Aronson, 1976.

_____, with P. Meadow. *Treatment of the Narcissistic Neuroses.* New York: Manhattan Center for Modern Psychoanalytic Studies, 1976.

Stearns, P. N. *Jealousy: The Evolution of an Emotion in American History.* New York: New York University Press, 1989.

Steiner, Z. Review of *King Edward VII* by P. Ziegler, *The New York Times Book Review,* February 10, 1991.

Steinmetz, S. *The Cycle of Violence: Assertive, Aggressive and Abusive Family Interaction.* New York: Praeger, 1977.

Sternberg, R. J., and Barnes, M. L., eds. *The Psychology of Love.* New Haven, Connecticut: Yale University Press, 1988.

Stevens, A. *The Roots of War.* New York: Paragon House, 1989.

Suttie, I. *Origins of Love and Hate.* London: Kegan Paul, 1935.

Tanner, T. *Adultery in the Novel: Contact and Transgression.* Baltimore: Johns Hopkins University Press, 1979.

Tweedie, J. *In the Name of Love.* New York: Pantheon Books, 1979.

Walsh, A. *The Science of Love.* New York: Prometheus Books, 1991.

Watson, J. B. *Psychology from the Standpoint of a Behaviorist.* Philadelphia: Lippincott, 1924.

Webster's Third New International Dictionary. Springfield, Massachusetts: Merriam-Webster Inc., 1971.

West, R. *Living Philosophies.* New York: Simon & Schuster, 1940.

Winnicott, D. W. "Aggression in Relation to Emotional Development." In *Through Paediatrics.* New York: Basic Books, 1950, pp. 204–218.

_____. "Hate in the Countertransference." In *Through Paediatrics to Psycho-Analysis.* New York: Basic Books, 1949, pp. 194–203.

_____. *The Maturational Processes and the Facilitating Environment.* London: Hogarth Press, 1965.

_____. "Symptom Tolerance in Paediatrics." In *Through Paediatrics.* New York: Basic Books, 1953, pp. 101–117.

Index

Breinigsville, PA USA
07 January 2011
252878BV00001B/9/P